THE LAST RIVER RAT

Kenny Salwey's Life in the Wild

By J. Scott Bestul & Kenny Salwey
With Pen-and-Ink Illustrations by Mary Kay Salwey

Voyageur Press

Edited by Michael Dregni
Designed by Kjerstin Moody
Jacket designed by Andrea Rud
Printed in China

First Hardcover Edition
04   05   06   5   4   3
First Softcover Edition
05   06   07   08   09   5   4   3   2   1

Library of Congress Cataloging-in-Publication Data
Bestul, J. Scott, 1960–
    The last river rat : Kenny Salwey's life in the wild / by J. Scott Bestul & Kenny Salwey.
        p. cm.
    ISBN 0-89658-457-7 (hardcover)
    ISBN 0-89658-749-5 (paperback)
    1. Salwey, Kenny, 1943– . 2. Naturalists—Wisconsin—Biography. 3. Floodplain forest ecology—Mississippi River Watershed. I. Salwey, Kenny, 1943– . II. Title.
    QH31.S16 B47 2001
    508.775'092—dc21

                                00-050274

Distributed in Canada by Raincoast Books
9050 Shaughnessy Street, Vancouver, B.C. V6P 6E5

Published by Voyageur Press, Inc.
123 North Second Street, P.O. Box 338, Stillwater, MN 55082 U.S.A.
651-430-2210, fax 651-430-2211
books@voyageurpress.com
www.voyageurpress.com

Educators, fundraisers, premium and gift buyers, publicists, and marketing managers: Looking for creative products and new sales ideas? Voyageur Press books are available at special discounts when purchased in quantities, and special editions can be created to your specifications. For details contact the marketing department at 800-888-9653.

ACKNOWLEDGMENTS

MANY THANKS TO my friend and budding river rat, J. Scott Bestul. This book was his idea. From the start we hit it off, and I'm grateful for his expertise and his passion for the land.

I would like to thank Reggie McCloud and all the folks at *Big River Newsletter* for allowing me to create five year's worth of monthly almanacs for them—excerpts of which appear in this book.

Also a big thank-you to my editor, Michael Dregni, and the staff at Voyageur Press.

Lastly, I want to thank the reader for taking more than a passing interest in nature. During the time it takes you to read this book, we will be fellow travelers in the great Circle of Life. There is no greater gift than the sharing of one's time with another. The critters and I say thank you from the bottom of our hearts.—Kenny Salwey

I'D LIKE TO thank Michael Dregni for his unflagging support during this project, and Mary Kay Salwey for her wonderful drawings and honest input. To the thousands of folks who, through volunteer or professional effort, keep the Upper Mississippi River one of the world's natural wonders, a heartfelt appreciation. But my deepest gratitude goes to Kenny, who showed me a beautiful place and a way of looking at things that I hope I'll never lose.—J. Scott Bestul

DEDICATION

I DEDICATE THIS book to all the river rats who have gone before me, from the ancient people who first saw the Great River to those of just yesterday. I follow them all in the wake of their canoes.

Most of all I dedicate this book to my beloved wife, Mary Kay, who sorted through my longhand scribblings and painstakingly drew the remarkable illustrations for this book. She is the light and the love of my life. She kept me on task and gave me the motivation to complete the book.—Kenny Salwey

FOR SHARI, WHO reads every word before they escape our house.— J. Scott Bestul

CONTENTS

Leaning on his walking stick, Kenny pauses to watch the woods. (Photograph © Mary Kay Salwey)

INTRODUCTION

Of River Rats and the Big River

Along the Mississippi River, old-timers often speak with reverence of a fabled fraternity of men and women who not only know the Big River, but have made it part of their lives and counted on it for a livelihood. Riverfolk have a name for this dwindling clan: They are known as "river rats." While the name conjures images of a sodden, bedraggled critter living in a mud house, it's considered quite a compliment around these parts, and unlike most names, it's one that's earned, not given at birth. Wresting a living, or even part of one, from the river is hard business. As locals are quick to point out, there are no dumb river rats who are very old; the Mississippi does a tidy job of weeding out those who make mistakes at the wrong times.

River rats are a respected bunch, and until a generation or two ago, they were fairly common. Every rivertown claimed a handful—and in some cases entire families—who looked to one of the world's greatest rivers for sustenance, income, and recreation. In the summer there were fish to catch and clams to dig. Come fall, ducks and deer provided meat for the smokehouse and dollars for the wallet, as there were always out-of-towners willing to hire a guide for a day. As fall gave way to winter, traps were set for beaver and mink, muskrat and otter, all of whose furs would bring the money needed to make it through until spring. And when the snow and ice left the river, the cycle began again. Theirs was a life lived close to the water.

Today, river rats are few and far between. Unspoiled stretches of the Big River are hard to find, and it's not a lifestyle that will earn you the keys to a fancy house or a big car. Living off the river is a dying way of life.

This is not true everywhere, however. Along the banks of the Mississippi where the waters separate Minnesota from Wisconsin, people speak still of a legendary modern-day river rat, the last river rat. This man is Kenny Salwey.

Kenny grew up on a small farm near Cochrane, Wisconsin, at a time when the river rat's way of life was still attractive. As a prospective river rat, he had no shortage of role models. Although he already spent his days outdoors doing farm chores, he longed to learn more of the natural world—of the plants and creatures living in the hills surrounding the river, and of the fish and turtles and ducks that called the backwaters home. Farm life was better than town life, but it was also tedious. Kenny wanted to live according to nature's rhythms, to let the seasons dictate the work that needed to be done. River rats seemed to have captured that essence perfectly—calling no person "boss" and relying only on their resourcefulness, ingenuity, and knowledge of the country to survive. He could think of no better life.

Kenny had rudimentary training from family members, whose French-Canadian roots remained strong. "I was taught young how to gather mushrooms, dig ginseng, setline for catfish, hunt ducks," Kenny recalls. "Those activities were part of my heritage. Not all of my family worried about gainful employment, and many of our activities were driven by the rhythms of the seasons. When certain times of the year came, there were important things to do for our survival, and these were the things I loved, even as a young boy."

Of course, acquiring enough knowledge to be a river rat was not accomplished overnight, and most river folk guarded their secrets jealously. "I hung around whatever river people would let me, listening closely to what they said and watching what they did," Kenny says. "I learned a lot that way—from the old ones. But they weren't willing to share everything. Each knew different places: favorite fishing holes, the best creek bank to trap a mink, the wild celery beds where the ducks came each fall. You could pick up a little bit from each person you knew, but most things you still needed to learn on your own."

Kenny made his home in the Whitman Swamp, a 6,000-acre swampland south of Buffalo City, Wisconsin, that is shut off from the modern world in the Big River's backwaters. And, in over four decades of roaming the Whitman, he has come to know the swamp almost as intimately as any of nature's creatures who live there.

The Whitman Swamp was separated from the main channel of the Upper Mississippi River by a dike built by the U.S. Army Corps of Engineers in 1933. The dike consisted of five miles of earth and rock beginning just downstream of Buffalo City, and was part of the vast complex of dams, locks, and levees meant to channel the Mississippi's power; the system was engineered to protect rivertowns from flooding and make commercial navigation safer and more successful. That was the dike's expressed purpose, anyway.

What the Whitman Dike actually did was shut the swamp off from the modern world. On the river side of the dike, tugs push barges full of grain and coal between New Orleans and Minneapolis–St. Paul, pleasure boaters steer yachts and sailboats up and down the channel, campers pitch tents on sand-mountains of dredge spoil, and jet skiers steer whining machines into their own chop. From ice-out until autumn's end, the main channel seems little more than a water-filled freeway carrying a mix of riders: businesspeople, commuters, sightseers, and Sunday drivers.

On the swamp side of the dike, however, time has nearly stood still. Whitman Swamp is a classic floodplain forest, an ecosystem that dominated the Upper Mississippi River watershed for hundreds of years. As the name implies, a floodplain forest is a largely wooded environment subject to the mood swings and vagaries of a

River Rat Country

Wisconsin

Buffalo

Cochrane

The Mississippi River

Dike

Big Lake Shack

Big Lake

● **Tent Camp**

● **Marsh Shack**

Minneiska

The Whitman Swamp

Minnesota

Lock & Dam No. 5

Minnesota

Mississippi River

Wisconsin

St. Paul

Minneapolis

La Crosse

river. When snowmelt and spring rain swell the Mississippi, Whitman Swamp becomes a smaller version of the river itself, full of swirling current, lakes and pools, eddies and ponds. The river flows into the swamp to cool off and calm down, to stretch and rage and bellow until it can re-establish control of itself and flow where it normally does. Once the Mississippi has had its temper tantrum, the swamp becomes a swamp again: a vast and peaceful place where small creeks and sheltered lakes form a tapestry; where white oaks and silver maple and cottonwood grow on the small ridges that weave among the water; and where birds and deer, musk-rats and turtles are insulated from the bustle on the business side of the Whitman Dike. The quiet backwater seemed part of another time and place to Kenny.

Swamps like the Whitman were common in the days before the lock-and-dam system. But damming the river forever changed the shape and appearance of the river bottoms, inundating hundreds of acres of floodplain forest above each dam and channeling the flow below each lock to a trickle of its former self. The river has never been the same. Channelization has, for the most part, pro-vided consistent water depth and flow for large boat traffic, and most of the towns and homes along the river are safer from flood-ing than they were in the past. But these improvements have come with a price, and one of those costs is the loss of places like the Whitman Swamp. For riverfolk who can remember the Mississippi before dams—and the number of those people is shrinking—it's a questionable trade at best.

But the Mississippi is only part of the river rat's home range. Included in his territory are the steeply wooded bluffs that stretch away from the Big River for miles to the east. Escapees from the terrain-flattening glaciers that leveled much of Wisconsin during the last Ice Age, the rugged hillsides are as much a part of the river system as the channel itself. Rising five hundred feet or more above the river bed, the hillsides gather snow in the winter and send it coursing downhill as runoff in the spring. The water freshens creeks and streams, which wind through scenic coulees and verdant meadows and quiet marshes until they feed the river itself.

Life flows back to the hills, too. Deer and ducks leave the river bottoms when the Mississippi floods or when swamp white oaks don't provide the acorns they relish. Fish from the Mississippi run up tributary streams to spawn their next generation. And the people who saw the river as their life's blood followed suit, alternating their time between backwaters and bluffs, responding to whatever activity was in season at the time. For a river rat, separating the hills and coulees from the river itself was unthinkable, like divorcing a sea from the shore it caressed.

Kenny finished twelve years of school by the skin of his teeth and then set off into the backwater classrooms to learn the lessons he wanted to learn the most. He lived in the swamp for weeks at a time, staying in three small shacks he'd built as outcamps. He fished and sold his catch. Dug ginseng for the valuable roots. Trapped muskrats and beaver and learned to handle fur. Shot ducks and guided hunters. He had no truck with those bent on making money for its own sake or elevating their social station to impress others. "I had little use for people back then," he remembers. "I'd be down in the swamp, listening to their cars go by on the highway and I'd think, 'Good! Let them go!'"

He was not, however, completely isolated. In 1961, he was drafted by the Army and stationed in the Pacific Northwest, where he immersed himself in the towering forests they visited in training exercises. Returning home, he married and bought a home in Buffalo City. But at heart, and for most of his time, he remained a riverman who would not be forced into a normal life. Kenny spent his days in the swamp, sometimes returning home in the evening, some-

Kenny stands in the entrance to Big Lake Shack. (Photograph © Michael Dregni)

times staying in one of his shacks for days at a time. If the civilized world was a swimming pool, he only dipped his toe in it.

While the freedom was exhilarating for a young man, the solitude came with a price. "I was suspicious of people," Kenny remembers. "Hated authority. I did whatever I needed to get by. If I was hungry, I shot a deer. If I wanted more ducks than the limit, I took them. I was just a taker. I hoarded the outdoors to myself."

Of course, the local game wardens knew that Kenny wasn't wasting time reading their regulation books. "One of the wardens was named Jim Everson," Kenny recalls. "Last of the old-time river wardens—very tough and smart. Jim'd come up to me when I was young and say, 'I ever catch you breaking the law, you'll get a ticket or an ass-chewing!' He gave me both several times." But admonitions and fines did little to slow the reclusive riverman. One citation was posted proudly on the wall of his shack for all to see.

Kenny didn't know it, but things were about to change.

"It was a summer day—hot as hell—and I was just laying up until evening in my tent camp. I'd just about drifted off when I heard an airboat coming through the swamp. Wardens were the only ones using airboats then, and as it got closer I started looking around camp—you know, making sure I didn't have anything laying around that wasn't supposed to be.

"Sure enough, it was Everson, and when he landed the boat and started walking to me, I started thinking what he could want me for—I couldn't remember doing anything wrong lately. But he wasn't looking to bust me that day. He just came up and settled down, making small talk. I was getting kind of suspicious when he finally come out and told me why he was there. He'd been scheduled to give a nature talk to a group of teachers up in Wabasha, [Minnesota,] but he couldn't make it. He wondered if I'd go.

"Well I couldn't believe my ears. I thought for a minute, then I let him have it right there. I said, 'I should go there? I hate schools.

I hate teachers. Hell, I ain't so sure I like game wardens, either. Why should I go?'

"Jim Everson looked me right square in the eye and said, 'Kenny, you are one of the most selfish, orneriest persons I ever met in my life. You do nothing but take, take, take from nature. You hoard all your outdoor experience. How about sharing, giving something back for a change?' Then he added, 'Not only that, but it's worth twenty-five bucks and a free meal.'

"He had given me a true butt-chewing, but what he said was true.

"'OK, I'll do it,' I told him."

Kenny came for the money and the food, but the experience would change his life forever.

"I took along a bunch of skins and a box of stuff: turtle shells, deer antlers, whatever. I was as nervous as a long-tailed cat in a room full of rocking chairs." But the shy riverman conquered his nervousness and talked, simply and quietly, about the things he knew and cared about: the patterns of nature down in the swamps and up in the bluffs, and how he felt people fit in the picture.

Somewhere in the midst of his stories, Kenny looked up and realized that the teachers were listening intently, absorbing everything he had to say. When he was finished, hands were in the air and questions followed. Before he left, Kenny had received invitations from several teachers, asking him to address the children at their schools. The response literally drew Kenny out of the swamp. "I still remember how good that felt," he says. "For the first time in my life, my heart was opened up to other people."

Since that epiphany, Kenny's life has been anything but reclusive. His schedule soon filled with talks to schoolkids, teachers, nature groups, resource policy makers. Instead of just reaping nature's harvest, Kenny began giving back, teaching people about the Upper Mississippi River and how he felt it should be cared for.

Kenny looks out over the waters of Big Lake while Spider takes it easy.
(Photograph © Michael Dregni)

He also became a voracious reader of conservation and nature writers, and could quote John Muir, Aldo Leopold, Sigurd F. Olson, and Henry David Thoreau with ease. He co-designed an environmental learning curriculum for an entire school district and once shared keynote-speaker status with Earth Day founder (and former Wisconsin Governor and Senator) Gaylord Nelson. It was heady stuff for a man used to speaking only a few words in a given day, and most of those to a dog.

There were, as one might suspect, times when Kenny questioned the life change. "I remember when I'd be days away from the swamp," he recalls. "The time commitment, the crowds, the busy schedule were almost too much." He considered fleeing—back to the river bottoms, away from scheduling people, apart from calendars and commitment. At about that time, a friend of his, the local school principal, talked to Kenny. "He told me I couldn't go back forever anymore," Kenny reflects. "That I'd touched too many lives, that people depended on me now. He said it wasn't fair for me to take that away from the kids who might need me in the future."

It seems a harsh sentence for a man who lived about as freely as one can in the tail end of the twentieth century. There had to be a rising sense of panic, however small, growing in his chest at the thought. He'd made a tentative stab at the civilized world, like a kid poking at a snapping turtle with a stick. But the turtle's head had lunged and his jaws had snapped and now those jaws would not let go of that life he once held so dear.

In the end, of course, Kenny sided with the principal. Had the groups he talked to been bored or hostile, Kenny might have considered retreat. But he was amazed at their reception; they hungered for the knowledge that seemed second nature to him. And he had the gift of a storyteller: a kind, rich, pleasing voice, a sense of the dramatic and of the humorous, the ability to look people—even hard people—in the eye and let them know he was sincere.

He was good at so many things that he did alone, it felt good to shine at something that required an audience.

So Kenny has struck a balance. He continues to give nature talks to a broad audience of students and their instructors, state resource managers, troubled kids, nature groups, women's groups, sportsman's clubs, and more. Yet when he's not speaking somewhere, Kenny's back home in the backwaters and bluffs, knee-deep in muck or clinging to a craggy hillside, part of the river world that once earned him a living, but still gives him life.

Like so many who've met him, I'm glad that Kenny made the choice that he did. Had he not come out of the swamp, much of the lore and the lifestyle of the river rat may have vanished. The towns lining the Mississippi don't produce river rats like they used to; the promise of a better education, a higher-paying job, a nicer neighborhood, and a faster-paced, more elegant lifestyle continually lures youngsters away from Minnesota and Wisconsin towns like Alma, Buffalo City, Winona, Fountain City, Reads Landing. . . . The way of the river rat is hard and the rewards few. Forty years ago, people didn't expect so much; these days, a kid who made the choices Kenny did in his youth would be told to see a career counselor and re-evaluate his options. So river rats are a dying breed, yet Kenny's rich oral tradition has ensured that at least some of the lifestyle will be remembered and, hopefully, appreciated.

I'm also glad Kenny came out of the swamp because he's my friend, and I'm a writer, and this book, we hope, will capture in print some of the traditions and practices he's included in his talks for years. I've tagged along with Kenny as he set beaver traps, hunted ducks, dug ginseng, whittled walking sticks, followed deer trails, listened to geese, and canoed down sloughs. In the process, he taught me a different calendar, one that is not driven by days or weeks, but according to the wind and the weather and the whimsy of nature. It's a calendar that river rats—and few others—know well. This book is designed to capture those events and seasons and chronicle the passage of swamp time.

And finally, I'm grateful to Kenny for showing me the Whitman Swamp. In this special place, shielded from time and progress, I've been able to catch a glimpse of the Mississippi before the lock-and-dam system. In that era, swamps like the Whitman were everywhere on the upper river, and in every swamp there was a river rat—or family of river rats—living by their unique calendar. But just as we can eliminate a species by despoiling its habitat, the river rats have shrunk to a fraction of their original number because places like the Whitman Swamp are now gone. In the void left by these secluded marshes are treeless, grassless, backwater lakes.

Most rivertown old-timers are philosophical about these changes. There is no denying progress, they say, and whining about channelization is like bemoaning the presence of automobiles. Sure, life was different before them, but was it better? Every year there are fewer folk who can remember the bygone era, until finally the last witness will no longer be around to testify. But the Whitman Swamp is there for most anyone to see. It is a vivid, beautiful, wild reminder of the floodplain forest of not so long ago, and it's also the second home of one man who lived there in a way that is also being forgotten. This is their story.

April

River Rat Almanac

APRIL IS A soft and gentle time. The wild, untamable winds of March have been exiled to the far north. In their place have come the mild, warm breezes of April, the month of promise. It feels good to sit on a driftwood log and enjoy the sunshine caressing your face.

The last vestiges of winter disappear from the river a little each day. You can smell the mud as it comes alive again, smacking of skunk cabbages and marsh marigolds, red-wings and killdeer, bullheads and turtles. The river is alive, vibrant, and pulsing.

The river is spring housecleaning now. It flows high and muddy, waters filling every lowland nook and cranny. Logs, barrels, and other flotsam drift in steady currents. Bluffs watch this parade pass on its way to the sea.

Riverfolk keep watchful eyes on levees and dikes as the river creeps a little higher each day. April showers come and go, giving the river new life. If the showers don't become deluges, our thoughts turn to fishing, gardening, and birding; otherwise thoughts of sandbags, dikes, and sump pumps come to mind. Patience and perseverance are necessary survival skills for riverfolk and wild things alike.

The New Year Begins in the
Three Camps

Anyone doubting that the modern calendar is hopelessly out of whack need only look at two obvious shortcomings: Leap Years (if the system is so great, why the constant corrections?) and Mondays (even the name sounds depressing). But the real kicker—the proof the emperor wears no clothes—is January. Why anyone would think to start a year in such a cold, foreboding season is proof positive there's more madness than method in this date-recording plan. Delivering Baby New Year on January 1 is like marketing a new luxury car in the height of a depression—you might have a great concept, but people just aren't in the mood.

If you're serious about starting things off right, lead off with April. That's when Kenny recognizes that the new year has begun: when the greening hills and awakening swamp tell him that growth and change are imminent. Lilac trees show the faintest hint of their colorful buds. Oak leaves are mouse-ear size and a pearlescent green they'll exhibit at no other time of year. Mallards and wood ducks add vibrant splashes of color to the marsh, which was a sea of grays and browns only days before. Muskrat and beaver, which have been traveling beneath the ice all winter, seem to take a sudden delight in cutting a V-wake across open water. Whitetail does appear awkward, their necks and hips thin and scraggly from a long winter, their bellies round with the fawns they're growing. And the most important harbinger of all, the sun rises early, stays late, and shines with a power it hasn't exhibited in months. New life, or at least omens of it, are everywhere.

While the long, warming days are welcome relief for the swamp animals that have survived a long winter, a careful observer will notice very little lazing about. April finds nearly every creature either courting, breeding, nesting, or preparing to deliver offspring. When summer arrives, when trees and grasses are their most lush and verdant, then animals can take a slight break in their frenetic activity to frolic. But April, for all its beauty, is a time to get down to business. There are mates to woo, homes to find, food to gather.

River rats follow the same rhythms as the animals of the swamp, and April is a busy time for them as well. While outdoor activities never cease no matter what the season, biting cold, deep snow, and fleeting light do reduce their intensity. When the new year arrives it's time to get out and explore the nooks and crannies of the world that went unvisited during the winter months. And, as I would discover, there is work to do as well.

"You interested in helping with some spring cleaning tomorrow?" Kenny asks me over the phone one evening. When I accept, his reply is one I'd come to know well in the year ahead. "Meet me at Big Lake Shack about nine o'clock."

The twisting two-track that leads to Big Lake Shack is an inviting entrance to the Whitman Swamp. There are other access points, of course: From the main channel of the river all one has to do is cross over the dike just upstream from Lock and Dam 5 northeast of Winona, Minnesota. Downstream there's a public landing where folk launch boats loaded with fishing tackle or hunting gear. But Kenny's drive is one of the best routes to reach the Whitman, traversing a low, scenic hardwood ridge that serves as a gradual transition from the bluffs, valleys, and farmland into the isolation that only a big backwater swamp can provide. In all but the worst flood years, you can drive the first three-quarters of a mile to Big Lake Shack, a small, dark hut that sits on the shores of Big Lake.

The first time I saw Big Lake Shack it struck me as somehow familiar, although I'd never seen it before. The shack is small, fourteen foot square at the most, with dark-stained, rough-sawn boards for siding. Small windows are cut in three sides, more to let in light than to capture any views. A small sign reading "Le Maison de

Salwey" hangs by the sturdy door, the antlers of a whitetail buck nailed above. Other decorations adorn the shack's exterior: snapping turtle shells; driftwood; a massive, coiled rope from a river barge; more deer racks. Glancing at the memorabilia, I wonder what special events they commemorate.

It hit me then: The shack is like the clubhouses and forts I built as a kid. I relished such retreats, as much for their impermanence as the shelter they provided. They were simple but serviceable, decorated with totems and symbols, and hosted some of my most memorable boyhood hours. If weather or an enemy laid them low, I was out nothing except the time spent rebuilding them. While infinitely more sturdy than anything I'd constructed in my youth, Big Lake Shack has the same feel—an exciting, cozy base camp for adventure.

Kenny pokes his head out the door as I ease the truck to a stop in front of the shack. April is only a few days old, and already Kenny's face, neck, and arms are a steer-hide brown—his French-Canadian lineage and years of outdoor living combine to make his skin bronze as soon as the sun hits it.

"Good morning, Scott."

His black Lab Spider echoes Kenny's greeting by thumping her tail against the cabin wall.

"Morning. Some kind of weather we're having, hey?"

"The rich men ain't the ones working today, that's for sure." We both laugh, thinking of images of poor souls chained to their desks on a day when even kids know they should be playing hooky.

The morning sun coats the shack with an auburn glow, but stepping inside is like entering a cave. The interior walls of Big Lake Shack are as dark as its siding, and it takes several seconds for my eyes to adjust to the dim surroundings. After they do, I scan the interior of the cozy shack. The wall immediately left of the heavy door is lined from floor to ceiling with four, sturdy bunks made of rough-sawn lumber. Old quilts, heavy blankets, and the occasional pillow are piled on the bunks. Spider, after nosing my palm in greeting, hops on her favorite bunk and curls into a corner.

On the west wall, sitting between and beneath two windows, is a rugged table and two benches. Small tins of condiments clutter one end of the table, as does a note scrawled by a visiting friend on a pad of paper; otherwise the table is clear and relatively clean. A cast-iron stove stands just in from the north wall, its sheet-metal stovepipe rising to the roofline. Skillets, pots, and cooking utensils hang from nails driven into the wall, within easy reach of the camp cook.

If the exterior of Big Lake Shack is adorned with totems, then the interior is a veritable museum. Dried herbs and flowers, photos of friends and loved ones, old tools, turkey feathers, Indian dream catchers, newspaper clippings, more turtle shells, another deer rack—items hang from each wall and the ceiling, too. In fact, there are so many that it's difficult to concentrate on just one and attempt a guess at it's origin and significance. When I drop my gaze, Kenny is looking at me and smiling. "Lot of memories hung in here," he says wistfully.

"I'd like to hear them sometime."

"You will. Have some of your own in here before long, I'd bet."

I let my concentration drift back to the wall behind the table, where I scan a yellowed newspaper clipping summarizing citations issued by local law enforcement officers. The third line reads, "Ken Salwey, Buffalo City, $25, leaving waterfowl decoys overnight." I point to the story and turn to Kenny. "You were famous."

"Ha!" he snorts. "Or infamous, depending on who you ask. When they wrote that, you didn't ask Jim Everson."

"That the warden who wrote that ticket?"

"Yup. Last of the great old-time river guys. He nailed me a few times like that in the old days. But mostly he missed me. That was a long time ago."

It's tough for me to visualize the Kenny I know in one of the epic struggles I relished reading about in my youth: the battle of wits between a grizzled woodsman who makes his own game laws and the straight-arrow warden intent on enforcing a stricter version. Of course, the man who struggled with Everson wasn't the Kenny that stands before me today—that was a different man, the one before the epiphany.

"We should get to work." Kenny's voice snaps me out of my reverie, and when I look toward the door, he's pulled a rug from the floor and is shaking it outside. I hop to and grab another, a woven rag throw with sand and mud grubbed into its colorful fibers. Stepping outside, I snap it several times in the fresh air, the dirt swirling about my head and shoulders. I'm looking for a place to hang the rug when Kenny clears his throat behind me. When I turn, he stands in the doorway, leaning on an ash walking stick.

"Cut you a walking stick the other day," he says, looking more at the stick than me. "I always use one, hiking this swamp and these hills. Surprising how handy they are. My dad always said to watch a guy carrying a walking stick—he's usually a good woodsman."

I thank him for the staff, then run my hands down its smooth, hard surface. Peeled ash, Kenny explains, is perfect walking-stick material: Strong as iron, it weathers slowly, yet still takes the luster of the user's hand as he or she grips and leans on the staff. "And it's nothing special, you know. Leave it somewhere and what have you lost? Not some fancy store-bought thing with carvings and inlays. Come on, let's go try it out."

"But I thought we were spring cleaning today."

"We're done!" Kenny announces. "I wanted to get those rugs shaken out and we did. You think I'm staying inside and washing windows on a day like this? Besides, we got two other shacks to visit."

As we pull on hip boots, Kenny explains that he'd like to show me his two other outcamps: the Tent Camp and the Marsh Shack, which both lie deeper in the swamp. Each camp provides convenient lodging as Kenny hunts, fishes, and traps in different areas of the Whitman.

Kenny tosses a burlap shoulder bag filled with water, apples, and sandwiches over his head, and Spider morphs from a bunk-lounger to a whirling dervish, eager to lead whatever journey we're embarking on. Kenny leads me down the quiet path as it winds north past the cabin, then ends abruptly near a narrow slough. Several canoes are tied at a rickety dock jutting into the water, but Kenny ignores them and we cross the head of the slough, our boots slipping through the still, cool water and into the muck beneath it. "Going to write a song about this black, boot-sucking mud some-day," Kenny insists, probing the slop ahead of him with his walking stick. "Ain't going to be Top 40, but folks that've been down here'll appreciate it."

Once we ford the slough, the walking becomes easy as we follow a long, dry ridge angling to the west. Silver maple, swamp white oak, and river birch bristle along the ridge, their crowns budding waxy green. Along the bank, cattails and bulrushes sprout and emerging beds of wild rice poke from the water's surface. We note deer tracks, the lumpy scat of raccoon, a scattering of owl pellets beneath a large maple. On virtually every bend we round we flush ducks, dozens and dozens of them: mallards, widgeon, teal, wood ducks, a pair of Canada geese—a cornucopia for waterfowl watchers.

And on the far shore of the slough, high in the branches of a cottonwood tree, is an eagle's nest. "Occupied for the last three summers," Kenny explains, pointing to the monstrous bundle of limbs and twigs resting in a sturdy crotch several dozen feet from the ground. "Wonder if they'll fledge a chick this year." As if on cue, a mature eagle wings over the water, rests briefly on a branch, then launches again and glides to the aerie, its huge head appearing as a white speck poking up from the center of the nest.

Two hundred yards past the eagle's nest we reach an old beaver dam that crosses the slough. The ends of the dam are clearly visible as they meet the wooded shore; mud and grass have grown over the jumble of sticks, making each end of the dam a part of the ridge. But the center of the dam has dissolved into the slough over the years, the water reclaiming its course. Nothing, Kenny points out, is ever permanent in nature.

On a small, oak-covered knoll shortly after the dam crossing we come to Tent Camp, Kenny's second-most-remote outpost. It is also the least permanent. While Kenny built Tent Camp on "the highest point in the swamp," he assumed correctly—this site in the Whitman is mere feet higher than the surrounding, flood-susceptible, terrain. Consequently, Tent Camp can float: Its foundation is a quartet of fifty-five-gallon steel drums that now rest on the forest duff, but have bobbed on Mississippi backwash through several spring floods.

Atop the barrels a simple, plywood decking serves as the floor, and log walls rest on the decking on three sides. One slender, sturdy oak log serves as a ridgepole that runs from back to front; over this Kenny has thrown a single sheet of military-spec tent canvas to serve as the roof. Another piece of canvas serves as the front wall. While Tent Camp is solid and sturdily built, I sense that the simple shelter is little more than an industrial-grade tepee in the midst of the swamp.

Despite its simple nature, Tent Camp has served Kenny well. A handy place to store supplies and equipment, the camp is also a welcome spot to rest after a long day of hunting or trapping the swamp. "Spent many an evening watching a fire here," Kenny says as we nose around the camp. "And laid up on a few hot summer days, waiting for the sun to cool off before heading back home."

It's then I remember that Kenny's conversion from reclusive loner—inspired by the simple request of the local warden—happened on a sweltering afternoon as he rested in camp.

"This where Everson visited you that day he wanted you to do the nature talk to those teachers?" I ask.

Kenny nods, grinning at the memory.

"How in the world did he ever know you had this spot back here?" Surrounded by a dizzying maze of sloughs, ridges, and marsh, Tent Camp would be hard to find even after someone had led you there.

"Remember what I said about those old wardens? Jim knew what was going on. Had an airboat that could go anywhere, and he used it. . . . Knew this swamp as well as I do."

I try to picture Kenny lounging around Tent Camp that day, hearing the approach of the whining airboat, knowing it had to be the warden, and wondering what trouble he'd face when Everson got there. They say you're least prepared for the things that change your life the most—a homily that surely proved itself true that hot summer day.

We spend a few minutes checking that Kenny's supplies and gear are intact, as well as mouse- and waterproof, then Kenny grabs his stick again and points it southwest. "We better go, if I'm going to show you the Marsh Shack."

We follow another twisted slough as it winds through the swamp, its banks lined with button brush, a woody shrub that bears dozens of round, seed-filled pods on its limbs. The bush grows in the water, and when the buttons fall they become instant duck food. Kenny recalls flushing dozens of mallards and wood ducks out of small sloughs choked with this unique plant. As we approach the end of the slough, Spider's tail begins wagging furiously and a trio of woodies launch themselves out of the water, their wings whapping button brush as they climb.

The ducks twist among tree limbs to gain altitude, then speed off. We follow their flight, and as they disappear, I notice the horizon ahead changing. The treeline fades and is replaced by azure sky and cirrus clouds. "That's the big marsh out there," Kenny says. "Looks different, don't it?"

"It does," I nod. "Makes you realize how big the swamp is."

The vast expanse of cattails, bulrushes, and reeds is dizzying, like seeing the prairie for the first time. Kenny points his stick toward the end of a small ridge, adorned by large oaks and maples.

"Marsh Shack's over there. You can see the roofline if you look close."

Staring hard, I can barely make out a horizontal line. We walk toward the shack, Kenny plodding surely ahead while I—eager to reach the cabin—prance impatiently behind him. Finally I settle for a simple sidestep so we can walk side by side. While Kenny's pace seems frustrating, I'll learn in the months ahead that he moves like a turtle: slow, but steady and sturdy regardless of terrain, weather, or fatigue.

We reach the Marsh Shack long after I feel we should. Then I realize that the change in topography has made me severely underestimate the distance and the time required to cover it. "Seems like this was closer than I figured," I offer. "When you first pointed at it, I thought we were almost there."

"That mistake's been made before, Scott. That's one reason I treasure these shacks; they kept me from sleeping on the ground more than once when I got caught out here."

Distances, I'm learning, are all relative in the swamp; even if you calculate your yardage well—and most folks can't—the terrain promises you probably won't get there in a hurry.

The Marsh Shack is the only one of his three shacks that Kenny did not build. Its former owner was an old-time river rat named Kermit Spieth who held title to a chunk of the Whitman for many years, and the shack was his getaway. Kermit was a trapper and duck hunter himself, and as Kenny was learning his way round the swamp, Kermit was out there roaming his own land. Kenny recognized Kermit's ground for the paradise it was, but wouldn't set foot on it out of respect for the older swamp-runner, who was a family friend. It wasn't long, however, before Kermit's age began limiting his travels; his acreage was deep in the Whitman, and accessing it, much less shooting ducks or setting traps there, was meant for those with younger, stronger legs. One day, Kermit approached Kenny and asked if he'd be interested in trapping his land and using the shack. Kenny jumped on the offer like a mallard piling into wild rice, and he used the shack for many seasons, eventually patterning the construction of Big Lake Shack after Kermit's marsh abode.

Consequently, the Marsh Shack seems like a hybrid between the shacks we'd just visited. Like the Tent Camp, Marsh Shack rests on barrels, ready to ride out the high-water seasons that visit the Whitman with regularity. But Marsh Shack resembles the Big Lake Shack's more finished appeal with its sturdy roof, four walls, and windows. Ironically, Marsh Shack, which lies nearly dead-center in the Whitman in some of the Upper Miss's most remote habitat, is made with stud walls and clapboard siding. The shack is still a bare-bones structure with no insulation and few creature comforts, but it does look decidedly civilized for such a remote, harsh neighborhood.

As Kenny searches the backside of some nearby trees to find the key he's hidden, I look around at the open cattail marsh surrounding the Marsh Shack. Mallards quack and gabble in the nearby reeds, and I spot several pairs of Canada geese skating across patches of open water. Red-winged blackbirds dance on the ends of nearby cattails, flaring their gorgeous wings and crying their joy—or displeasure—at our presence. I'm staring at a copse of willows on the far end of the marsh, about a half-mile away I guess, when Kenny steps up to my side.

"That's where this shack used to sit, you know."

"There? Across all those cattails and water? How'd it wind up over here?"

"Good question. Happened several years ago, shortly after Kermit sold his land to the state. I was in town one day when a friend came up to me. He worked for the DNR, liked to hunt and trap, too. He pulled me aside and said, 'Kenny, you didn't hear this from me and I know nothing about it, but the department's going into Kermit's land before ice-out and burning down that shack. They don't want a building like that on state property—too much liability if someone gets hurt in it.'

"I thanked him and went home to think. It was dead of winter then, but I knew I had to do something to save that shack. So I called a friend, Mike Roach, who hunted with me and stayed in the shack during deer season. He and his dad, who was an engineer, took a couple of evenings and made a twelve-foot-long pair of steel skis, or runners, that would fit under those barrels. Then they drove up here in an old Willys Jeep that Mike's dad owned. That afternoon, Mike's dad managed to drive that old Jeep out to the shack, me leading the way, poking the ice with a spud to make sure it was strong enough, Mike sawing logs with a chainsaw and clearing stuff in front of his dad. By nightfall we were froze and exhausted, but we cooked supper in the shack and rolled into the bunks to sleep.

"In the morning it was freezing cold, but after breakfast we went out and jacked up the shack and slid those skis under the barrels on each side. Then we took a cable, hooked it to two corners of the shack and ran it back to the Jeep. Then Mike and I went across the marsh, clearing a path between the shack and this spot right here, well off the state boundary. Most of it was clear—just ice and snow and cattails laid down—but there was a stand of big willows that'd been chewed by the beaver. The ends of those willows was like little spear points sticking up through the ice. So we had to saw them all off flush with the ice so the Jeep wouldn't get a flat tire.

"When it come time to go, Mike's dad started up that Jeep. I looked at him and said, 'Once you get that thing moving, don't stop for nothing or that shack'll keep going and wind up in your backseat.' He just smiled and revved that engine, then started creeping forward, getting the shack started. Well he followed my advice real well, because once he got going he never looked back; the Jeep grinding across that ice and the shack coming behind, swaying back and forth so much I swore it'd tip on its side any second. Mike and I ran ahead, cheering him on and praying he wouldn't get stuck. But he kept plugging across that marsh, heading for the spit of land we're standing on right now.

"When he reached the edge of this little ridge, Mike's dad give her hard, knowing he had to not only get the Jeep up the bank, but have enough steam to pull the shack behind him. Mike and I stood behind and watched as the Jeep disappeared into the trees and held our breath. The shack hit that bank so hard it sounded like an explosion, the shack swaying hard right, then back the other way as each of those skis hit the solid ground. I thought the shack would cave in on itself just from being jerked around so bad; I could picture the roof falling in and the siding ripping off right there. But all of a sudden it came to rest, right at this spot, and it's been here to this day.

"When we walked up to check on Mike's dad, he was still in the driver's seat, staring behind him, his face as flush as a tomato. That shack had come to a stop about a foot from his rear bumper."

I roar at the tale and Kenny nods in delight, grateful I can appreciate the herculean task that was performed that cold winter day. Some might view skiing the shack as stealing. Most around these parts, however, would figure the state bought the land, after all—not the shack. And even if the DNR did own Marsh Shack, it was destined for razing, so what did they care if it had mysteriously moved a half-mile onto private property? Whatever the case, the cross-country relocation was a subtle, but firm, act of defiance; a trump card that showed an old riverman could still play cat-and-mouse with the best of them.

Kenny opens Marsh Shack and waves me in. The bare, clean interior is light and airy, like this fine spring day. Spider crawls onto one of the bunks and curls up, asleep almost instantly. Kenny opens the burlap sack and we have our lunch: dense rye bread, slabs of venison sausage, and chunks cut from a round of smoky cheddar cheese, all washed down with cold water from a jug. The meal is as simple and satisfying as can be. We eat and talk and look out the windows, watching a heron wade in the marsh, hunting frogs and fish.

While the April sun is gaining power, it's still not in the sky very long this time of year. As it begins to descend toward the Minnesota bluffs, Kenny and I grab our walking sticks once more and begin a leisurely walk that will lead us back to Big Lake Shack. Spider, sensing our purpose, wanders farther ahead now, leading the way and setting a firm pace. Kenny leads me on a slightly larger loop this time, into a large stand of white oaks known as the Big Woods.

"Good deer hunting in here when the acorns are falling," Kenny promises. "You'll have to give it a try this fall, learn how to hunt these 'wet-tails.'"

I smile and thank him, but right now fall seems so far away, both in distance and in thought. Right now we're celebrating the New Year, and I want the revelry to last as long as possible.

RAT TALE

Big Boy and Beauty

KENNY TELLS THE TALE: In the marshy lands of the Whitman Swamp rests a body of water called Big Lake. On the shores of this lake I built a little outpost shack one summer. Solid, sturdy, earthy, yet homey, Big Lake Shack sits nestled in the forest on a small grassy bank near water's edge.

I laid out the shack about five long paces, squared, on top of four large, squared-off chunks of hill-country limestone that support each corner. The walls I crafted from home-sawn, green, oak lumber, and not one board is the same thickness as the other. The gaps in the horizontal wood siding are covered with narrow baton boards. The floor is double oak-plank with sand-filled cracks. Not one lick of insulation can be found anywhere. Four, hinged windows, two on each wall opposite the others, let light in through the east and west. A double-thickness door with a leather-strap handle is set between the two windows in the east wall. It serves as entry and exit, and swings outward on three long, wide, barn hinges. Several railroad spikes held in place with nails keep the door shut when I'm away from the shack.

Along the interior south wall stand four, single-width wooden bunks covered with a hodgepodge of blankets, quilts, and sleeping bags. Hinged to the west wall is an oak-plank table, supported by two collapsible legs and skirted on either side by rough-oak benches. On the north wall, I've hung an array of kitchen gear—cast-iron frying pans, pots, lids, and such—along with the necessary eating tools. In one corner, a woodbox is filled to the brim with seasoned firewood. About three feet out from the "kitchen wall" sits a heavy, firebrick-lined, wood-burning stove with a stovepipe chimney going straight up through a metal-lined hole in the roof boards.

Used tin covers the roof, which overhangs all four sides by a foot or so.

Once built, I coated the entire outside surface with used motor oil, which accounts for the dark, mahogany color of the wood. All around the outside walls hang traps, hand-woven nets, deer antlers, old canoe paddles, and the skeletons of several thirty- to forty-pound "mud cats"—flathead catfish.

Inside, the shack's rafters are a virtual museum of swamp natural history. Turtle shells, dried roots, herbs, jars filled with special stones, and practical as well as whimsical memorabilia of all kinds hang everywhere.

The wild fragrance that permeates everything is perhaps the most unforgettable aspect of Big Lake Shack. A mixture of catnip, dank old clothes, wild ginger, swamp water, wild sage, and woodsmoke give one a strong hint of the life that's been lived here.

I called this shack home for many years when I trapped day after day and sometimes even into the night. I got to know Big Lake and its critters mighty good. The lake and its surrounding marshes are home to lots of animals. I've killed some of the critters that live on Big Lake, but never once did I do so just to watch them die, to see the fire of life leave their eyes. I killed them so that I, myself, might live. Perhaps a strange concept. But in the end I was taught many lessons by the critters on Big Lake. And I will never forget those lessons: They are set solidly in my heart.

Goose hunting is quite popular in the Big Lake Country of the Mississippi River. But it wasn't so long ago that there weren't any such birds living here. Back twenty or so years, the only wild geese we saw were those of the migrating kind. Each springtime and autumn they would follow the ancient pathways in the sky along the Big River. What caused them to begin nesting here, to become full-time residents as some are now, I cannot say. All I know is what I am about to describe.

Big Boy and Beauty were a pair of giant Canada geese—but much more than just a pair of geese as it turned out.

One day, I was out trapping spring muskrats on Big Lake. I guess I heard them before I saw them. They came in low, talking to each other. They made two or three circles, ever lower. In perfect unison they'd turn, like a pair of fighter planes. They settled down with a *swoosh* on Big Lake. They talked back and forth contentedly and swam off into the cattails and bulrushes along the shore.

From that day on, I began to observe Big Boy and Beauty, as I called them, the first pair of giant Canada geese to nest on Big Lake. I came to understand their life cycles, their habits, their personalities. Every spring, in the years that followed, I looked forward to seeing them come back to Big Lake. I watched them in their mating ritual. I saw Big Boy chase off intruding ganders. Beauty would build her nest with great care on the little island that sits in the middle of Big Lake, relatively safe from predators and intruders. I watched as they hatched their goslings. Like little yellow cotton balls, they would float about on the water with mom and dad to their front and back. Soon they started feeding on insects in the high grasses.

One year the water was high and Beauty built her nest on top of a deserted muskrat house. The water rose enough to float the muskrat house. Day in and day out, week upon week—twenty-nine days to be exact—she rode that nest, back and forth across Big Lake, whichever way the wind blew. When I'd approach her with my canoe, she'd lay her head and neck flat on the muskrat house, trying not to be seen. I heard her fight off the raccoons, mink, and owls. A goose is a formidable fighter, let me tell you.

Several years later on another spring day, I was once again muskrat trapping. I placed a trap on an old muskrat hut on the island in Big Lake, never thinking of the consequences. I stuck the trap in place with a forked stick. As Spider and I came around the point of the island, we saw that the stake was gone. The muskrat house was leveled—nothing left of it. But goose feathers were everywhere, and I knew immediately that I had caught one of my friends. I followed a trail of feathers off into the bulrushes. There sat Big Boy, thoroughly water soaked. Exhausted. As I approached, Spider jumped out of the canoe. Big Boy summoned up enough strength to flap and flop his way out of the bulrushes, pulling the stake and trap behind him. I was able to make out that the trap had Big Boy caught only by the webbing of one foot.

If I could just catch him and get a hold of that trap, I thought, I could set him free and he'd be none the worse for wear. So the chase began. I loaded Spider back up, and she showered me with water spray. I told her to sit and stay in the front of the canoe. We chased Big Boy out into the middle of Big Lake. Every time I got close enough to grab the stake or trap chain, the big male goose would dive. In the clear, spring-fed water, I watched him. He couldn't swim, but he used his wings to literally "fly" under the water. His underwater flight was almost dreamlike as I drifted and paddled with the canoe and watched him. When he came up for air and I'd get close to him, he'd dive again. Finally, I was able to grab the trap chain. Big Boy began to splash and fight. All the while, Beauty circled overhead, six, eight, maybe ten feet off the water. A few times, she almost took the hat off my head. Crying, squawking, complaining, begging, encouraging her lifetime mate to keep trying to get away, to keep on fighting for his life.

I managed to get a hold of the trap spring and press it down. Big Boy swam away. Slowly he made his way to a nearby muskrat house and crawled up to the top of it. Beauty came swinging in, a foot or two off the water, and landed right beside him. Contentedly they began to rub their heads and necks together, almost as if they were hugging. They preened each other's feathers. I just sat there in awe, drifting with the gentle springtime breeze. The sun broke through the clouds and the two geese stood highlighted on top of the 'rat house. They turned in unison and looked at me as if to say, "There, you big ugly critter! We're still together. No matter what!"

From that day on, I no longer hunted geese at Big Lake. Not because I feel it is wrong to hunt geese, it's just wrong for me. I learned how loyal geese are to each other. They mate for life. When they say "We are one!" they mean it. No questions about it. No ifs, ands, or buts. In my years as a guide, I had seen many a hunter shoot a goose down. The survivor would swing back around and fly right over, looking for its fallen mate.

And so, now, even today, Big Boy and Beauty live on. They are getting up there in years. And I know that one day, only one will come back. Maybe neither one. But they have raised many young, and those offspring come back to this marsh because they know the path to their roots, their heritage. They will carry on.

When the raw, fierce winds of March fill this great river valley and the winter's ice lies black, honeycombed, and rotting upon the waters of the swamp, I know a milder, gentler day will soon come. The ice will disappear beneath quiet, rippling waves carried by a warm south breeze. A redwinged blackbird will foretell of April showers from its perch atop a swaying cattail. Beyond the melody of the red-wing's song, I will hear the call of the wild goose. There will always be a Big Boy and Beauty on Big Lake.

MAY

River Rat Almanac

IN MAY, THE Big River promises new life, lushness, and growth by scouring, cleansing, and rejuvenating all that its homeless waters touch. Snow waters from the north make the Big River angry and restless, but now it's starting to relax and enjoy its journey in the warm sunshine.

The Big River has gotten bigger, deeper, broader, and swifter since the mid-April snow melt began along its tributaries. Water has inundated every island, lowland meadow, and backwater marsh, as it has done for eons. The river is seeking its own course.

After a flood, some of us riverfolk go on daily treasure hunts, picking up barrels, lumber, and such, but the most precious treasures are the wild, natural ones. One can once again smell the earth and the waters and the green things. Bloodroot, skunk cabbage, marsh marigolds, and many varieties of sedge grasses are springing up along the backwaters.

April showers have brought May flowers in gay profusion. Color is everywhere—shades of green, blue, and white, with a touch of yellow, pink, and brown added in just the right places. Wild violets, May apple, and wild ginger grow in almost every glen and hollow. The fragrance of plum and apple blossoms, flower blooms, fresh earth, and old leaves wafts upon the breeze. A short hike through the hills and dales makes me feel like I'm browsing in an art gallery, perfume shop, and greenhouse all rolled up in one.

Trout Fishing and Morel Picking

If you're not a river rat, May is a beautiful month in the river valley. Hillsides that only days ago seemed barren and brown are
suddenly full of summer's promise. Stately oaks leaf out in pale-
green splendor. Violets, trillium, and orchids add splashes of color
to the bluffs. Songbird pairs work madly to feed their hatchlings,
their vibrant plumage and melodic singing impossibly beautiful. If
June is the month when people marry, then May seems ripe for
proposal—a period of hope, beauty, and the promise of renewal.

But if you're a river rat, May is a month of deception and secrecy. Sociable folk for the rest of the year, rats skulk about in May,
avoiding their friends if they can, and lying brazenly to them if
they can't. Reclusive to the point of paranoia, a late-spring river rat
makes Howard Hughes seem like a gadabout and the Yeti an exhibit in a carnival freak show. Come May Day, a rat will turn himself inside-out to avoid you on the street. Chase after him and he'll
flee like a Hollywood star with tabloid photographers on his heels.

The reason for this suddenly odd behavior? The answer can be
found in any remote valley laced by a cold, free-running stream. To
divine the reason explaining these springtime shenanigans, one must
visit such a valley in May, shuck off socks and footgear, and stand
in the stream. The initial shock of cold water will, at first, make
certain parts of the anatomy switch places, but then a gentle numb-
ness takes over and the mystery is revealed. If you've chosen your
location well, there will be fish finning gently against the stream
bottom, their sleek outlines undulating in the current.

They're trout, of course, and May marks the peak of trout fishing in bluff country. For some folk, trout fishing is recreation, a chance to cast a line on beautiful water and maybe catch a fish or two. For folks like Kenny, trout season is like Lent and his best waters are cherished temples—locales so closely guarded his own mother wouldn't stand a chance of gleaning their whereabouts from a deathbed confession.

That Minnesota and Wisconsin bluff country hosts four-star trouting is no secret; any number of pamphlets, maps, and tourism brochures can tell the neophyte where *salmo* can be found. But those are the places everyone knows. What the guides don't show are the shaded sections of stream most anglers overlook, the locations of deep, dark holes that plunge beneath tree roots, the braided currents pushing against grass-covered banks. These are the spots where big trout live, and finding them involves miles of walking in hip boots over rock and root, stone and stump. They're not divulged cheaply, and the lengths some will go to protect their secret spots are legendary. While it's generally acknowledged that all anglers are liars, fanatical trouters take dishonesty to pathological levels.

So when Kenny calls, inviting me on a mid-May trout safari, I know better than to ask where we'd be fishing. This is a faux pas akin to querying newlyweds on what they did during their honeymoon; you might get an answer, but don't be hurt if the blushing bride lies like a felon to your face.

"Meet me at the junction of Trout Run Road and HH at three o'clock," Kenny says. "We'll go in my car from there. Bring a spinning rod, your hip boots, some hooks and sinkers, a sandwich, and some water."

"Am I getting blindfolded?" I ask, half in jest.

"I'll think on that," he replies sincerely.

I am early for the rendezvous, knowing that such meet-times can be crucial, as hard-core trouters frequently have tails—not like a dog—like someone who follows them. These tails have to be eluded, and the timing for a clean getaway can be critical. When Kenny's dull green Catalina pulls in behind my truck, I whisk my gear from the front seat, pop open my door, and call to my golden retriever Cody to follow me. Kenny is looking nervously in the rearview mirror as we wriggle into the vehicle, and the car is rolling before I slam the door shut.

"Good switchover," he whispers. "I see you've done this before."

"Once or twice," I pant out the window.

Since Kenny doesn't mention the blindfold again, I don't either, but after a few minutes of driving it's clear I'm being given the roundabout tour to muddy my recollection of our route. It would have worked too, except when we pull down a slight grade on a sand road, cross an old iron bridge, and park by some cottonwoods close to an abandoned farmstead, I know exactly which creek we are on. I'd never fished it, but had chased turkeys and deer in the surrounding bluffs and knew its name well. Out of respect for Kenny's elaborate approach, however, I never let on.

We rig our rods as we stand together by the trunk, Spider and Cody frisking each other, eager to explore. Upon Kenny's advice, I'd rig my spinning reel with eight-pound test line, and following his lead I pull it through the rod guides and tie on a size ten hook. Kenny pulls a snuff tin full of lead sinkers from his shirt pocket and rattles it. "Put one of these about a foot up from your hook," he instructs. "Then take one of these."

When I look up, Kenny's bronzed hand holds a wriggling, squirming red worm toward me.

"These your magic trout bait?" I ask somewhat incredulously.

"Sometimes they are," he replies matter-of-factly. "But today they're for catching bait. You ever trout-fished with a chub tail?"

I had, but it had been years since I used the technique. Actually, most of my recent trout fishing had been with a fly rod, a pleasing way to catch fish, but sometimes maddeningly complex and full of rules of etiquette, either expressed or understood. Like most trouters, though, I'd learned—and fell in love with—the sport while fishing with bait and keeping most of my brooks and browns instead of catching and releasing them. For some reason, I now find the prospect of returning to those methods most refreshing and relish the chance to relearn from Kenny.

With red worms impaled and gyrating on our hooks, we wade through short grass to get to the stream. Roosevelt Creek (which, you should assume, is an alias) is running slightly high and a little off-color—nearly perfect bait-fishing conditions. As we slip up on the stream, the dogs bounce past us and dive in, pushing waves ahead of them, sure to spook fish for many yards up and downstream. I am about to holler my displeasure at Cody when Kenny chuckles softly. "Just look at them. Running and swimming just for the fun of it. Always give the first hole to the dog, I say. Let them enjoy themselves, then we can get on with fishing."

Spider finally chases Cody out on the bank, so we walk a few steps upstream of their frolic to a small pool marked by riffles and emerging stones. "This is a good place to get chubs," Kenny says. "Throw that red worm in there and see what you can find."

I click the bail on my reel, keep a finger on the line to check it, then pitch the worm to the deep water on the far side of the bank. In an instant I feel a frantic tapping and set the hook, only to feel the light squirming of a chub on my line. Reeling the small fish in, I grab for it with my left hand, press it in my palm, then turn to Kenny for instruction.

The first step in making a good chub, or sucker, tail bait is to find a fish of the proper size, Kenny explains. Too small and the point is lost: You may as well use the minnow itself for bait. Too large and your offering will intimidate the trout. The wriggling chub I grasp is about three inches long, a perfect sucker-tail candidate. "Why don't you show me how this is done?" I ask Kenny, thrusting the minnow at him.

"No problem. Got a knife?"

I produce a small jackknife as Kenny leans his rod against a nearby bush and grabs the chub by the head. Taking the knife from me, Kenny makes a vertical cut reaching down to the chub's backbone, just behind the dorsal fin. Turning his knife ninety degrees, he then follows the backbone out to the tail to complete the cut. The finished product, then, suggests a smaller minnow that's more trout-sized than the whole critter. Chub tails also appeal to trout—especially big ones—because they smell like fresh meat and, naturally, have the flavor and texture of the real deal. Any comparison to commercial lures is a far greater compliment to the artificial than the other way around.

Kenny hands the chub tail back to me with instructions on properly hooking the thing. "The secret is to hook it just once, starting on the underside with the hook point, then burying it in the meat as you go. You don't want the trout to feel the hook when they grab that bait. And this ain't like chucking hardware or floating dry flies—the take will be real soft, not an explosion around the lure like you're probably used to."

Using Kenny's ample supply of homegrown red worms we catch several more chubs, saving them in a small jar Kenny carries for that purpose. Three rough fish into our trout outing and I am already enjoying myself. Part of it is the simple joy of catching fish, the rest is the ease of it. While some veteran anglers liken fishing to a religious quest—where the size of the quarry or difficulty of fooling them is elevated to the near-spiritual, all anglers secretly want to catch lots of fish, all the time. And while it's a hoot reeling in sophisticated, moody fish, anyone who tells you there's no joy in catching some of the gullible species is lying through their polarized glasses. I've caught everything from stunted bluegills to trophy muskies, and reeling in these little dace was as much fun as I'd had fishing in a year.

After collecting a half-dozen chubs, we move on in search of big trout. Indeed, the very section of stream we're standing in is de facto trophy water; no signs are posted or stories written about it, but Kenny and a handful of others knew the pigs were here. Three miles above our parking area is a glorious section of stream known for its perfect (and manmade) habitat and ice-cold, burbling currents. Signs proclaim the first-rate fishing area, and fancy vehicles driven by well-equipped dudes are parked by those markers throughout the season. But as one hikes downstream, things change. The water is slightly warmer and more sluggish; the only habitat work is done by grazing cattle. Each evening, trout dimple the surface of the upstream section as they slurp flies. Downstream the creek remains serene, twisting its way past abandoned farmsteads and rusted machinery. There are fewer trout here, but they are bigger, and very few people know about them.

So the tracks of hip-booted anglers end far upstream, where the signs pronounce official trout water. "We won't see anyone here today, or any other day we come back here," Kenny winks at me as we wander upstream. "Besides the big fish, that's the other advantage of fishing where trout aren't supposed to be."

This downstream section of Roosevelt Creek twists through pastures and meadows, thick brush growing on banks too steep for cattle to graze, stately cottonwoods shading the stream elsewhere. Kenny stops where the creek snakes against a brushy bank, the water curling under a pair of rotting logs that had fallen in midstream. "Good place here," he says quietly. The dogs, sensing our change of attitude, sit close to our knees and watch as Kenny lobs a chub tail upstream of the logs.

"The trick is to have enough weight on the line to get the bait down to the big trout, but not so much that it can't drift naturally," Kenny says. "I'll work this side of those logs, you pitch onto the other, if you can."

Following Kenny's lead, I make a short, arcing cast to the far bank, where the current gently pulls my bait toward the logs. The water slows as it deepens and the chub tail follows suit. I can feel it bumping along the bottom—hanging up for a second, pulling free again, tumbling in the current. I imagine a big brown finning among the logs, catching the scent of the freshly cut minnow.

Large brown trout are, for the most part, meat-eating predators. While juvenile fish readily chase insects throughout their stages of growth, adult fish are like any wolf or coyote—they want as much food for the effort as possible, so they concentrate on large prey: minnows, sculpins, mice, sometimes even small birds or ducklings. Once a brown reaches adulthood, it changes from an enthusiastic, flamboyant fly-chaser to a skulking, sullen ogre afraid to move in daylight. Hugging the bottom of deep pools or tucked among sunken root and stream bottom rock, its life is so secretive that most anglers never know the big brown even exists.

The process of catching such monsters with bait is, in terms of tackle, simple. But the execution is anything but. The trouter must sneak to known lairs, keeping his or her foot tread light and shadow off the water. The angler will ignore water occupied by lesser fish, concentrating on specific big-brown pools and runs, cutbanks and eddies. And the trouter will exercise a steady patience that few can muster. His or her take of fish will be a fraction of most trouters, but even the average fish will be ones to remember. It is not an endeavor for the weak of heart.

On my sixth drift, I feel my bait hesitate slightly. It's only a slight hitch, a momentary interruption in the natural drift I've felt a half-dozen times before. My first guess is the chub tail has hit a rock, but when I gently lift the rod tip to free it, the line moves slightly upstream.

"Something's got my bait," I say softly.

"Sure it's not a snag?" Kenny asks calmly.

"Yes." Keeping my index finger on the line beneath my reel, I feel a gentle thrumming, assurance that something very alive is attached to it.

"Don't tighten the line or he'll spit it out. Just reel in some slack so your line is pointing at the fish," Kenny says. I follow his directions, but can no longer feel the tapping. "Raise your rod tip slowly and keep your finger on the line. Can you feel him now?"

The gentle tapping returns for a second, then stops. "I think he's still there."

"Good. Give him some time. Sing 'Three Blind Mice' twice through. Then reel in the slack and haul back and set the hook." I search my memory for the lyrics to the children's song, then launch into a soft chorus. I'm repeating "See how they run" when I notice Kenny grinning.

"Better stick to your day job," he teases.

"I'm fishing here!" I retort.

I finish the second chorus, slowly reel the line taut, then yank back on the rod. The resistance is immediate and intense—the trout bulldogging for the cover of the logs, bending the rod tip with sharp raps and steady pulling. I see a broad, butter-colored flank flash once, then disappear. It's a good trout, not a great one. Realizing I'm not fast to a trophy, I shorten the battle, horsing the brown out from the logs on his next run. Cody presses against my legs and whimpers, his head cocked puppylike as he watches the flailing fish. When I kneel by the bank and scoop the trout onto shore, Kenny laughs as both dogs stick their noses in to investigate. The sixteen-inch brown is broad and strong, a good eating size. I hold the fish up for the four of us to admire: The red spots on his side are like dollops of paint on a cream-colored canvas. Kenny murmurs approval as I slip the fish into his creel. "Couple more like that and we'll have a meal."

"Let's get them then," I say, suddenly full of confidence.

But it will take a solid hour for us to tangle with another. We try several promising holes with no luck, then we each miss strikes from trout that swim off with our carefully prepared bait. We dig into Kenny's red worms and collect a few more small suckers, then tromp upstream again. When we reach a dark, chocolate-colored pool pushing against a cut bank, Kenny nods and tells me to fish on. "Sorry," I murmur. "Got to visit the bushes for a minute. You go ahead."

"You sure? I can wait. This hole's always got a good one."

"I bet it does, but you'll have to show it to me—I'm past desperate."

The dogs follow me back to the tree line, and I've barely snuck in the woods when I hear splashing water back at the creek. I'm too far into the woods to see Kenny, but the tip of his rod, bending and jumping above the stream bank, is clearly visible. "What've you got down there?" I yell over my shoulder. Only the sounds of splashing greet my query.

Rushing to finish business, I hurry down to the stream to see

Kenny land a long, slab-sided trout half-again the size of mine—its huge tail smacking the grassy bank in defiance, the broad flank as wide as my palm, its hook jaw giving the fish an eaglelike appearance. Most river valley fishermen wait a lifetime for one fish such as this, a wild brown grown so large it barely resembles a trout. Kenny is breathing heavily as he kneels by the monster. "He hit that chub on the first drift. I was halfway through the song when he swam downstream toward that brushpile. Knew I had to set the hook before he got there."

The dogs crowd in on Kenny, trying to lick the flopping trophy. Kenny brushes them back, trying to unhook the fish. The dogs wag their tails happily, enjoying the game, and playfully slam against Kenny, knocking him backward on the bank. I yell at them to come, slapping my hand against my thigh, as they look toward me. When I look back at Kenny, he's on his haunches and staring at the water. Following his gaze I see the monster trout, which has flopped free from the line and lies in the shallows, struggling for deeper water. Kenny leans forward, hands outstretched, and lunges for the fish. With a spasmodic slap of its tail the trout is gone, torpedoing toward the middle of the stream and spraying Kenny in the face as it escapes.

I can't think of a thing to say. Kenny stares dully at the creek. Even the dogs are silent and look from the water back at us, seeming to sense the improbability of what they've witnessed. How do you explain such a fish tale? It's as if a mermaid had jumped out on a rock, granted a wish, then disappeared before you could grab a camera.

Kenny finally breaks the silence, laughing—as only he seems capable—at something that would break most men's hearts. "Guess now I can tell folks about 'The One That Got Away,'" he says, making the little quotation marks in the air with his fingers.

"How big was that fish?" I ask. The trout seemed as big as a salmon as it splashed away, and had only grown larger in my mind in the moments following its escape.

"Twenty-five inches, maybe longer," Kenny sighs. "Too big to eat. Good thing we lost him!"

In the next several minutes we'll each retell the trout story as we saw it, Kenny shaking his head at the quick strike and strong run of the brown, my tale of interrupted personal business adding comic relief to the frantic battle. While Kenny had caught bigger trout in his forty-some years of wandering these streams, he knows the years and miles that separate such fish. "I'll probably be an old bastard before I tangle with another one like that," he finally says. I'd like to comfort him, but know he may be right.

What most anglers learn the hard way is that botching a trophy is not the worst thing. The worst thing is putting your line in the water again. You know your chances at another monster are nearly zero. The prospect of tangling with something smaller is disappointing. You may fish on, but your mind is no longer that of an angler: Instead of a heart full of hope and anticipation, you watch your line and replay the recent past with a melancholy tune for accompaniment.

So we continue up the creek, trying to screw our enthusiasm back up before reaching the next hole. We climb a small rise, leaving the streambed as it oxbows and going overland to rejoin it further upstream. The dogs lead the way, chasing each other for short bursts, then throwing themselves to the ground to roll and dry themselves. The May sun is resting on the western hilltops, and we hear the distant gobble of a turkey heading to roost.

"Would you look at that!"

I snap my head toward Kenny, who had stopped in midstride to stare at a tree in front of him. I follow his eyes and catch my breath in a little gasp. We had stumbled onto a bunch of morel mushrooms, standing like little sentinels around an aging elm. We kneel slowly in front of a springtime bonanza as wonderful as they come.

"Look at the size of these!" I chortle. "How many do you think there are?"

"Hundred, anyway." Kenny says, eyeing the bounty before us. "Enough for supper, that's for sure."

Morels are no secret to river valley folk. Perhaps the tastiest wild mushrooms in the area, they're also among the easiest to identify: Their elongated, spongelike cap resembles a "brain on a stem" in one guidebook's description. Few outdoor lovers who venture forth in spring have failed to pick a bunch of morels, and some 'shroomers hunt them with true zeal. Most folk keep them for personal use, eating fresh mushrooms as long as they can find—or stand—them, preserving bigger harvests by drying them for later consumption. Some even pick for profit: The going rate for morels, which are shipped to big-city restaurants, may be as high as ten dollars per pound. Kenny and I are surrounded by some serious pocket change, but our thoughts are on anything but money.

Kenny reaches into the back pocket of his trousers and pulls out a wrinkled grocery sack, sliding a hand inside it and smacking it open. "Never go anywhere in May without one of these," he says, winking at me. Until he produced the bag, I'd given no thought to how we were going to transport our bounty. But we quickly set to the task of picking, sliding our fingers down to the base of each mushroom stem, pinching it firmly between thumb and forefinger, and twisting it off. One by one we slide the brown, earthy-smelling morels into the sack, crawling around on our knees to reach the fungi as we finish picking the candidates nearest us.

We are only halfway through our harvest when I realize something wonderful has happened: We have forgotten, or at least stopped talking about, The Fish That Got Away. Morels can do that to a person, partly because they're so treasured, and partly because this is such a windfall crop. You can know all about where mushrooms are supposed to grow—by just-dead elm trees, on south-facing slopes, in well-drained hillsides—but fungi don't read books or listen to theories. Finding morels can be done through lots of hard work, but the best batches I've plundered have been the result of luck. Following this fence line instead of that one. Looking right instead of left. Stopping to tie a boot and peeking up just so. One minute you're just walking through the woods, the next you have a reason to invite friends over for a feast.

The haunting *Who-cooks-for-you?* cry of a barred owl echoes from the hillsides as we pick the last of the stand. The dogs, who've waited patiently as we played in the dirt, are now anxious to go. They know the way back to the vehicle and demand we follow them. Light is fading quickly as we meander down the streambed, retracing our tracks by feel as much as sight. A lone whippoorwill is calling urgently as we reach the bridge, and the shrill chanting of spring peepers increases in volume to meet the rising moon.

The ride to my truck is slow and quiet, the frantic pace and backward glances of the sneak out noticeably absent. We are at ease with ourselves, a good way to end a fishing trip that could have been remembered only as one where a trophy was lost. The warm air of the May evening pulses through the windows, and in minutes the dogs are snoring their contentment from the back seat. Kenny takes no diversionary roads this trip, and we reach my truck in a fraction of the time it took to find the stream.

"You plan on coming over for supper tomorrow night, Scott," Kenny says as he brakes next to my pickup. "We got some good eating to take care of."

"I'll do that. You name the time and I'll be there."

"Six o'clock. And bring an appetite."

I nod and smile, then grab my gear to go. Kenny waits to make sure my truck will start. I'm about to wave him off when it occurs to me that I should reassure Kenny I won't tell anyone where we've been this special night. I slide out of the cab and walk quickly to his open window.

"I just wanted you to know I knew the name of this creek, but won't ever tell anyone."

"I know you won't," Kenny smiles and nods.

"You do?"

"Wouldn't have taken you there if I'd thought you'd tell someone. All that crazy driving before is for the folks that would. You can see why I'm particular about who I take here."

For the first time since we'd found the morels my mind returns to the giant fish. The disappointment in not catching it is softer now, easier to take. The monster brown is still there, his hook jaw and enormous head waiting to swallow another chub tail, another day. Maybe the next time we will catch him. Or maybe not. But slowly I feel an angler's hope returning—and that feeling alone is better than anything we came home with that night.

RAT TALE

That Black, Boot-Sucking, Mississippi Mud

KENNY TELLS THE TALE: For as long as any of us could remember, our whole family used to make our way each spring down to the Big River's backwater sloughs in order to catch, cook, and eat some of those dark-backed, yellow-bellied, whisker-faced, culinary delights called bullheads. Fresh fish was a welcome supplement to our ordinary diet of home-raised pork, beef, and garden vegetables, and the bullhead fishing trip was a sign of spring. Our family—Grandmother Mary, Grandpa Adolf, Ma and Pa, Brother Gerald and me—spaced ourselves a cane-fishing-pole length apart, so nobody would be prone to being slapped alongside the head by a cold, wet, airborne bullhead once we started hauling in the big ones.

Round about dark the skeeters and bullheads began to bite in unison. For some while, we were kept fairly busy taking fish off the hooks, putting the bewhiskered prizes in the metal wash tubs, baiting up with earthworms, and watching our lines for another bite. Our in-between-bite time was spent watching so we didn't get too many bites from the hovering, humming hoards of backwater skeeters.

Now on this particular evening, when the fish catching slowed up I decided to move a short ways down the slough to where I figured there'd be more fish. I hadn't gone more then twenty feet when I felt this strange sucking sensation on my left foot. I looked down and realized that said foot was lost in the mud. I figured by planting my right foot up alongside the left one I'd get enough leverage to pull it loose. Wrong! Now I was halfway up to my knees with both feet in that black mud. My seven-year-old frame was skinny as a rail—Pa often teased me about needing window weights in my pockets to keep from blowing away on a windy day—but suddenly I felt like I weighed a ton. The more I pulled and strained the deeper I sunk. At first I struggled in silence, not wanting the folks to think I was too young and foolish to go off on my own in the swamp. I stuck the butt end of my cane fishing pole down into the mud alongside me for some added help but got none. The skeeters were meanwhile carrying out a full-scale attack, and all around me the night air was as black as the inside of a cave. That ungodly mud had a hold on me clear up to my knees, and to make matters worse I presently felt like I was going to tip over. That's when I came completely unglued.

My quiet struggling turned to screaming, yelling, and thrashing. To heck with the folks! I wanted out of the mud now! The feeling of being off balance became a face-first reality. My screaming, yelling, and thrashing turned to blubbering, crying, and wallowing. I even used some words I heard my Pa say when he hit his thumb with a hammer. My dilemma seemed to go on for hours, but it was most likely only a couple of minutes until I felt strong hands take hold of me. I thought my arms and legs were going to come plumb off me as Grandpa Adolf and Pa dragged me out of that sump hole and up the slough bank to high, dry ground where I lay in a soggy heap, blubbering, sniffling, and whining.

The whole family gathered around to see what fine shape I was in. Ma was peeved and said that I was just too darn careless and swore she'd never let me out of her sight again. Brother Gerald pointed his finger at me in the glow of a flashlight and cackled with raucous laughter. Pa and Grandpa Adolf recounted all the gruesome details of how they had to dredge me up from the bottom of Rohrers's Slough and drag me out like a derrick boat does a bridge piling.

Grandmother Mary, however, put her comforting arm around my mud-caked shoulders and allowed as how it wasn't something a little fresh water and a good night sleep wouldn't cure. Her dark eyes twinkled in the summer night's moonlight when she said that everybody there had such a happening or two in their own time as well. "If you travel these Big River swamps often enough, that black, boot-sucking, Mississippi mud is bound to find you," she said. "This was your first chance—and it probably won't be your last, Kenny boy." She smiled down at me and patted the top of my mucky head.

Then, it was off to the spring holes for Ma and I where I received one whale of a scrubbing. Such was my introduction to what lies below the quiet waters of the Whitman Swamp.

During the half century since that night, I must honestly say I have had what I consider to be more than my fair share of close encounters with that mud. Each time I meet up with the mud I remember Grandmother Mary's prophecy about that long-ago night being my "first chance" to deal with the mud, but it wouldn't be the last. How right she was!

As I grew into my teens, my forays into the Whitman Swamp became more frequent, and so did my experiences with the mud. In fact there were so many spills and thrills that I couldn't begin to give accurate count.

One that stands out in my mind is when I was on a mid-November duck hunt and slipped from a fallen log while trying to cross a narrow, marshy creek in the predawn darkness. During the ensuing scramble to gain dry ground I lost my shotgun. Now I realize that a shotgun is a fairly large object—it isn't as if it were a set of keys or a jackknife—but I had to crawl back into that quagmire three different times, groping about until the shotgun was recovered. The ducks were safe that day as I hightailed it for home.

The years from age seventeen to twenty are recalled with sheer bliss. Not one mud-filled nightmare occurred throughout this period. Military service time. I was no where near the stuff.

Oh, but it ended all too soon. I was back again and began to eke out a living in the Whitman. Not only was the mud still there, it had gotten deeper, slimier, stickier, and had spread out. It found me in places where, to the best of my knowledge, it had never lurked before. I had written off most of my previous mud-bath accidents as my being young, foolish, and inexperienced about traveling that unforgiving country. Maybe I was hoping more than anything that as the years wore on my dunkings would lessen. I would learn the ways needed to avoid being caught up in it. But that awful oozing black goop found me, grabbed hold of me, and gave me a good going over every now and then just to keep me humble. And humble I was whenever I came in contact with it.

There were canoe rollovers, where the mud waited patiently below for me to try standing up in it. And there were more log-crossing slips, where I gyrated about like a tightrope artist before accepting the inevitable plunge into its murky depths.

I began to recognize the more obvious signs of the mud's presence, like large flats of shallow water that sported a lush growth of aquatic plants. Or small ponds where the water's edge was an orange, mineral-like color. But there were also plenty of weird, bizarre, unexpected happenings when I exercised great caution only to have it find me anyway.

Take the time I was traveling the winter icepack in search of fresh fish for the dinner table. With the coming of dawn I had loaded aboard my toboggan a couple of homemade willow ice-fishing poles, a fish sack, ice chisel, some venison jerky, and a bottle of wild ginger tea laced with honey. I set forth toward Maple Leaf Marsh, which lay an hour's walk to the south and east of the Tent Camp. It was mid-January and colder than a well-driller's butt on a lonesome ridgetop. When I turned to look back at the snow-covered Tent Camp, the smoke coming from its crooked stovepipe seemed to hang in one place like it was frozen in time and space and would stay there until spring. The sky was a deep, cloudless blue that faded to a whitish hue near the horizon. A brilliant yellow-orange haze filtered through the trees to the east as the morning sun began to rise from its nighttime slumber. The snow crunched and squeaked beneath my feet as I trudged across the vast, open reaches of the windswept marsh. My toboggan pulled easily across the snow, and soon Spider and I were in the Maple Leaf Marsh.

We spent the entire day chopping holes through the ice in various places, fishing a while, then moving on. Mostly we found a foot or more of good ice beneath the deep snow that covered the landscape. About an hour before dark I took a notion to try one more place before heading back to camp. When I chopped the hole I noticed the ice was much thinner than usual. My habit was to get down on my hands and knees, cup my hands around my face and peer down the hole to see if there were any fish finning around down there. I was doing that when I heard the ice begin to crack. Oh no, I whispered as I began to crawl toward my toboggan. *Whomp!* The ice broke. A fleeting thought crossed my mind—bet there's mud under this water! A split second later I found out. Yup, there's mud all right.

After a fair amount of slithering, sloshing, and slogging, I managed to haul myself out onto solid ice. Whoa Nelly, what a sowish mess I was! There was mud all over me; it was just that it was a little thicker in certain places, like the inside of my pants, my ears, and between my fingers. Why not wash off in the water you ask? Because as soon as I crawled out onto the ice, that cursed facsimile of black wallpaper paste froze onto me in a heartbeat, that's why! My old pal Spider found the whole thing rather amusing. She simply stood there looking at me, wagging her tail with a sort of lopsided grin on her face. All the way back to the Tent Camp I talked to myself about that darn old mud. My ungainly gait, plastered with frozen mud, could have been likened to a cowboy with a bad case of saddle sores walking the slippery deck of a sailing ship.

Perhaps the worst feature of that slinky stuff is how downright sneaky it is. More than once I've followed a game trail across boggy areas by stepping from one grassy hummock to another, poking my walking stick down to make certain the mud isn't too deep. The next day, while traveling the same trail, I slipped off a hammock only to find myself mired down in muck up to my belly. Overnight the stuff shifted itself and snuck alongside my trail to lay in wait for my poor hapless self—I swear it did!

And so it is that I have come to respect, or hate, or maybe even fear that black, boot-sucking, Mississippi mud. Every pore of my body and spirit has been assaulted by it. It's strange stuff. Throw a gob up against the ceiling, it'll kind of hang there until it decides to ooze itself on down the wall. When dry, it's the finest dust, like talcum powder. When wet, it's down-right scary stuff; it's so blasted unpredictable it must have a mind of its own.

On the one hand, I'd have to say that Grandmother Mary, if you're up there in that big old swamp in the sky, hear me now: I don't want anymore "chances" to deal with that darned old mud. I've done had all the chance I can stand for one lifetime.

Then again on the other hand, I guess there is something kind of special about that awful goo. It won't find you except in certain wild, lone-some, beautiful places where the Circle of Life is filled to the brim with wonderful things of all descriptions. It thrives where the arrowhead, lotus, and pickerelweed grows tall and lush, where the red-wing blackbird, the Canada geese, and the coyote talk to each other. That mud lies deep in the sloughs as the northern pike, muskrat, and beaver swim above it and the frogs and turtles sleep winter away beneath it. These are the places where the morning sun shimmers like a big orange ball through a curtain of fog, and the moonshadows dance among the white swamp oaks while the sum-mer breeze sings a lullaby amidst the cottonwoods. I guess I wouldn't mind having one more "chance" to deal with that black, boot-sucking, Missis-sippi mud after all.

JUNE

River Rat Almanac

JUNE IS SUCH a verdant, lovely, peaceful time along the river. The air, sky, and water seem to melt into a deep azure. Leaves, grasses, and aquatic plants display so many shades of green. Flowers and birds in full plumage add brilliant color to this perfect landscape tapestry.

Bird songs fill the air from dawn to dusk. Robins, orioles, sandhill cranes, and Canada geese all sing at once with great joy. Some are background singers, like song sparrows, red-winged blackbirds, swallows, and catbirds. Each sings a different song in a different key, yet somehow they blend into a beautiful chorus.

The fish are filled with joy and energy as well. Sunfish guard their spawning beds, swimming round and round in a tight circle over a bowl-shaped depression in the sand. Carp are bumping, wallowing, and splashing about in the backwaters. Bass and catfish wriggle slowly back and forth along rocky shores, less frenzied than other finny folks.

Spring and summer become one. Almost without notice, the longest day of the year comes and goes. The plants take full advantages of the extra daylight. The fruits of the trees begin to form, and the Big River is lined with lush foliage. The cottonwood trees sing their lovely lullabies. Turtles seek their traditional egg-laying grounds in sunny, sandy spots near the backwaters—most fairly close to where they were born. The trilling, croaking, and snoring of frogs and toads along the backwater ponds can be deafening and soothing at once.

The Snake Hunters

I don't recall the reason Kenny and I met in the Whitman Swamp today, but it is not a pleasant place to be. The sun is shimmering off the water like a reflector oven, and swarming deerflies hang on my hat like sticktights in a retriever's coat. Mud, as ripe as barnyard muck, sucks at my boots. With sweat streaming down my back, I look down for water, tempted to douse my hat and let the splash run over my hair. But duckweed covers the mud-brown swamp water like a lime-green veil. The swamp seems claustrophobic, with no trace of wind and a wall of cattail and willow around me. I figure I'd rather be just about any place else right now.

Instinctively I look to the surrounding blufflands for relief. I knew the tree-covered hillsides held little promise; singing mosquitoes and junglelike humidity would make a trip there a poor trade. But my eyes scan the ridges and settle on a small patch of bare ground on a southwest-facing slope. The treeless knob seems inviting, promising a grand view and, perhaps, a face-cooling breeze. I stare long enough to feel transported, when Kenny clears his throat beside me.

"What do you see on that goat prairie?"

"Huh? Oh, nothing. Just looks like a cooler place than here, right now," I groan.

Kenny laughs and nods. "Most anywhere seems cooler than the swamp right now. That goat prairie might be. Depends on the breeze. If one's blowing, maybe so. If not, might be hotter than Hades up there right now. Snakes, too, probably."

"Rattlers?" I ask.

"Yup. They like it there. Sun on them if they're cool, shade nearby if not. Mice to eat. Grass and rocks to hide in. Good place for a snake to live."

I stare for a while longer at the treeless point. While I'd heard these small openings called goat prairies before, I never could trace the origin of the nickname. Domestic goats were in short supply on area farms, and no wild cousins had ever called these ridges home. "Why do they call them goat prairies?" I ask Kenny, hoping finally to solve the puzzle.

"Good question. Don't know as anyone really knows. Maybe they're so steep, folks figured only a goat could climb one. One of those 'local color' deals, I guess."

"Is there a good chance at finding a rattler in a place like that?" I ask, pointing dully to the distant bluff.

"Used to be. Still might. Not so many snakes around these days as before."

"Before when?"

This was a semi-loaded question. I knew that, in decades past, there'd been a bounty on rattlesnakes and people had taken advantage of them. Some took to killing snakes regularly and became semi-professional at it. Other folks just killed rattlers whenever they saw one, any debate in their mind about doing so erased by the knowledge that the local government provided a monetary stamp of approval. Between the temptation of the bounty and folk's near-universal revulsion of reptiles, I imagined an epic slaughter of serpents. But I also knew that declines in animal populations are rarely caused by just one factor. Besides, the snake bounty had been eliminated decades ago—why hadn't rattlers bounced back?

"That's tough to pin down," Kenny says softly. "Maybe we should hike up there and check it out. Might find us a snake if we poked around a bit."

I gaze hard at Kenny for a moment, wondering if he was trying to duck my question. I consider pressing the issue when another deerfly zaps me sharply on the neck and I nearly fall into swamp muck trying to slap him. Kenny grins as I recover my balance, and the sweat that had been beading on my forehead finally rolls into my eyes. Suddenly, I don't give a muskrat's patoot why Kenny wants to hike to a goat prairie—if it gets me out of this bug-infested quagmire, I'm up for it.

"You lead, I'll follow," I say.

Reaching a goat prairie is never easy, partly due to where they grow, and partly due to what lies between you and it. The prairie in question is on the end of one of the longest, tallest ridges in the area. We are fortunate in that a paved road twists to the top of the ridge so we can drive to blufftop level rather than hike the near-vertical slope from the valley. Our luck runs out on the walk in, however, as a recent logging crew had left a jumble of oak tops in our path. Nettles and vines were woven among the tops, and we slither among the dense growth, probing ahead with our walking sticks. Though our pace is slow, we pause several times to sip water from a canteen.

Stepping onto the goat prairie from the dank, thick woods is like emerging from a tunnel. There is a slight breeze wafting across the opening, and we stand on the edge of the prairie, leaning hard on our sticks, letting the wind play on our sweating faces. The view is magnificent; the green fingers of adjacent hills stretch out around us, the narrow ribbon of a trout stream snakes through the valley below, the broad swath of the Big River and the island-laced backwaters sprawl in the hazy distance. Heralding our intrusion, a red-tailed hawk screams and launches from a giant oak downslope.

Goat prairies are one of the most unique, and least appreciated, habitats in the Mississippi River valley. Virtually a tallgrass prairie in miniature, these openings occur most often on southwest-facing ridgetops, and usually on the end of the ridge itself. Plants like big and little bluestem grow in profusion, as well as wild Canada rye and puccoon. Outcroppings of lime- and sandstone are common in goat prairies; some are as small as your hand, others large enough to crush a house if they dislodge and roll downhill. These rocks hint at the composition of the rugged bluffs themselves, as if the ridge was a giant arm and nature had peeled back just a little skin to hint at what lies beneath. And sometimes there are caves, darkened entries into the very bluff itself.

These qualities make a goat prairie a rattlesnake's paradise. Caves are perfect den sites, places for snakes to slumber through winter, warmed by the bodies of other rattlers drawn to the cavern by centuries-old instinct. Come spring, the bare, south-facing rocks are quickly and thoroughly soaked by sunshine, and cold-blooded snakes gather on such ledges to revitalize their lethargic systems. Goat-prairie grasses give rattlesnakes a perfect hunting ground for mice, voles, and other vermin. And as summer heat overtakes the ridgetops, rattlers can retreat to the cooling comfort of brushpiles and fallen logs in the nearby woods.

So it is with great caution that I follow Kenny as he slips quietly from the woods and onto the goat prairie. I should state here that I do not consider myself a snake-a-phobe. I captured and handled garter snakes frequently as a child, graduated to the odd bullsnake and racer as I grew, and once, as a ten-year-old, even got cuddly with a friend's boa constrictor. But I have also never kidded myself about reptiles returning my affection. While the wild snakes I caught in my youth seemed grateful to me for releasing them, none of them had the very real and possibly deadly option of whipping around and giving me a pair of venom-loaded fangs to the forearm for my trouble. So though I loved the *concept* of seeing a rattlesnake, I still wasn't sure how I'd react if I actually did.

I also know this about Kenny: If he takes you somewhere to look for something, you're getting escorted to one of the best places he knows, not just some offbeat locale where an encounter might happen if the moon and stars are lined up just so.

"Where do you usually find them?" I finally manage to ask as Kenny sneaks around the goat prairie, using his walking stick like a blind man's cane to poke in front of him.

"Harder to tell, now. Earlier, a month ago maybe, they might be laid out on these rocks soaking up sun. Been warm lately. They could be out hunting, or maybe holed up in this little cave, keeping out of the heat."

When Kenny says "this little cave," I instinctively stand on tiptoe to look around him. The cave is, indeed, small. A small toddler could wriggle through the blackened entrance in the small escarpment of limestone. That same toddler could not, however, expect an easy exit if trouble—like an edgy 'coon, bobcat, or snake—greeted him or her. Kenny probes gently into the opening with his stick, then straightens up. "No one's home today."

"How do you know?"

"No rattling," he says flatly. "People call rattlers 'The Snake That Talks' because it warns you with its tail, and it's a speech you know the meaning of without a translator! We'll poke around this little goat prairie for a while. If we don't see anything we'll just pack up and go to another one."

Kenny's agenda proves to be a tall order. We work across the small goat prairie thoroughly and in silence, Kenny looking in likely spots for a snake coiled in hiding or stretched out enjoying the sun, me following cautiously behind. Though this place has been a snake utopia in years past, today we see no trace of a rattler. "That's all right," Kenny sighs as we complete a thorough loop of the two-acre prairie. "We'll go look at another one."

But we visit a similar prairie with identical results, and another, and when we drive to a fourth, I sense Kenny's frustration mounting. At least part of this is due to the diminishing number and size of goat prairies themselves. If forests were content to stay forests, there's a good chance goat prairies would thrive. But woodlands have a way of encroaching on these important grasslands; one year there's suddenly a small patch of sumac on the edge of the goat prairie, a few seasons later a gnarled-but-hearty red cedar—an invading tree species not native to the prairie—pushes up through the thin, dry soil. Perhaps in another decade a pair of oak seedlings have taken root, and the beginnings of a forest takeover are in place.

Before bluff country was settled by European immigrants, periodic fires ensured the health and survival of these little prairies. A lightning strike would ignite a hillside, and the fire would spread quickly across the south and west slopes, where the soil was thin and dry. Shrubs and emerging woody vegetation would burn, shrivel, and die in the flames, but the charred grasses and forbs would regenerate after time and rain had worked some magic. Tender green shoots would emerge, stronger and more tenacious, and the goat prairie would be as lush and vital as ever.

Curiously, early farmers in the region continued this process for years after settling in bluff country. While they fought every wildfire that broke out, many farmers conducted controlled burns to maintain goat prairies. Cattle were turned loose to graze on these naturally occurring grasslands, and in doing so, farmers saved themselves several weeks of buying feed for their hungry herds. While any visitor to the region would marvel at the prospect of a herd of cows munching contentedly on a nearly vertical slope, old-timers attest that such sights were common not fifty years ago. They'll also describe some of the springtime burns—of an entire hillside, glowing red and smoky-white in the evening—as one of their most vivid memories.

Eventually, of course, herdsmen learned they could keep their bovines just as fat and healthy—and save themselves a lot of work—by confining them in a barnyard or smaller, less-rugged pasture close to home. So the burning of hillsides ceased, and in the years since, goat prairies—and the rattlesnakes that called them home—have waned.

And so have the snake hunters, Kenny tells me as we walk to

another of his old "snaking spots." They were a rugged, independent lot: river rats and others who refused to work a regular job, but could keep money coming in through a long, hot summer by hunting vermin for bounty. Farmers paid bounties on pests like pocket gophers, which dug up hayfields and pastures, leaving them pockmarked and rugged. And the county paid for the rattles off a snake's tail: anywhere from fifty cents to five dollars, depending on where folk sold them. No one got rich being a snake hunter, but these were people who counted freedom as their biggest asset, and who was more free than a snake hunter?

Kenny learned to hunt snakes from a pair of river rats who happened to be his cousins: Wilmer—who was always known as "Whimpy"—and Ed Salwey, who were recognized as seasoned veterans of the goat prairies. In a good summer, each of these men might collect bounty on as many as five hundred rattlers—an accomplishment that took a lot of time and countless miles of hiking the steep, craggy bluffs that rattlers loved. Ed and Whimpy were standout members of a small, secretive fraternity of snakers that roamed Wisconsin's "west coast" and the wooded hillsides of Minnesota. Snakers were a furtive bunch, and Kenny's opportunity to learn from two of the best gave him a rare look into a way of life that was soon to disappear from the region.

"Snakers spent as much time hiding their hotspots as they did getting to them," Kenny tells me as we drive to another secluded goat prairie. "Most folks knew which vehicles belonged to who back then, and a good snaker would park a mile or two from his place, then hike over one or two ridges to reach it. If he got followed, whoever came after him would check out the first hill he came to, find nothing and hopefully go home. It took a lot of hiking to protect a good place, but it was worth it."

Snaking tools were simple: something to capture the rattler with and something to carry snakes or their rattles back home. The former implement was largely a matter of preference. "Some guys carried a long forked stick, measuring from four to six feet," Kenny explains. "You could use it for a walking stick while you climbed the hills—its main function—and when you found a snake the fork was used to pin his head to the ground. Some guys carried a frog spear, a four-tined gig with barbs at the end of each tine. But cousin Whimpy had no interest in those spears. 'Kenny, I got enough things to worry about while I'm walking them hills,' he told me once. 'I don't need to add falling on them tines to the list.' Good advice, I thought."

The majority of snakes were killed on the spot, as a snaker only had to produce the rattles to collect the bounty. Most snakers carried a large knife for killing the snake, and after pinning the rattler's head firmly to the ground with the stick, they'd sever the body just ahead of the stick, then immediately step on the writhing tail to prevent it from slithering downhill. Once the snaker had collected the rattles, he or she laid the carcass neatly out in the open so hawks, owls, and other scavengers could have a good meal.

"But not all the snakes were killed," Kenny stresses. "For many years there was a good market for live snakes at a place called Reptile Gardens out in Rapid City, South Dakota. They kept a supply of live rattlesnakes, not only for display, but to 'milk' them for venom to use in making snake-bite serum. Most of the snakers I knew kept a bunch of live ones and brought them to Rapid City once a year. Those snakers tended rattlers like pets, kept them in a chicken-wire pen with food and water in a basement, garage, or woodshed. You see, Reptile Gardens wouldn't pay for any snake in bad shape, and if you drove all the way out there with a bunch of sick ones, you were better off just killing them at home. So they made life pretty easy for them snakes while they kept them."

Naturally, catching a rattler and taking it home without either party getting hurt took a lot more skill than did a simple goat-prairie beheading. "It's important to get the forked part of the stick as close to the snake's head as possible," Kenny recalls. "That way the rattler can't reach back and bite you. Then you get a good, firm grip just behind the head and let up on the stick. When your stick hand is free, you reach down and grab a sack you brought to put them in. Some guys liked grain sacks with little airholes punched in them. Most just used a plain old burlap sack. You just lift the snake and slide them into that bag, give the bag a quick twist, then tie it shut with a piece of baling twine."

The dark bag kept the captive snake content while the snaker hiked off to search for other rattlers. Any additional snakes were slipped into the same bag as the first, until it held four or five adults. "You get that many and it's too heavy to carry far," Kenny says. "So generally we'd leave a full bag in the first cool, shady spot we could, then pick it up when the day's hunting was over."

Some snakers, men and women who'd caught hundreds of rattlers and were looking for new challenges, would live-capture a snake with their bare hands. "Two of them known to do that were Bobby Fort and William Wensul—called 'Black Bill' for his swarthy complexion," Kenny remembers. "They say Fort would wait to catch a snake out in the open and wait for them to coil up. Then he'd crouch in front of the snake and start making slow circles in the air with one hand. When the rattler had focused on that hand, he'd grab like lightning with the other hand for the snake's neck, then pop them in the sack."

Kenny looks at me to ensure I'm properly amazed. I am.

"There's one key to catching a rattler that way," he continues, then arches his eyebrow for dramatic effect. I bite.

"What's that?"

"Never doubting for a second you can do it."

Kenny's tales make it seem like finding snakes in the old days was about as difficult as tripping over a log, and when I say so, his laughter fills the car. "That's because I'm telling you highlights, like they do with the news on TV these days. Mostly, snake hunting was just like you and me are living it today—lots of tough walking and not much finding. The best days for snaking are the hot, windless ones—great if you're lying on a sandbar or getting dragged across the river on water skis. But you've felt it up here. No water about, your tongue lying like a slab of wood in your mouth. Cousin Whimpy always said the best snakers were part camel."

There were other hazards as well. Poking around the nooks and crannies of a limestone ledge with a forked stick, the snaker might bust into a beehive. Such an encounter was fraught with danger. The instinctive running path was, naturally, downhill—where the steep grade made freefalling a good bet and the trail was booby-trapped with obstacles tailor-made for breaking a limb. Running uphill made for safer footing, but gravity slowed the escape and gave the bees plenty of time to find their target. Hiking a couple of miles back to a vehicle after a multiple-sting bee attack was an arduous task and potentially life-threatening if the victim was allergic.

And of course, there was the constant threat of a bite from the snake itself. While few of these were fatal, even a minor bite was a cause for concern.

"One of the first times Cousin Whimpy took me snaking, we sat down for a minute to grab a drink," Kenny recalls. "I'd killed a snake on a piece of flat sandstone just before and was feeling pretty proud of myself. But Whimpy says to me, 'Kenny, I watched you reach down to cut the rattles off that snake and you didn't sweep your stick through the grass first. That's a good way to get yourself bit.' And for emphasis he rolled up his shirtsleeve and pointed at two small white circles about an inch apart on his bronze arm. 'I reached for a dead rattler in high grass once and didn't check for his companions first—this is what I got for my trouble. My arm swelled up like a stovepipe and it throbbed so bad I could feel my heart-beat in the hairs of my head. Later, all the skin from that arm peeled off. So don't go thinking all them snakes are going to warn you before they bite.'"

Kenny finally pulls the car to a stop on a remote, gravel road, and we grab our walking sticks to check one more goat prairie before we call it a day. The heat of the day has settled in now. The temperature is the same, but somehow more intense, like the dull, sapping ache of a hard sunburn on the second day. Thankfully, the walk out to the small goat prairie is an easy hike, a well-used deer trail providing a fine path down the ridgetop. We walk without speaking, Kenny leading the way while I follow, visions of bare-handed snake-charmers dancing in my head.

We stop just feet from the edge of the goat prairie. Unlike the others we'd visited, I stare hard at the ground immediately, resist-ing the temptation to take a panoramic view from the blufftop vantage point. Kenny is scanning the right side of the opening so I turn my gaze to the left, letting it sweep over a small limestone knob, through a patch of bluestem, toward a short stand of sumac. An oak branch lies on the ground near the edge of the sumac, pale-brown and barkless. It stops my eye for a split second, but I con-tinue to sweep my gaze until it reaches the edge of the woods. It is then that I realize why the oak branch looked so odd—the tree line is full of birch and aspen! When I look back for the branch it is gone.

"Kenny."

"Hmm?"

"I think I saw one."

"A snake?"

"There was a branch there a minute ago and it's not there any-more . . ." I begin walking to the sumac slowly, and I hear Kenny a step behind me. The grass is short there, the ground sandy. Nowhere for a snake to go in the second or two my eyes left it. Surely I couldn't have imagined it, some dream-serpent in a bluff country mirage?

"Look here," Kenny says, pointing with his walking stick to a slight impression in the dry soil in front of me. It is a curving "S," two fingers wide, a hand long, neatly sculpted in the duff.

"Was it a rattler?"

"Hard to tell. Might be."

"Where could it have gone?"

Kenny laughs and points with his walking stick to a nearby brushpile, a rock outcropping just down the hill. "Where couldn't he?"

I daydream, just for a second, that I am a snake hunter. This is not hard to do, for I've been a hunter since I was young. What would I do now? Grab my forked stick and bag and start probing the brush, the rocks, the grass, until I found the snake? And if I could find it, how would it feel—to study the snake carefully, wait for the right moment, then pin its head with a quick jab of his stick? Being a hunter, it takes little imagination to envision the tension, the excitement, the fear at such a moment. And also, how it must have been to have a dozen, a hundred, five hundred such encounters in a summer. In the handful of minutes since I saw my first wild rattlesnake, it is easy for me to imagine being a snaker.

But it is also easy for me to realize what Kenny has taught me today, and I doubt his lesson is one a good snaker would miss, either. Our visits to the small, remaining goat prairies of Kenny's past prove that the timber rattlesnakes that once thrived in this special habitat are becoming a rare creature indeed. It is true that snakers killed thousands of the rattlers whose progeny could now be sunning themselves on limestone shelves all over bluff country. But if there were no goat prairies for them to live in, could they thrive as they did when they were hunted?

When someone cuts down a forest, even the dullest among us notice and grieve. But the loss of one goat prairie, or all of them, is such a prolonged, piecemeal death that few are even aware of the loss. And as these hillside savannas ebb, so do the snakes that inhabit them. Perhaps one day the bluffs that guide the Upper Mississippi's course will hold no more goat prairies, and probably, not long after, no more rattlers. Most people won't notice, a smaller number will not care, and a few may even be glad.

But the snake hunters, and those of us who understand them, would know that something wild and crucial had been lost.

Rat Tale
Frog Tears and Rabbit Coffee

Kenny tells the tale: "The tree frogs are singing: It's going to rain soon."

How many times did I hear Grandmother Mary say these words? She'd stand there in the hot-summer dust, all brown and wrinkled, apron covering the front of her printed dress and cock an ear toward that gnarly oak tree that stood in the meadow just south of her rambling old farmhouse. After listening for a moment, she'd point her well-worn walking stick toward the oak tree and utter her proclamation about the frogs singing in the tree.

It wasn't really as if she were telling me about the tree frogs and the impending rain. It seemed as though she was thinking out loud, musing to herself about this genuine fact. There wasn't even a hint of doubt in her voice. I simply took it for granted that the rains would come soon and continued to tag along behind her in the potato patch to pick more bugs off the leaves and dust the plants good and proper with wood ashes. And sure enough within a day or so the rain came and she would say, "Yup, the rain is the tree frog's teardrops, yes siree, my boy, it sure is." Grandmother and I would have to go back to the potato patch and ash the plants again because the rain had washed them clean.

Now it never occurred to me that Grandmother could have missed with her prediction. She was old and wise. She spent her entire life living close to the natural things and paid attention to the signs and omens of the weather. She was a teenager at the turn of the twentieth century, a mother and grandmother before the end of the 1920s. Her roots were deeply embedded in the ancient habits, ways, means, and methods of cooking, agriculture, medicine, and weather forecasting. I had seen her medicinal remedies work, and I had seen her weather predictions come to pass far too many times to question her in any way. So when Grandmother said, "The tree frogs are singing: It's going to rain soon," I not only listened, I believed.

A lot of tree frogs and rains have come and gone since that day nearly half a century ago when Grandmother and I stopped to listen to the tree frogs sing. Over the years, I have continued to take note of those same signs and omens nature has to offer, and it is truly surprising how often they have proven to be correct. Take the whole business about rabbits cooking coffee for example.

My little, six-year-old, sun-tanned finger was pointing up into the hills that surrounded our wood-framed farmhouse when I popped the question. "Pa, what's making that smoke up in the woods?" Pa never cracked a grin, "Why, that's because the rabbits are cooking coffee today." My eyes grew wide as I thought over that piece of information for a moment or two before asking sort of a half question: "Naw, rabbits don't start no fires do they?" Pa chuckled a bit, then confessed, "Guess they don't, my boy, but that's what my Pa told me and his Pa told him. All us hill folks say that because it looks a lot like the thin smoke from a small campfire is rising up out of the hollows."

After mulling things over in my mind, I asked, "Why does that happen, Pa?" He gave me the answer directly. "It only does seems to happen after it's rained for some time. When it lets up or quits altogether and them thin wispy streams of 'smoke' start to rise up from the wooded hollows in the hills, you can pretty well bet your boots it'll rain again that day and most times quite soon as well." Then he added, "Now, let's get on with the day's work before it rains again."

I walked a few steps, stopped, and turned to ask another question I'd thought of only to find old Pa standing there watching me with a half-smile on his face. He said, "Kenny, we talked enough for today about hills and hollows, rain and smoke, and such. Let's just say the rabbits are cooking coffee and it's going to rain some more today. Now get going before them poor chickens starve to death."

I did as he said but my mind wasn't on the chickens. It was filled to the brim with thoughts of woods and hills, campfires and smoke, rain, rabbits, and coffee. From that day on I watched for the signs of any "cooking" going on during rainy days.

Did it rain later that day so long ago, you ask? You can bet your best bullfrog it did—and almost always does every time the rabbits are cooking coffee in the hill country along the Mississippi River.

I am in no way implying that the ancient methods are better than the new technological methods. What I am simply saying here is: Pick up as many of the old and new ways as you can. Examine them. Try them. Keep what you feel are right and good and enjoyable. Leave the rest behind. Whether they are old or new does not make a difference. In this manner, all of the ancient ways will not be forgotten and all of the modern ways will not be accepted. We will have integrated the best of both worlds, the natural world and the artificial world. We cannot help but benefit from such a marriage in terms of culture, knowledge, and enjoyment. The next time a tree frog sings, I will be listening, and I'll surely be taking note of the smoke when the rabbits are cooking coffee in the hills.

Here are some other ancient bits of wisdom I've picked up listening to the old-timers here in Buffalo County.

Spring peepers are harbingers of weather to come. When the peepers' chorus sings, it's a genuine spring concert, and you can count on one thing for sure: Spring is here.

When you hear the deep, throaty croak of the bullfrog, you know warm summer nights are in store.

Flying and hopping critters like crickets, grasshoppers, and cicadas are also weather barometers. Grasshoppers generally appear toward summer's end. A large population of 'hoppers means a hot, dry end to summer. Cicada bugs or seventeen-year locusts usually "sing" the loudest and longest just before and during extremely hot, dry periods as well. If the crickets quit chirping, a storm of some sort is usually approaching. Crickets are most times associated with warm, clear, dew-filled nights and a clear, sunny morning lies ahead.

Mosquitoes attacking with a blood-thirsty gusto means a warm, still night. They don't like cold or wind.

If you go barefoot during a summer's dawn and your feet are dry, rain will be heading your way within the day.

When the shiny, lighter-colored undersides of oak leaves turn and oscillate back and forth in the wind, rain is sure to follow.

Of course, there is the well-known saying: "Red at night, sailors sleep tight. Red in the morning, sailors take warning." This refers to the pleasant day to follow a colorful sunset. But if the sunrise is rosy, the weather will turn foul.

Another old adage: "Wind from the west, fishing's the best. Wind from the east, fishing's the least." Anytime the wind is blowing from the east—northeast, southeast, or due east—the weather patterns are generally unsettled and precipitation is likely. Fish do not bite or feed much at such times, although they sometimes feed voraciously just before a storm.

Sometimes you may see hazy circles around the moon or sun that we call moon dogs or sun dogs. These signs usually mean a long-term change in the weather lasting anywhere from three days to three weeks or until the next full moon.

Whenever Buffalo County folk see deer or wild turkeys feeding in larger numbers than usual or at odd times of the day, we know that these feeding frenzies are signs that a change toward rougher weather is coming. Fish and birds also feed heavily prior to an approaching storm front. The critters must know; their survival depends upon this instinct.

The full moon seems to have the greatest impact on the weather. If the weather is to change, it will be around the time of the full moon. Whatever conditions are present during the full moon, these should continue for a week or ten days.

Short, choppy waves are an indication of fair, cool weather. Whitecaps most times will signify windy, dry conditions. The water's color during either type of weather conditions ranges from light blue to dark, azure blue. Large waves, rollers, combers, or swells that have long distances between their crests are a sure sign of impending storm. The water's color under these weather conditions ranges from dark gray to almost pitch black.

Fluffy, puffy white clouds mean bright, clear days. To see such clouds along with a red sunset is to be assured of a clear night and most likely a clear, dry day tomorrow.

High, thin, streaky, white clouds means a change in the weather will come in about forty-eight hours.

The huge, towering thunderheads of summer, with little or no wind, suggest heat, heat, and more heat. This is the time when the leaves hang limp and birds walk about with their wings held out from their bodies.

A red sunrise, followed by wind and dark clouds, will bring rain.

In the winter, an unbroken, steel-gray sky along with a stiff north, northwest, or northeast wind will bring snow.

"Rain before seven, quit before eleven" means that if it starts raining before seven in the morning, it should quit before 11 A.M.

Clear skies after a snow will most certainly result in cold temperatures. How cold will depend on how close it is to the full moon.

Low, dense clouds that seem to hang on to the horizon usually mean moisture—rain or snow. Heavy, thick fog along the ground in fall or spring will mean a clear, bright, sunny day once the fog has burned off. Ground fog in late winter means warm weather for the next several days. Fog or mist rising from creeks or springs will bring another hot day tomorrow.

Anyone who has spent a fair amount of time around woodstoves and campfires knows that woodsmoke has a mind of its own. It will drift wherever the homeless winds have a mind to go, which oftentimes seems to be back in my face, no matter which side of the fire I move to. This means unsettled weather. Heavy air. When the smoke rises straight up, it's going to be cool and clear. If the smoke hangs close to the ground, it will rain or snow within the next day or two.

Folks say no two snowflakes are alike—might be true. One thing's for sure, if the snow flakes coming down are those large fluffy kind that look like tiny parachutes swaying from side to side, not to worry; the snowstorm will end soon. On the other hand, if the snowflakes are the smaller, harder variety—wind-driven and in a hurry to hit the earth—look out! You might be shoveling big time tomorrow morning.

The same holds true for raindrops. The larger the drops, the less chance there is for a long, heavy, gully-washing downpour. I guess one could say bigger does not always mean more; in the case of raindrops and snowflakes it means less.

When muskrats build their winter houses larger than normal, it generally means that a colder winter is upon us.

The size of the beavers' feed beds is another way to gauge the severity of the coming winter. If after checking a number of beaver colonies, you find the majority have more brush or feed piled up in the water by their lodges than usual, it will be a long, hard winter.

Beaver dams can also tell us something. If the beavers suspect a cold winter, they will oftentimes build their dams higher in order to increase the water depth behind the dam. Once the winter ice forms over the beaver pond, it is too late to build the dam higher. If the water is too shallow, the beaver will not be able to swim about under the ice to get to their feed beds.

The depth of muskrat and beaver runs, or underwater trails gouged into the mud, can also be an indicator of the severity of the coming winter. Deeper runs mean colder weather.

Where there are few hollow trees, the squirrels will build nests made of leaves in the treetops. Here again, the earlier they build them and the bigger they are can foretell the coming of an early, cold winter.

Skunks, raccoons, and opossums are the kind of critters who sleep during the cold, nasty periods of winter. On the warm, thawing nights, they wake up and roam about foraging for food. When you notice these critters denning up in hollow trees or holes in the ground, you can be sure cold weather is coming; conversely, if you see their tracks in the snow, you can assume a warm spell will linger for a while.

A thick critter pelt with long guard hairs early in the year is unusual. Scientific studies have shown that the length of daylight hours has a definite bearing on the pelts of critters. If this happens in early fall, it could mean an early winter. If it happens late, it could be a mild winter. If they shed early, it might be an early spring. Yet muskrats seem to "hold" their guard hairs until early spring no matter what. An exception to every rule? Birds of all species feather out in winter and early spring. If one observes closely when this occurs, one can sometimes detect the coming of various weather patterns.

Much weather information can be gleaned from taking note of critter and bird calls. For example, coyotes generally howl and bark a great deal just before a storm whether it's winter or summer. They, like dogs, seem restless and nervous at such times.

Squirrels bark and chatter more before and during mild stretches of weather. Horses whinny and nay and cows moo and low most in mild, dry times. They are dead silent during rain and snowstorms and huddle together to turn their backs to the wind.

Birds also fall silent in stormy times, before and after. With birds, one should always be aware of when you first hear their various mating calls and observe their mating rituals. By understanding each bird's habits and calls and nesting timetables and recording these observations in a journal or calendar, you can compare notes from year to year. This will give you an indication as to whether they are early, late, or about on schedule. Weather conditions will have had a great deal to do with these things.

Some critters will not mate or breed at all if weather conditions are adverse to their survival. Wise, is it not? Some folks call this instinct "conditioned response." Call it what you may, I call it a good plan.

Migration patterns or movements are another way in which critters and birds supply us with information about weather conditions both short and long term and nearby or far off. Some of the conditions foretold may be occurring at the other end of our continent. Nevertheless, they are on the way.

As our natural world disappears, so shall our dependence upon it. As our dependence disappears, so will our bond with nature disappear, and it naturally follows that the ancient ways of weather forecasting and all other forms of natural folklore will disappear as well.

JULY

River Rat Almanac

JULY ON THE mighty Mississippi; heat, bugs, and humidity seem to be everywhere. If one rides slowly along in a boat with an arm outstretched, beads of moisture soon form. The searing sun bakes the sandbars. Vegetation is so lush, green, and thick that most things would not try to penetrate it.

Thunder claps and lightning strikes resound from hill to hill, flashing across the hot, humid, nighttime sky. Flickering campfires dot the sandbars. Nights are short. By the time the last shadows of darkness have disappeared the Big River is alive and vibrant. Great blue herons, snowy egrets, kingfishers, bald eagles, and flocks of cormorants stake out their favorite fishing holes. Riverfolk do the same.

The Big River seems lazy and peaceful as it slides gently past the sandbars and towheads of countless overgrown islands. Life is good on the river in July. Find an old rope hanging from a cottonwood branch over the water, and you'll soon find a group of kids, with black, boot-sucking, Mississippi mud squishing up between suntanned toes and sticking to soles. Guess anybody who grew up on the river knows that black mud sticks to both kinds of souls for a lifetime.

To Catch a Cat

Some fisher-folk like to brag up the Mississippi's spring and fall walleye fishing, or how smallmouth bass go berserk in late summer, or places where you can catch bluegills and crappie through the backwater ice come winter. The fishing—and occasionally the catching—can be fine for all these sexy, mainstream gamefish, but despite the best promotion efforts of fishing writers, tournament promoters, and local tourism officials, such widely admired species will never be the signature fish of the Big River. That title resides firmly on the flathead catfish—or as it's locally known, the "mudcat." A bewhiskered, smooth-skinned, beady-eyed critter, mudcats sport a cheesy grin suggesting that, while you may have just lifted him into your boat or slid him onto your bank, he's not done fighting yet and might at any moment smack you in the face with his tail just for spite.

This is not the kind of demeanor that inspires anglers to wax philosophical about, or even snap photographs of, flatheads. But catfish don't care about that, of course, and would gladly trade a sharp, pectoral fin-stab to an angler's palm for a *Field & Stream* cover shot any day.

So mudcat aren't sleek or gorgeous, but saying you've fished the Big River without landing and eating a flathead is like saying you're proud of your wife's family, but you keep cropping her goofy Uncle Chester out of every family photograph. And—like most Uncle Chesters I've met—folks who take some time to get tight with catfish are rarely disappointed. An old, broad-bellied, river-worn flathead is a veritable poster child for the motto: "There's more to me than meets the eye."

Which is why I happily accept when Kenny phones with an

invitation during a July hot spell. "You need to see how to setline for cats," Kenny says evenly. "Got an afternoon and evening free to haul some in with me? Swamp's fishing is good right now."

"I'll be there tomorrow afternoon," I promise.

The next afternoon, as the truck bounces down the sand roads leading to Big Lake Shack, I am eager and excited. That is, until I notice a strange, mistlike cloud around my windshield. I turn on the wipers briefly, hoping that will clear the shimmering vapor obscuring my view. No luck. So I stop the truck to figure why, on a sunlit, slightly humid day, I can barely see the road in front of me. I was about to swing open the truck door when I realize the mist is not a singular, unbroken shroud, but one made of thousands of independent particles. "Deerflies" I breathe. "Unbelievable swarms of deerflies."

If there's a common denominator among enchanted forests in literature, it's the presence of a guardian of the wood. Gnomes, sprites, ogres, trolls, merry men—all appear in tales as gatekeepers who taunt, tease, harass, and sometimes injure or kill folk who enter their realm. It's easy to dismiss such notions as the fantasies of some addled writer, but those who do so just aren't paying attention during their woodland visits. Every wild place has a creature who ensures trespassers endure some character building; in the Whitman Swamp, deerflies and mosquitoes carry the torch during mid- and late-summer. By the time I reach the shack, I have an eerie empathy with lobsters, who must surely sense the intentions of the folk who stare and point at them from the other side of the glass.

Kenny holds open the shack door as I emerge from the truck, duck my head, and make a sprinting dive for safety. It is an athletic move for someone my age, but the insects are unimpressed. The awaiting deerflies, accompanied by a whining host of mosquitoes, descend on my face, neck, and wrists in a stinging fury. I'm fond of telling people that a good part of the irritation of insect bites comes not from the wound itself, but the hovering, singing, and lighting of the attacker. Those homilies, however, were told before I'd been assaulted by the vermin of the Whitman Swamp. These bugs mean business, and before we slammed the shack door shut on their charge, I carried numerous welts on my neck, face, and arms. The common deerfly doesn't carry the dramatic appeal of a gnome or troll, but make no mistake, they're every bit as effective when it comes to guarding a wood.

It takes a minute for my eyes to adjust to the shack's dark interior, but when they do I notice Kenny thrusting a soiled, long-sleeve cotton shirt at me. "Put that on," he says, as he pulls a similar tunic from a box and lays it across his knee. "We'll need them to make it to the canoe landing alive!"

Before I slip into the shirt I notice scrawling print across the back of the collar. "Bug Shirt" is the magic-marker inscription. "What's this?" I ask, showing the label to Kenny.

"I write that on there to keep them out of the laundry," he explains. "Secret to keeping bugs off is to not be so clean. So I get a couple shirts started every spring—get them good and sweated up, full of the oils we got naturally in our skin. Years ago, we didn't wash our clothes or ourselves so damn much, and bugs weren't such a problem. Now we shower every day, and they like that. We smell better—sweeter—to them, I guess.

"But I just load a bug shirt up with dope every time I go out, and it gets good and saturated, with the repellent and the sweat and what-not. By the time the deerflies are swarming, that shirt's about the best protection I got. Other than the repellent I make, of course. But I ain't had time to mix any of that this year."

"What goes into the repellent?"

"Simple recipe. Just mix hog lard, citronella, garlic, sulfur. Makes a paste you spread on your face, neck, and arms."

"And it works?" I ask, trying not to make a face. I imagine spreading a vile, sticky goop across the nape of my neck with something stout, like a tongue depressor or putty knife.

"Damn right. It not only keeps the bugs off, you can clear a café if you walk in there at high noon on a busy day. Come on, let's head to the canoes, I got most of the gear waiting down at the landing."

The walk to the canoe landing goes surprisingly well. The extra layer of the long-sleeved shirt is warm and constricting, but I don't notice the smell much, and if I ignore their constant hum, it's clear the deerflies and mosquitoes have become more docile—zipping and flying between us, but rarely landing for a full-bore feast. I make a mental note: When wandering the Whitman in mid-summer, I'll gladly trade the freshness of a morning shower for a stinking bug shirt any day.

We reach the landing, and Kenny rights an overturned canoe and starts loading gear.

"I call this boat the *Queen Mary*," he explains. "Took the back thwart out for room while trapping. Had Mike Roach weld these other braces in for support. Built that padded box up front to make it comfy for the dog. It ain't the lightest canoe in the swamp, but there's none sturdier or can haul more gear."

After Kenny pushes the *Queen Mary* to the water's edge, Spider and I slip into the bow, and Kenny pushes off the bank from the stern. Once away from the bank, the miraculous occurs: The bugs give up on their assault, finally repulsed by our shirts, or simply unwilling to leave the warm, dark woods to chase us across the water. Relieved and excited, I reach for a paddle, but Kenny insists that I enjoy the ride. As Kenny's paddle dips and dribbles behind me, I feel a long-held tension slide from between my shoulders. I'm easing into swamp time.

The bow of the canoe slices quietly through the water, pushing through undulating beds of coontail, pondweed, and arrowhead. We leave the narrow slough of the boat landing, make a graceful left turn, and enter Indian Creek, a flowing waterway that transverses the Whitman for over seven miles. River birch and silver maple lean gently over the creek corridor as it winds through the swamp. Kenny deftly steers the canoe around sharp bends, past fallen logs, through a small bed of wild rice that towers over our heads.

One of my first, and most lasting, surprises about the Whitman Swamp was the quality and temperature of the water itself. The very word "swamp" conjures images of still, dank, cocoa-brown water that's part coffee, part quicksand. While there are stagnant puddles and oozing muck in abundance in the Whitman, there's a surprising amount of clear, flowing water that feels as cool as it looks. Take a swim in some of the pools in Indian Creek—even at the peak of one of the hard, humid summers the river valley is famous for—and you'll scurry to shore looking for something warm and dry to wrap yourself in. Or as Kenny is fond of saying, "You'll sing the national anthem in octaves you never dreamed of." On this day, after the sun has had hours to soak into every pore of the swamp, all I have to do to cool down is trail my hand in the water beside the canoe.

It's glass-clear water, too. We watch schools of minnows dart in unison to escape our approach. Bluegills, small bass, and an occasional northern pike speed across the shallow flats, seeking cover in the dense beds of pondweed. And as we approach a broad stand of wild rice, the pale yellow seed heads of several plants shake and quiver as a larger, unseen fish bumps the bases of the rich green stalks below the surface.

While I'd enjoyed the ride up to this point, it's clearly time for me to grab a paddle. The rice bed forms a wall that stretches the width of the creek and offers no easy channel, even for the sleek nose of the *Queen Mary*. Kenny grunts and heaves from the stern, using his paddle as a pole. I grab a long paddle and do likewise. Spider pokes her nose out the bow, trying to sniff a path through the dense growth. Though later we'll rejoice at the lushness of the rice bed and remark on its potential for October duck hunting, right now it's an obstacle of seeming epic proportions. Suddenly, my bug shirt is heavy, constricting armor, and the sun feels like a branding iron between my shoulder blades. But after several moments of hard pushing and slow progress, we emerge from the rice.

Here the creek widens and slows, its banks lined with large white oak and the occasional elm. Small sloughs enter the channel from each side, and Kenny names them as we paddle even with each. "That's the Tent Camp Slough to the left. You remember that from when we walked to the three shacks this spring." I nod, recalling how the slough narrows to a trickle by an ancient beaver dam we crossed, then widens again once past it. "This one coming up on the right is the Lumber Slough, that comes through the culverts in the levee. And up there is where we'll set the line out—that's the Devil's Elbow—a good place for catching mudcats."

The Devil's Elbow is a wide, deep, switchback of Indian Creek; a place where the water doubles back on itself and forms dark, forbidding pools. It's a spot that seems ripe for fishing, with elm logs and oak tops leaning into the water from the grassy bank— woody cover that offers protection to fish of all kinds. Kenny slides the *Queen Mary* around a sharp right turn, paddles hard left to get out of the current, and eases the canoe into a quiet bay. Then he reaches for a long, shallow, wooden box lying at his feet.

"This here's a setline box," Kenny says, shifting a new pinch of snuff under his lower lip then setting the box on a canoe paddle that he rests across the canoe's gunwale. "In the old days, this was how all the river people would catch catfish to eat or to sell. It's a simple way to fish—and effective, too. We'll run out a short line now, leave it out tonight, check it in the morning. Maybe have a mudcat for breakfast tomorrow."

The setline box is about two feet long and ten inches wide, with short, slanting sidewalls. Small notches are cut at one-inch intervals along the walls, and from each notch dangles a pre-baited hook—for this trip Kenny has chosen small chunks of dogfish meat. The hooks are attached to short, twelve-inch-long lines of braided dacron, which connect by a swivel to a single, longer line of the same material. The short leaders and long main line are all draped neatly, though loosely, in the bottom of the box, which is made of coarse, galvanized screen. The screen allows the wet lines to drain and dry, preventing rotting. Each setline box contains fifty hooks, Kenny explains. "We used to be able to have hundred-hook boxes, but those are illegal now. You're allowed to put out four hundred hooks per license per day, so in the old days four boxes, nowadays eight. Not many put out that much anymore."

To start the line, Kenny shoves a long willow stick in the muddy creek bottom next to shore, then ties the beginning of the main line to the stake with a slipknot. Then he backs the canoe gently offshore, allowing the main line to feed slowly out of the box. As it does, he gently feeds the short lines and baited hooks out of the box as well, and they dangle from the main line at right angles. This process continues until a half-dozen hooks have plopped in the water, followed by an oval-shaped wooden float, or buoy. "The float will keep the line closer to the surface," Kenny explains. "When you're working deep water, you use a sinking line. Keep it weighted down with a window weight or railroad shoe. But since this is a shallower channel and the fish are working towards shore, we'll want to keep it higher."

Kenny deftly backs the boat a few more feet, keeping it right at the seam where the main current meets the quiet water of the eddy. He feeds six more hooks out of the box, then plops another float onto the water. "They're pretty," I say, pointing to the rich luster of the wooden buoy.

"Antiques, too," Kenny says. "Hand-carved by my old friend Ottmar Probst. Not many wood ones around these days. Most of the setlines you see now have plastic or foam floats. Ottmar made these with a jackknife. He could make about anything with his hands and a few simple tools."

"He teach you to do this?"

"He was one of them. Like I said, most river people did some setlining for food or money. You could drive into any rivertown in the summer and buy fish. We'd either dress them out or keep them alive in a washtub full of water. Some folks wanted to buy them still alive and do their own cleaning. The fish we didn't sell ourselves went to markets in Winona, La Crosse, Pepin. But that's died, too. Catfish farms supply the restaurants now. Cook wants a hundred five-pounders for a fish fry, all a farmer's got to do is go to a pond and scoop up a bunch—all the same size, all PCB-free—anytime he wants to. Not many making their living fishing this river anymore."

Kenny has only half the box—twenty-five hooks—out when the bow of the canoe bumps shore at the downstream end of the small bay. "That's perfect," he says. "We're not looking to make a haul, just get a few for eating, so we'll tie this off and call it good." Kenny wraps the main line around another willow stake he sets next to the bank, then tucks the box into the heavy grass on shore.

With a wink at me, he glances over his shoulder at the sun, now resting over the Minnesota bluffs. "We got a little time to fish for supper if you want, before we head back," he pronounces.

We paddle hard upstream, pulling against the current flowing through the Devil's Elbow, until we clear the hard dogleg and nose the canoe against a tangled elm top leaning in the water. Kenny hands me a long, fiberglass fly rod rigged with yellow dacron running line, a split-shot sinker, and a bare hook. He has an identical outfit for himself, and we bait the hooks with one of the red garden worms he's raised in his basement for over a decade. We dangle and drift our baits around the elm limbs, and within minutes we're each fighting a pan-size bluegill. It's fishing at its best and most basic: simple gear, eager bluegills, a stringer to slide them on, and the anticipation of a fish fry. When we stow the gear and begin paddling back to the landing, eight shining sunfish dangle from our boat and a bronze sunset plays on our shoulders. We are rich men indeed.

The paddle back is easier. We find our original path through the wild rice bed and slice through the towering stalks. We see a young whitetail buck near one bend in the creek, and a pair of wood ducks flush with a squealing whistle from another. Before I know it we are nosing into the landing, turning the *Queen Mary* over for the night, and hauling fish and gear back to Big Lake Shack. Though the whining hum of mosquitoes accompanies our every step, the bug shirts keep most of them at bay.

Once inside the shack, we light a half-dozen oil lamps, which send up bright orange flames that flicker and glow on the shack walls. I set to cleaning fish while Kenny readies the cookstove. Spider finds her spot in a lower bunk and curls up with a groan. "Work hard today, did you Spider?" Kenny teases. "That's a good dog."

We both chuckle as Spider turns to face the wall and escape the mocking.

"Wasn't it Ottmar who gave you your first duck dog?" I ask.

"Yup. That was Spook. Ottmar taught me a lot, and not just about dogs," Kenny recalls. "He was one of the last old-time rivermen. Could make just about anything he needed. Had a mind like an engineer; he'd just get something in his head and figure how to build it. Had huge hands—fingers like sausages—but was nimble as could be. He made his own gill nets from scratch. Got the braided line from Memphis Net & Twine Company—same place those setlines we strung today come from—and had no pattern. Just tie them up over one knee, each little square the same size as the last. I used to watch him mend those nets in his backyard; he'd string them between two trees and his fingers'd just move through those nets like he was a seamstress.

"Ottmar made moonshine in a little shed by his garage every year. Good corn whiskey that he cooked in a copper kettle and run through charcoal to give it a little color. He drank that whiskey and chewed snuff—make that *ate* snuff. He'd put a pinch in his mouth before he went to bed, and when he woke up it wasn't there no more—every day of his life and lived to be eighty-eight.

"Ottmar had his first shot of whiskey when he was six years old. His Dad took him into the tavern in Buffalo City one day; he was so small he had to stand on the foot rail just to see the bar. But the bartender seen him peering up at the bottles and called over to his Dad. 'Say, this little guy says he wants a shot a whiskey!' Well, his Dad never missed a beat, just shot back, 'Well, give him one!' Can you imagine!"

We howl at the tale, then Kenny motions for me to start handing him fillets. As he tosses the first of them into the grease simmering in the cast-iron fry pan, Kenny recalls another memory of his river rat mentor.

"Ottmar and his wife lived almost completely off the land. When they were old enough to draw social security, the checks weren't more than a couple hundred bucks—he probably never made ten thousand in his best year of working—but they hardly knew how to act. 'What we going to do with this extra money?' he'd say to her, like they'd just won the lottery!

"When he got older, things got a little tougher for Ottmar. His still caught on fire one day and nearly burned the garage down. That convinced him to quit making 'shine and live on the gallons he'd stored up. Then he got cancer. Found a lump on his . . . well, a place where a man don't want to find no lump. So the doctor said, 'We ain't taking no chances, Ottmar. We'll just remove it.' So they did, and being as tough as he was, he did just fine. But it bugged him he had to take his pants down to pee. So he made himself a little tin funnel he kept in his pants. That solved that problem.

"But he wasn't afraid to laugh at the whole thing. Fell out of his boat in the swamp one summer day and got soaked from head to toe. So he just peeled all his clothes off, rolled them in a ball under his arm, and walked home, right across the highway on a Sunday afternoon, cars buzzing past and folks staring. Wife yelled at him, but Ottmar didn't care. 'What've I got for them to look at anymore?' he says to her!"

Our laughter fills the shack once again, but then Kenny signals that the fish is ready, and we dig hungrily into the meal, prodding forks into the dusty, golden-brown batter covering the white, flaky fillets. We wash the fish and chunks of dark raisin bread down with long pulls of water from an old Minute Maid orange juice jug.

"That's the Elixir of the Gods," Kenny says as he thrusts the water jug at me.

Unable to remember the last meal I'd had that tasted better, I can only nod in agreement.

We talk briefly after eating and while we make a quick cleaning of the cabin, but the day and the heat have settled on us and we both look enviously at Spider as she snores from her bunk. Kenny snuffs all the lamps but one, then crawls in next to his sleeping Lab; I take the other ground-level bunk, slipping under an old, hand-tied quilt and propping a tick pillow under my head. As Kenny whiffs out the final lamp the cabin turns dark as a cave, and the strident singing of frogs and the occasional screech owl is all that I hear before drifting off.

* * *

Another serenade wakens us in the morning, but the owls and frogs have been replaced by songbirds, geese, and sandhill cranes. We listen to the chorus for a while before rising, but Spider has rested and needs to greet the day and chase off any intruders who've accumulated on the grounds since nightfall. Kenny rises to let her out, and we both dress, don bug shirts, and follow her out on the lawn.

The sun is hanging low over the eastern bluffs when we reach the canoe landing again. A pair of Canada geese honk their displeasure at our arrival and fly down the slough, gabbling to each other about our intrusion. We flip the *Queen Mary* once again, Spider hops in, and we launch it to retrace our path to the setline waiting at the Devil's Elbow. The morning air is cool, and a slight breeze stirs across our faces, making us appreciate the extra layer the bug shirt provides.

When we reach Devil's Elbow and paddle into our small bay, I notice the wooden floats skating oddly across the surface, first pulling one direction, then another. "That's a good sign," Kenny says. "Looks like we got fish on!"

And he's right. The fifth line from the upstream bank holds a nice sized mudcat of four or five pounds, and two more downstream hooks hold slightly smaller fish. Kenny reels each in, hand over hand, then slides the cat onto a stringer.

"If we were doing this with more line, or sets, I'd have a pair of metal washtubs in front of me right now," Kenny says. "You want one for the turtles you might get—those are a bonus, especially snappers—the other one for mudcat. But I'll just string these up. We had a good night's catch for what we put out."

Kenny retrieves the rest of the set, gently laying the line in loose coils on the bottom of the box. When he's finished, he lays the box gently at his feet, pulls the willow pole from the stream bottom, then grips his paddle for our return trip to the Big Lake Shack. There's where we'll have our second fish meal in less than twelve hours, the firm flesh of the mudcat just as tasty, if not more so, than the sunfish so noted for their flavor. Somewhere in the middle of breakfast—with my mouth full of mudcat and Spider waiting by my knee for her share—I realize just how many Whitman Swamp fillets I've consumed in the last few hours. By rights I should be sated, but all I can do is eat and pet the dog and look fondly out over Big Lake toward a deep, dark pool called the Devil's Elbow.

RAT TALE

Passing the Flame: The Marsh Shack

KENNY TELLS THE TALE: When I first started roaming the Whitman Swamp, it was already home to an old-time river rat by the name of Kermit Spieth. Now Kermit was not your "normal" river rat. He had gone to business college as a young man and was well read and soft spoken. He and his wife Florence operated a small general store in the tiny village of Cochrane a mile east of the Big River. Most of his spare time was spent smack in the middle of the Whitman Swamp on 120 acres of "land" that he owned. Here, Kermit exchanged his dress pants and white shirt for bib overalls, a wool coat, and hip boots. His pen was set aside and replaced by a canoe paddle, walking stick, gun, trap, or fishing pole. Kermit was one of the few people I knew who was a businessman and an authentic, old-time river rat—and he was respected as both.

By the end of the summer of 1953, Kermit and several of his longtime duck hunting partners from around the state had completed construction to their satisfaction of a hunting outpost in the far reaches of the Whitman on some of Kermit's land. This outpost became known as the Marsh Shack. It was not a work of art by any means, but it was a labor of love. It was functional, rough hewn, and weather worthy; a shelter from the elements, it was also a place to hang their hats when enjoying the sunrise whisper of migrating wings over the open porch, the "lights out" announcement from the mallard hens at dusk, and the questioning *Who, who, whooo me?* of the hunting owl after dark.

By the time the Marsh Shack was a few years old, I was already hunting ducks close to the perimeter of Kermit's private land on which it was built. I was in my early teens and was just beginning to understand the ins and outs, dos and don'ts of the intricate maze of Whitman wetlands. Some of the land, which was privately owned at that time, one could hunt on; some land, one couldn't hunt, and the Marsh Shack land was definitely off limits. It was a code of ethics among river rats that made me stay off Kermit's land. To be caught there would bring repercussions that I did not want to experience in any way, shape, or form. Even though that territory was teeming with ducks, muskrats, and beavers, I steered clear of it out of respect. Kermit, his wife Florence, and their daughter Marylyn were family friends, yet I never approached them about going out to their land or the shack. Nobody I knew had ever even been inside of that mysterious place. Sometimes on late-autumn nights when flocks of migrating ducks crossed the harvest moon, I dreamt of living in the Marsh Shack, dining upon wild rice-fattened mallards, and running long lines of muskrat traps in the vast marshes beyond. It never came to more than that. I stayed away.

About ten years later, after having been in and out of the army, I was running long lines of traps, hunting, fishing, and trying desperately to carve out a meager living with the land. One fine day I happened to meet Kermit in town. After chatting a bit, he came right out and asked me point blank if I'd be interested in trapping on his swampland. He added that I could use his Marsh Shack as a base of operations, if I'd like. Interested? If I'd like? Was I interested in seeing one of my fondest dreams come true? Would I like to be standing in the middle of a swampman's paradise? I began to shiver and shudder, stammer and stutter. Finally I composed myself enough to tell Kermit that I'd need a little time to think it over, seeing as I was so busy and all.

About twelve minutes later, I pulled up in front of Kermit's house. We agreed that we would split the fur checks right down the middle. He gave me a key to the shack, and I floated out of his house and back to my car. Somebody slap me! Life couldn't be this good!

The very next day I turned the key in the front door of the Marsh Shack and stepped into another world, a time gone by, a way of life that was already then beginning to disappear. The shack was built to combat the nature of the terrain in which it stood. It was a dark, rectangular building that measured about a canoe-length and -width square. The shack stood on top of a dozen barrels, which served as a floating foundation in case the waters of the Whitman Swamp rose high enough to lift it off its footings—which was indeed a common occurrence. It was a lovely place, a place of shifting winds, no trees yet lots of marsh, a land that was more water than earth.

Inside, a medium-sized, wood-burning stove sat quietly in one corner with its stovepipe chimney extended perhaps eight feet straight up through the front-to-back slanted roof. Next to the stove was a pile of dry firewood, ranked up in short rows, neat and well cared for. Along the east wall were four wooden-framed bunks; each held a bed spring with a small mattress resting upon it and some blankets, quilts, pillows, and such to top them off. Against the south wall stood an LP gas–fired cook stove sporting four burners and an oven. Alongside of it was an old-time wash basin with a looking glass mounted on the wall above it. A drop-leaf table fit tightly to the west wall, directly below a large, rectangular, hinged window. Above the window hung an empty, notched gun rack; a couple of duck calls dangled from it along with an old, battered, weather-beaten, felt hat. A mouse-chewn burlap bag held half a dozen wooden duck decoys in the far corner. Imprinted upon the rough plank floor were several muddy footprints. A rubber patching kit along with a few empty shotgun shell casings lay strewn about on the table and a goodly number of mouse droppings as well. It was as if the hunters had just left a moment or two before, yet the place hadn't been used for years. I felt an eerie sense of having been there many times before—and I guess in a spiritual way I had been.

From that day on, I have found shelter, comfort, and warmth within the old shack's walls. Many a catfish has been skinned and staked up on a hot summer's night upon the rickety mosquito-infested front porch while the southern breeze sang its song in the nearby river birch leaves. How many times, on a crisp autumn night, have I sat reading near the window by the glow of a kerosene lamp and heard the gabble of ducks a stone's throw away and thought of the promise of whispering wings at dawn.

When the white winds of winter blow and bluster their way around every tar-papered inch of the outside walls looking for a crack to sneak through, and I lay in my bunk listening to the crackle of the fire, the creaking and groaning of the weathered boards, and the soft reassurance of my own breathing, morning seems far, far away. The sparkling hopes and the perilous fears of the trapline shall come soon enough. For now, I am safe and happy.

Spring in the marsh is unmatched in its glory. The snow and ice melt on the roof, steadily dripping onto the ground. The smell of tar paper being heated by the growing sun wafts through the air. For the first time since early autumn one can actually open a window to breath in the scent of a regenerating earth. You can hear the happy singing of the red-wing blackbird and the far-off talk of the wild goose. Now the wind brings hopes and promises that I did not dare to think of for so long. And the Marsh Shack has withstood another year, another round of the four seasons, another full turn of the Circle of Life. And so have I.

The Marsh Shack was the first camp that I worked out of in the remote, rugged Whitman Swamp country. Although I did not build this camp it soon became home to me and I treated the shack as if I had toted every piece of it out there, drove every nail, and sawed each board myself. Each time I saw it from afar I experienced a feeling of comfort and adventure and a sense of pride in my heart. This was my first toehold, my first stepping stone along the path toward self-sufficiency. The Marsh Shack symbolized a passing of the flame from an old-time river rat to me.

AUGUST

River Rat Almanac

SUMMERTIME AND THE living is easy. Just some words to a song? Not at all. To river people these are profound truths. In August, the mighty Mississippi runs low and slow and easy. The dog days of summer are here, and dogs and folks alike seek shady places on the islands and river banks.

Life on the Big River has slowed to the pace of a laid-back snail. Riverfolk and their dogs concern themselves mainly with eating, sleeping, lying in the shade, and swimming—not necessarily in that order—with maybe a little fishing thrown in for good measure.

The *whir* of a male cicada pierces the evening air as he calls out his woes among the cottonwoods. In lowland meadows and riverbank prairies, the grasses are alive with hoppers of every size. From evening until morning crickets chirp their merry song. Mosquitoes hum menacingly, suggesting an imminent bite. I've always thought ear plugs might be as useful as bug spray when it comes to skeeters. It is August—the month of the insect.

Walking Sticks and Woodslore

Before I met Kenny I viewed the month of August with about as much anticipation as a trip to the dentist. August was when time stood on itself. The heat of summer dug in and the pleasing coolness of fall seemed eons away. Reasons to detest the month read like a laundry list: The fishing was poor, bees were ornery, humidity cloaked the river valley like a blanket. . . . Even some birds—swallows, most notably—started flocking up for migrations. I'd always admired the swallows for their early departure. I'd blow out of the river valley in August if I had the chance, too.

But that was my mindset before I met Kenny. Once I spent some time hanging around the seasoned riverman, I came to view August as an important month. This was a big step for a guy known for comparing August to Tuesday, a day of the week that wears mediocrity like an old shirt. Once Kenny took me under his wing, however, I began to understand that August is a month of preparation, excitement, and renewal, a deep, full breath of air before the frenzy of fall sweeps over the land.

My metamorphosis did not happen overnight, of course, and it began with something as simple as a peeled-ash walking stick. Kenny had called me for another rendezvous at the Big Lake Shack in mid-August, and I had to work hard to disguise the hesitation in my voice.

"What's on the agenda for tomorrow?" I ask.

"Nothing important. We'll just poke around and see what happens."

Given my already bad attitude toward late summer, and remembering the deerflies and other winged vermin that met me on my last trip to the swamp, and knowing the next day's forecast called for bright skies and a magnum sun, I am not particularly excited about poking around anywhere that didn't have air conditioning. But I'd signed on to see how river rats lived, and if all they did in August was poke, then I'd have at that, too.

The resident horde of deerflies meet me as I steer the truck from the blacktop onto the two-track, then escort me to the shack. They put on an impressive aerial display, buzzing and diving around the pickup like whining fighter planes attacking a groaning old bomber. But like watching a horror movie for the second time, some of the effect was lost. I also had a bug shirt of my own now tucked under my seat, and I slip into it immediately as I pop open the door, then release Cody from his spot in the truck bed. A group of deerflies make a strafing run at my head, smell the bug shirt and veer off, whining their displeasure. I chuckle and congratulate myself. I was finally smelling bad enough to keep bugs away.

"Back here, Scott."

Kenny's voice comes from behind the shack, and when I peek around back he's sitting on an oak stump by the fire ring. A small fire crackles beneath a cast-iron, three-legged kettle. Steam rises from the kettle and disappears into the warm August morning, and it's clear the water will soon be boiling. Kenny motions for me to sit on a stump near him, and as I do, he reaches out to shake my hand. The semi-formal greeting is a ritual that rarely goes unobserved at any of our meetings. Spider and Cody sniff each other in greeting, then romp off to play in the woods near the shack.

"Little hot for cooking, ain't it, Kenny?" I ask, pointing to the kettle.

"Hah!" he snorts. "Yeah, figured it was time to make some chili.

Ain't warm enough in the swamp without a fire! No, going to boil some traps today, get them ready for season." Then he motions to a mound of long, slender branches piled next to him. "Also peeling some walking sticks. Got a couple folks coming to the swamp later this month and I thought I'd get them each one." I smiled, remembering our April outing when Kenny gave me the walking stick I now keep in my truck permanently and use on many an outing. Kenny's visitors were lucky folk indeed. "If you got a knife, you can help me," Kenny says.

"I'd like that. Show me what to do."

Kenny explains that, like mine, these walking sticks will be made of ash he'd cut from the swamp months before. "Usually early spring is when I get out and harvest them. Cut some ash for walking sticks and a bunch of willow for trap stakes—we'll work on some of those in a little while. After I get what I need cut, I stick the thicker, or butt, ends of all of them in a slough to keep them from rotting. That saves them for now."

The fire has coaxed the water to a lazy boil. Kenny stands and lifts a batch of two dozen traps attached to a stout wire and gently lowers them into the kettle. "That kettle water's full of silver maple bark and the hulls from black walnuts," Kenny explains as the traps disappear into the dark soup. "That'll dye the metal on the traps, and de-scent them too. We'll leave them go for awhile while we work on these sticks."

Peeling walking sticks is a pleasant, leisurely activity that I fall into easily. Being a devout whittler since receiving my first jackknife as a boy, I follow Kenny's lead almost mindlessly, starting at the tip end of the walking stick and shaving the tight bark off the pole with my knife. Whittling is a deceptively simple craft that requires only a sharp knife and a feel for how bark lays against the wood. Some trees sport a thin, tight, skin that must be shaved delicately from the sapwood. Others have coarse, chunkier bark that resembles a thick hide. Peeling bark off a pole is not brain surgery, or even wood carving, but a deft whittling job is a thing of simple beauty that produces a smooth, barkless pole with no nicks—in the wood or the carver.

We work in silence for a time, and the dogs, finally tired of their play, throw themselves at our feet. Cody sniffs the pile of shavings at my feet, then sighs heavily and stretches out against the ground. "You better get rested up," Kenny says, smiling at Cody. "Next month we'll be ginseng hunting, and you'll need to run them hills with us."

"I don't think he'll have much trouble with the resting part," I admit. At nearly ten years of age, Cody is a typical old retriever; if his legs could only match his heart, he'd set the woods on fire.

"Maybe we can cut you a walking stick to help you up and down these hills," Kenny coos at the now-sleeping dog. "*I* sure can't imagine getting along without one."

One of my earliest impressions of Kenny was that he did, indeed, have a walking stick with him nearly everywhere he went: on every hike, every hunt, while slipping down trout streams, even when talking to a room full of schoolkids. The peeled ash stick was always there to lean on, sweep debris off a trail, point to a buck rub or beaver slide. It was as much a part of Kenny as an arm or leg. I mention this to him, and his explanation comes easily. "Once you get used to using a walking stick, they kind of become part of you. There's practical reasons for that, and others that go deeper.

"A walking stick is like a third leg when you're going up or down one of these steep hills. It'll help you balance when you're crossing a log over a ditch or mucking through one a these sloughs filled with boot-sucking mud. With a walking stick you can clear a fallen branch from a trail without leaning over, or coax a snake to move from your path.

"I believe a person who uses a walking stick sees more of what's happening in the woods. Thoreau wrote about 'sauntering' with a walking stick, where he'd hike a ways, then stop and lean on the stick to observe what was around him. He got that right; I've noticed the same thing myself and so have other people used to using walking sticks. My uncle once told me to take note when I saw a man using a walking stick—that such a man probably knows what he's doing in the woods. And after a lot of years, I've come to agree with that."

I've always been interested in the fact that Kenny's walking sticks are not ornately carved. Nor are they initialed or fitted with a rope grip or lanyard to prevent loss. They're utterly simple: a smooth-shaven, mostly straight length of river-bottom ash that, ideally, reaches about as high as the hiker's armpit. When I query Kenny about the bare-bones nature of his staffs, his answer is as simple as the implement. "Partly because it's practical," he says. "I don't want something fancy if I got to shove it in some mudhole for balance, or worry about it if I'm banging through some thicket digging mushrooms or ginseng. Besides, if I put one down someday and forget where it is, what've I lost? Not some store-bought, carved-up thing. It's just a stick. I can find another."

Despite his speech, I know Kenny's appreciation for the walking stick goes beyond its practical value, and I press him on the point. "You don't seem to have lost one in awhile. The one you're carrying today is the same one you had when we met."

"And it's a good stick, too!" Kenny replies quickly. "Don't get me wrong. When I lose one, it's like losing an old friend. Every stick is unique; grips a little different in your hand, the bend is here instead of there, the wood's a little darker or lighter than the one your partner's using. And probably the main thing that sets every walking stick apart from the others is the way your hand moves along that stick when you walk. The oils you rub into the wood with every grip—you couldn't get such a beautiful polish if you worked that wood with sandpaper and varnish."

We've each finished a walking stick when Kenny stands again, lifts the traps out of the water using a long stick with a metal hook on the end, and drops them on the ground. Then he stokes the fire, reaches for another batch of traps, and drops them into the dark, steaming water. After sitting, then dipping some snuff, Kenny points to a small mound of willow poles behind him. "Since you got the hang of that ash, might as well set into these willows, too. Come in handy trapping this fall."

"Sounds good."

The bundle of willows consists of five-foot sticks of varying thickness. Kenny explains as we work: The poles will be used as trap stakes as he makes water sets for muskrat, beaver, and raccoon. Peeling the willows makes them resist rotting and weathering, an important consideration for an implement that will spend weeks either submerged in water or exposed to wind, rain, and snow. Removing the bark also makes them unattractive to beaver as a food source; the big rodents are known for their fondness for chewing the bark off any slender branch or twig near open water.

"Willow poles are light and easy to carry in the canoe," Kenny says as we begin whittling. "The other thing that peeling does is make them easy to handle. Your trapping gloves never snag on bark or little branches that'd be there if you didn't peel. And like walking sticks, they're simple. Why buy a store-bought stake when you can make something just as good for nothing but the time it takes to do it?"

We spend a good half-hour working on the slender willows, whittling the smooth, tight bark from the branches, this time taking care to leave a fork in the stick when possible. This fork allows Kenny to push the stake into the mud up to the trap ring—a metal ring on the end of each trap chain—to prevent animals from escaping with the trap. As we finish each willow we place it in a growing pile that will be stored next to a small shed near Big Lake Shack with other trapping supplies.

"Better get this batch of traps out of the fire, then call it a day for that hot job," Kenny says as he rises and lifts the second string of traps from the kettle and places them on the ground. Dripping and steaming, the legholds are a deep black-brown shade that will make them almost invisible to furbearers. While the majority of Kenny's trapping is done with water sets, and water is the best camouflage for any trap, he still boils a few traps each year that need the treatment. Like peeling walking sticks and willows, it's simply a tradition of the season.

There is still a small pile of willow sticks by Kenny's stump, but he doesn't return to his seat. "C'mon," he says, motioning me toward the shack. "Let's have something to eat."

I rise and stretch, my back stooped from too much time in whittling posture. After working out my carving kinks, I head to the front of the shack, kicking myself for neglecting to bring something to the lunch table. But Kenny isn't waiting at the cabin door, he's standing by his car, pointing to the passenger side. "Hop in. We're having lunch in the hills today."

After calling the dogs into the back seat, Kenny steers the car down the swamp road, onto the blacktop, and up a narrow route leading to a secluded hillside. Southerly breezes are pushing through the uplands, and the shade of towering oaks makes the country road seem like a covered bridge. We slide out of the car and grab walking sticks. Then Kenny lets the dogs out, slides on a shoulder bag containing some empty margarine tubs and a jug of water. He winks at me and slips off the pavement and into the dark, late-summer woods.

The walking is easy at first. Towering red oaks produce such gloaming shade that only a handful of tree species and almost no underbrush can grow beneath them. We walk noiselessly for several hundred yards through such a park, my gaze alternating between the arching treetops and the ground just ahead of my feet. The season's first acorns have begun falling, and the fat, abundant nuts seem to forecast a bumper crop; something to remember when it's time to chase deer and squirrels this fall.

Suddenly I realize the trees are casting harsh shadows at my feet, and I look up to see a small, but dramatic, opening in the timber ahead of me. The dense canopy has disappeared, and only small oaks and a few young basswood take their place. Bright sunlight streams on the forest floor, and lush saplings and brush are everywhere, pushing for the sky. The contrast in forest type and density is so great it's like entering another world. Kenny senses my wonder.

"Been some logging here a couple years ago. My nephew does it in winter—skids the logs out with horses. Easier on these hills than some of these skidders. Don't gouge no roads or trails, hardly. Makes use of some of this big old oak timber, and lets the forest grow up again. Good for the deer, rabbits, grouse, songbirds. . . . And of course, it makes lunch for guys like us, too." Then Kenny reaches into the burlap sack, produces a pair of margarine tubs, thrusts one at me, and points to the sunlit woods ahead of us. "Come on."

It takes me a second to recognize them, but when my eyes adjust

I realize we are standing in front of the greatest concentration of blackberries I've ever seen. Hundreds of black-purple fruits are drooping, hanging, and sagging from an impenetrable wall of brush and vine. But in the most surreal vision of berry picking I've ever experienced, this time there is no need to wade through berry brush to secure the juicy plunder. Without turning my head left or right, I spot enough accessible berries hanging just at eye level to cover several bowls of breakfast cereal, bake a couple of pies, cook some jam, freeze for winter, and still have enough to make a small batch of wine. This is berry heaven and we are standing at the Pearly Gates.

Kenny, of course, is not wasting any time assessing the situation; he is popping berries in his mouth like a kid who's just had his first taste of a blackberry and can't get enough. I am so overwhelmed by the bounty I can't suppress a belly laugh, which momentarily distracts Kenny from his munching. I squelch my chuckle, then explain myself: "There's so many, I don't know where to start!"

Kenny nods as a small stream of purple juice slides down his chin. "That can be a problem. Two schools of thought on it. Disciplined folks pick for the pot first, then eat. Me, I figure I'll eat all I want first, then settle down and fill some bowls. Who the heck knows how long you're are going to live? Could be struck by lightning before you get a bellyful. So which group are you in?"

I try to answer but my mouth is so full of berries I can only mumble. No matter. Kenny is back to his plunder, holding his tub to his chest with his left hand and plucking berries with his right. Near as I can tell, he's eaten enough to go into alternating mode; tossing one handful of fruit into the tub, the next in his mouth. I continue feeding myself for several minutes before I lay into making produce. The berries are so abundant I nab only the largest, ripest fruit, but I fill three tubs so quickly that my feet have barely moved since we started picking. Kenny has filled all his containers, too, and walks toward me, munching on a handful almost as an afterthought, obviously sated.

"Good year for berries, I guess," he offers.

"I'll say. Why is that?"

"Had rain when we needed it this spring and summer. Barely find them in a dry year. Also this patch is prime—plants are young and healthy. If they get water when they need it, they'll fill out some fruit."

"How'd you know this was here?"

"Didn't. Just knew about the logging Tim had done here a while back. Figured with the wet summer it might be good."

"You were right."

Picking blackberries is one of the simplest, yet most satisfying endeavors going in bluff country. Visit most local grocery stores or farmer's markets and you can buy wild berries for a reasonable price. But something—besides the sweat, scratched arms, and hiking—is lost in the process. I mention this to Kenny as we start a leisurely walk back to scout other berry patches for a return trip.

"It's the self-sufficiency," he says without thinking. "Sure, buying them's more convenient, but it takes you one step further away from the land. You can buy most everything pre-packaged nowadays. But it's getting rare to find anyone who knows enough to gather their own food in the woods, even this time of year, when it's like a big salad bar out here."

As we lean into our walking sticks to climb a hill, Kenny explains that simple foods, such as berries, are like a primer for people interested in wild edibles. "But most let their interest die at the blackberry vine," he says. "Too bad. There's wild strawberries in June—as sweet a fruit as you'll ever find. Blackcaps in early summer. Blackberries now. Wild apples ripening soon. Those are easy ones that anyone can identify with a little practice. But instead of being curious and searching for more plants they can use, they lose confidence. Then they wind up missing out on something like this."

Kenny stops and points to the ground ahead of us with his walking stick. There, scattered across the nut-brown forest floor like cue balls on a billiard table are a dozen cream-white puffballs, their softly dimpled skin reminiscent of tanned leather. "These are in the perfect eating stage," Kenny says, stooping by one of the larger ones and plucking it gently from its stem. "Wait a while and they turn brown and yellow. Then you can kick them and they live up to their name. Turn powdery and blow up like a bomb—that's how they release the spores they need to reproduce. But we'll take a few of these home and fry them in butter. Then we'll eat like kings."

As he carefully gathers a few of the puffballs, Kenny holds court on hunting fall mushrooms. "You can get all kinds of people excited about looking for morels in the spring, and it's easy to see why. Good time of year to stretch your legs, take a spring hike. And morels are good eating and easy to identify. But to me they don't eat near as well as the fall mushrooms, and there's so many more of them now. Better variety, different tastes. Trouble is, people get scared—worried they'll eat the wrong kind and get sick."

"Shouldn't they be?"

"Course they should! You can get sicker than a dog, maybe die if you get really reckless. That's why you go with someone who knows them. Or bring a good field guide—the kind with color pictures—so there's no doubt. Then learn one or two new ones each fall. Won't be long and you'll be able to head to the woods in August and live off the land for a couple months if you had to."

"What are some of the better-eating fall mushrooms?"

"I like the hen-of-the-woods," Kenny says dreamily. "They grow by old oak trees and stumps. Have a gray, ruffly appearance, like feathers. They can get huge. Biggest one I ever took weighed sixty-three pounds. Had to cut it in half to get it out of the woods! Neat thing about them is you can find them growing in the same places year after year. I cut off small chunks, then sauté them in butter.

"Button mushrooms are excellent eating, too. They look like the 'stems and pieces' you buy in a can in the grocery store. They grow near oak stumps in logged areas only a year or two after the cut. They'll be brown or tan, with a little cap—that gives them their name.

"Then there's the fairy circle, which looks like its name, and honey mushrooms, sulfur shelf . . ."

"Sounds like I need to tag along on a fall hunt so I can see some of these critters myself," I interject.

"Hah!" Kenny snorts. "Guess I was getting kind of carried away there. You're right. You do need to come again soon and we'll look for some of the different mushrooms. I got some good places to hunt."

"I'd like that."

"Next week then," he says, patting the puffballs that now bulge from his shoulder bag. "If you got time to go for a couple hours. We'll get the rest of them traps boiled, then sneak off in the hills for a mushroom hunt. Bring yourself a couple paper bags, case we get lucky."

Kenny leads a leisurely loop across the hillside that, somewhat mysteriously, leads us back to the welcome sight of the car. The woods remain thick with foliage and heavy with late summer air. Every so often, a mosquito hums in my ear or lands on my neck. And if I take the time to think about it, my T-shirt clings to the small of my back, sucked there by a growing puddle of sweat. Even the dogs, who've been largely silent all day, pant heavily and lap eagerly at the water we pour into our palms when we reach the roadside. It is August after all, and summer is still dug in hard along the Big River.

But somewhere on the hike, I seem to have lost some of my dander about the month I once compared to Tuesday. Was it the simple pleasure of peeling walking sticks and trap stakes? The incredible bounty of the blackberry patch? The portent of learning some fall mushrooms to serve to my family and guests? Not an easy question—and one that requires more thought and energy than I have at the moment. Perhaps I'll get to it in a slower month. But certainly not August, when the river rat world shifts into overdrive.

RAT TALE
Tent Camp and the Bad Bees

KENNY TELLS THE TALE: Out in the middle of the 6,000 acres of seasonally flooded hardwoods of the Upper Mississippi River backwaters in the Whitman Swamp I built a spike camp that I named simply enough Tent Camp. This hithermost outpost I called "home" during endless winter nights when I was running long lines of traps, or during spring and fall when I was guiding hunters, anglers, and, later, nature lovers out into the deepest parts of the swamp.

The old Tent Camp site is located about three quarters of a mile from the shores of Big Lake where my main shack sits to this day. In those years when the Tent Camp sheltered me from the winter's cold nights, snow squalls, and ice storms, I made my way to the camp from Big Lake by following a shallow slough lined with cattails and wild rice. The slough widens out in a long, narrow, shallow spot called Long Lake. Beyond Long Lake, I often stopped to admire a flowage dammed at one end by a huge, ancient beaver dam. I always pondered for a bit, How many generations of beaver have lived here in this wild place? How many generations have taken care of this dam? How many have cut their winter feed from the shores of this flowage? The lodge sits on the bank, plastered with mud for warmth. In cold months, the vent hole on top was frosted from the breath of the beaver curled up inside. After crossing the beaver dam, I walked along a high bank, which are rare in the swamp; most banks aren't more than two or three feet above water level. I built the Tent Camp at the highest point in the swamp where the bank is probably five or six feet above the water. On top of this "high" knoll in the heavily wooded ground was a small, open clearing, the perfect place for this spike camp.

After finding this place a couple dozen years ago, I began hauling out loads of supplies to build the camp. Having little money, I used recycled, bartered, or natural materials as much as I could. First, I hauled out four old, metal barrels with my canoe. I found these barrels on the shore of the Mississippi after a season of spring floods. On another trip, I hauled a load of rough, home-sawn lumber, an old hammer, saw, battered ax, baling wire, rope, and some old rusty nails that I'd pulled out of a ramshackle shed I'd torn down years earlier. With these few supplies, I built a make-shift wooden platform and wired a barrel under each corner. From the surrounding swamp, I then cut and peeled a few poles of young ash and put those up for rafters and walls. Later, I hauled out an old tarpaulin, salvaged for me by a friend who had worked at an army barracks. I stretched that old canvas over the poles, placed a few cut stumps leading up to the wooden platform, and the Tent Camp was born.

I outfitted the inside of the tent camp with a little, old, wood-burning, sheepherder stove, an army cot, and some plastic, five-gallon pails covered with lids where I kept dried fruit, smoked meat, and a couple sets of spare clothes. I spent many pleasurable days lying on that old cot, smelling the canvas and autumn leaves, listening to the ducks and geese and song-birds and the sharp winter wind. After many a long day on the trail, the Tent Camp looked like a Hilton to me.

When the springtime floodwaters came, ropes were tied from each of the four corners of the tent's platform to nearby trees. These kept the Tent Camp floating high and dry until the waters receded and the camp settled back down to its place on the forest floor. I remember one time, I was trapping spring 'rats and the water was higher than it had ever been; the Tent Camp was probably six feet higher than normal. I pulled the canoe over to it, tied it off, and went inside for a little noontime rest. I had an old pillow on the army cot, and when I got to laying on that pillow I felt something move. I sat up quickly and there was a big bull snake curled up under my pillow. I was startled to say the least! I looked around a bit more under some rags and other junk and I found a couple of water snakes and another bull snake. Then of course it dawned on me: There was no dry land out there in the swamp, and the Tent Camp was the sole refuge that those poor old snakes had. So I moved that old bull snake off the cot and lay down. I let the rest of the snakes stay where they were. I could tolerate those critters, and I hope they'd do the same if they had me in that position.

The Tent Camp brings back many memories. To the south and west of the site runs a spit of water called Tent Camp Slough. It's a narrow, muddy, little slough that meanders back through the swamp's white oaks, ash, and alders that line her banks. Thick, velvety green mats of duckweed cover the slough summertime through fall. I can usually find a few wood ducks sitting on old logs, the drakes with their beautiful plume, scratching themselves, preening each other, a belly full of acorns, mighty happy. I have many fond memories of laying inside the tent and listening to the wood ducks as they whistle and call to each other.

One day I was lying on the cot inside the Tent Camp for a little noon rest. I looked up at the ceiling, and I noticed there was a hole in the canvas. I made a mental note to come back later in the summer to patch that hole before everything started to rot. It doesn't take long, you know; when you got a hole in the roof, everything else goes downhill.

On a hot day in late July, I loaded up some tar and canvas for a patch. I put the old dog in the front of the canoe, and I made my way out to where the Tent Camp sat. When I got to the camp, I walked up the old wooden steps, went inside the tent walls, and immediately realized I was too short on one end to reach that hole in the ceiling. I got to looking around and saw there was a five-gallon pail tipped upside down on a stump not too far from the tent. It had been there all spring and summer. As I looked at that pail, a light bulb went on inside my old noodle and I thought to myself, You know, Kenny, you can go down there and you can get you that pail, tip it upside down on the floor, stand on it, reach that hole, and patch it."

The dog and I made our way down those old wooden steps and over to that pail. I no more than touched the pail—wiggled it a little bit—and the biggest swarm of bees you ever saw in your life came ripping out from under there. They weren't happy campers! Them bees wanted us out of there—not tomorrow, not later that day, but right now! The bees were all over me. They were all over the dog and they weren't just crawling—they were a-stinging, big time!

Now I don't have to tell you but there's only one thing you can do about that time and that's run just as fast as you can. Well, maybe there's two things you can do: run and scream at the same time. My focus was mostly on the running part of it. We started picking them up and laying them down, heading for the nearest slough. We were aiming to jump in that slough to get some relief from them bees.

Now as I mentioned earlier, in the summer, a Mississippi River backwater slough is covered with a thick, emerald green carpet of duckweed. They tell me duckweed is the smallest flowering plant around. Every single one of them little green specks is a separate plant all its own. Now, under the duckweed is some water. And in that water is some fish, snakes, frogs, turtles, and such. Under the water is that dread stuff called black, boot-sucking, Mississippi Mud. That's the stuff, when you're wading through it with rubber boots on and you get a funny feeling in one foot, you turn to look back and there—three steps behind you—is one of your rubber boots sticking in the mud. That mud'll suck the boots plumb off your feet. All things considered, however, with those bees on my tail I guarantee that backwater slough looked a whole lot like heaven to me!

Now you all know who Bo Jackson is. At one time, he was one of the fastest runners on earth. I could have beat Bo Jackson in a hundred yard dash about this time, though. The old dog was gaining speed. Funny how something like that'll limber up your old bones. The old dog passed me and left me with the bees. I heard him hit the water in the slough. I wished I was there with him, but I still had a-ways to go.

When I got to the edge of the bank, I leapt out into mid-air, did a belly flop, and made a water entry that would've done any black Lab real proud. The water sprayed and the mud flew and then the second worst thing of that day happened to me. I found out the water was too shallow. It wouldn't cover me. I had to lay down and roll in the mud—and the blood and the bees. When they got all done with me, I had to hold one eye open with my fingers so I could see to get out of that swamp.

Now I was never much of a student in school; I learned most of my lessons from nature. But I often thought about bees. Were bees bad or good? I guarantee you one thing, my friend, not being much of a speller, I could sure as heck have spelled my answer that day: B–A–D. They were all bad. But after a few days I got to thinking about how those bees make honey and how they pollinate all the plants. They were just trying to protect their home. Anybody would have done the same. That's when I got to thinking bees were both bad and good. And isn't that the case with all critters? Isn't that the case with all humans? You know there's a little bit of bad in the best of us and a little bit of good in the worst. I guess what one has to do is seek the good and praise it.

One day a couple years later down the road, I saw that the Tent Camp's canvas was rotting beyond repair from the many years of wear and tear in the raw elements of the swamp. Tree limbs had fallen on it after some rough windstorms. I realized I would also have to start replacing some of the skinned pole rafters. So, I came to the conclusion that the Tent Camp had served its purpose. By that time, I had acquired the Marsh Shack, which lay even farther out in the swamp. I still had the Big Lake Shack as well. Since the Tent Camp sat about halfway in between, I decided I could get along with out it any longer and that way I could avoid having to do some major repairs.

I'll never forget the day I tore down the Tent Camp. I peeled the canvas off and the Tent Camp stood like a lonely skeleton. As I tore each pole down I thought about some of the stories and the experiences she'd given me. My heart grew heavy. I got down to taking apart the platform. The barrels were the last to go. I hauled six or seven canoe loads of stuff back over to the high ground from the Tent Camp. I wanted to record the last load going out from the Tent Camp and I took a number of pictures with a camera I had borrowed from a friend. I had my dog posing in most of them. Funny thing about it, those pictures never turned out. But the pictures I had taken in my mind, in my memory, have never faded. You see, my friends, in the end, after all is said and done, all the wear and tear, all the crying and gnashing of teeth in this life, all the chasing of the rainbows, finding our dreams, all we are left with is our memories. I shall forever remember the Tent Camp and the summer of the bad bees.

SEPTEMBER

River Rat Almanac

IN SEPTEMBER, ONE'S thoughts hold both the passing of summer and the approach of autumn. This month is a kindred spirit to April. In April, winter grudgingly gives way to spring. In September, summer gradually dissolves into autumn.

An ancient blufftop cliff provides an eagle's-eye view of the great River far below. Following a chilly, damp night, the morning sunlight lifts the breath of the River to form beautiful white fluffy clouds that move slowly across a deep azure background. From my bird's-eye view, I can easily trace its tributaries by following the thick fog banks drifting lazily down the valleys.

Sound seems to travel farther these days. Bird songs are not plentiful— warblers, robins and their kin are busy getting ready for the long, hard journey south. Tree swallows are already winging their way. The squirrels and chipmunks work feverishly on their lay-away plan for winter. Many critters leave their family groups—sometimes driven off by their parents. Great hordes of blackbirds descend upon the backwater rice fields with reckless abandon. Migrating blue-winged teal and locally hatched wood ducks and mallards gorge their gizzards as they dip in the shallow backwaters, cleaning up the spoils their feathered kin left behind from feeding among the tall stalks protruding above the waters. The cold, wet spring produced late hatches of the wood ducks and mallards. The southern journey will be difficult, because their flight muscles are not so strong and their fat reserves are a bit lacking. How many will return next spring?

But in September, blue is beautiful—sky blue asters, New England asters, bluebells, blue cohosh, big and little bluestem, and leftover chicory plants. Grapes and elderberries hang plump and ripe along fence rows. Great blue herons, kingfishers and blue jays haunt the backwaters, along with large flocks of migrating blue-winged teal.

Ginseng Digging

For most residents of the Upper Mississippi River valley, September is a month for looking up. The haziness of the August sky is replaced by a blue so clear it's tempting to think your vision has improved. Leaf edges hint at the color show they'll unveil in the weeks to come. Birds begin flocking up, working out social problems and class rank before the big flight south. Keeping track of these changes is an ongoing process, like watching an extended aerial show, and in September it's not unusual to see people walking around with their heads tipped back and their mouths slung open, afraid to miss anything.

But for the river rat September is a month of looking down, stooping over, and scratching in the dirt. The first month of fall is ginseng time, and while the rest of world looks skyward, the crook in Kenny's neck bends the opposite direction. Wild ginseng grows well in the steeply wooded bluffs surrounding the Big River, and digging the roots of this elusive plant is not only a cherished fall ritual, it's a needed source of income.

Ginseng, of course, is a plant that's been prized by Eastern cultures for centuries. But Americans have hopped on the ginseng bandwagon lately, too. According to ginseng's proponents—an eclectic group ranging from Chinese philosophers to celebrity hawkers as unlikely as Rush Limbaugh—ingesting the root can cure diseases, increase energy, and, naturally, turn you into a love machine. Though ginseng is widely cultivated, the highest prices are reserved for wild plants whose hearty roots have weathered storm and drought and pushed their way past rock and clay and tree roots to survive. The root of a wild ginseng plant wears the signs of struggle on its gnarled and scarred surface—and buyers are willing to pay far more dearly for those badges of strength amid hardship than they do for the smooth, anemic product of its domestic cousin.

Prices for wild roots have spiked in recent years: Kenny recalls earning $35 per pound when he first started digging four decades ago; current prices have reached over $500 for sixteen ounces of dried root. Yet this is not easy money. Ginseng is difficult to find in quantities large enough to realize any profit, and even if you know where to look, its actual presence is never guaranteed. In dry years it may go dormant. In cold autumns the leaves (the easiest means of identifying the plant) can fall to an early frost. And like all valuable plants, it knows enough to grow where the brambles are thickest, the hills steepest, and the loggers have left enough oak tops to stop a Humvee. There are other challenges as well: whining, thirsty mosquitoes; tiny deer ticks carrying Lyme disease; and bees and wasps whose orneriness seems to peak when the calendar shows September 1. Veteran "shang" diggers swear that these pests guard the best ginseng slopes with maniacal vengeance.

Still, there's a heady allure to hunting something so finicky and ethereal. So when Kenny showed up at my door the first week of September, dressed for a ginseng hunt, I was jazzed.

"Like my purse and dress?" he laughs as I open the door. Kenny is wearing an army-issue, thigh-length, lightweight parka, and a battered woman's purse is slung across his shoulder. The parka is for warding off the chill of the cool, foggy morning; the purse is a ginseng-digger's survival kit. While I watch, he pulls out digging tools, plastic bread bags for storing roots, a canteen of water, another bread bag containing hard rolls and smoked venison sausage, and three old snuff tins. "Ginseng seed," he says, thrusting one of the tins at me. I twist the top off the container, which is packed tightly with aspirin-shaped, tobacco-brown pellets. "Ordered those from a commercial grower," he says.

My knowledge of ginseng could fit into one of the snuff tins with room to spare, but I know the price discrepancy between wild and cultivated root. Would these seeds result in a valuable plant, or a wimpy commercial version, I wonder.

"Once they take root and claw their way past stones and hard-pan over ten years, they will have become wild ginseng," Kenny assures me. I nod, then take one of the snuff tins from Kenny when he hands it to me and shove it into my pocket. I grab my walking stick, and follow Kenny, Cody, and Spider as they cross the fields into the deep September woods.

As we enter the woods, Kenny admits it's been years—a decade or more—since he'd "dug root" in the bluffs surrounding my home. "That's why I brought so many seeds," he explains. "If we don't find any plants, we'll make sure they'll be here in the future."

"Why wouldn't they be here anymore?" I ask.

"Dug up. With prices so high, some folks will wipe out a patch, trying to make as much money as possible."

Wisconsin state law prohibits picking immature ginseng plants; those with fewer than three prongs, or leaf petioles, projecting from the stem. This ensures that young plants have a chance to reach maturity and produce the seeds that will ensure the future of the stand. For this same reason, diggers are also required to plant the seeds of any mature ginseng plants they harvest. But ginseng dig-ging is a lonely, secretive business and enforcing such laws is so difficult that the vast majority of 'shang hunters have only their honor to guide them. Sadly, most veteran hunters agree that local stands aren't nearly as abundant as in the past, a sad byproduct of the booming market.

As I trudge behind Kenny I have a rough idea of what our quarry looks like, but feel completely reliant on my guide, who walks the woods slowly, pausing now and then to lean on his walking stick and scan the slope. I'd scanned a field guide the night before and read a few helpful clues about identifying 'shang: One main stem. Projecting petioles, from which three to five leaves hang. Mature plants sport at least three and may have up to five, petioles or "prongs." Leaves, which turn golden in autumn, are serrated along each edge, like the teeth of a saw. Plants stand one to two feet high and have a cluster of bright red berries at the end of the main stem. There was a drawing, too, but a picture would have been better. No matter, though; once Kenny showed me a plant, I was confident I could find them on my own.

I'm blundering behind Kenny so blindly that when he stops by a rotting oak stump I nearly pile into him. Following his gaze, I search the ground by the stump, at my feet, down the slope. I can't spot a plant even remotely resembling my manual sketch, and after a minute, I can't even visualize that. Finally, I can take it no longer.

"Is there a plant around here I'm not seeing?"

"Nope. All gone," Kenny says resignedly.

"Picked by someone else?"

"Maybe. Used to be a good stand here. It might be dormant, but with prices like they are, it's probably gone. We'll plant some here, though. It's a good spot for ginseng."

Kenny digs into his purse for the snuff tin and digging tool. Easing slowly to the ground beside the stump, he breathes out slowly, then explains where ginseng likes to grow. "We're on a north slope here. Plenty of shade. Cool temps in summer, plenty of drainage. The dead oak stump pumps nutrients into the soil. There's basswood trees around, too; they like to grow near them." Scratching at the leaf litter with his two-pronged digging tool, Kenny makes a shallow bed in the dirt, like a turkey scratching for acorns. Finished with the digging, he drops the tool—attached to his belt with a two-foot length of rope—by his knees. "Lose enough of these and you learn to tie them on," he chuckles.

Planting is so simple it's nearly thoughtless. Scattering the seeds across his half-inch-deep rakings, Kenny pushes each one gently into the duff with a dirt-stained fingertip. "Can't plant too deep," he warns. "In nature, they just fall to the ground, you know. But if you cover them, a few more will escape the birds and squirrels and grow up to be four-prongers. Camouflages the spot from other diggers, too," he winks. "Now it's just a matter of waiting."

"How long?" I imagine myself trucking to this secret garden, plucking out a few roots whenever a financial emergency should arise in September.

"You'll see the plants next spring, probably. But it'll be ten years before any three-prongers appear." Kenny sees me doing the math in my head and grins. "Maybe your kids can buy some milk money when you sell them. Who knows what roots will bring then. Or what the price of milk will be."

We chuckle at the uncertainty of the future, somehow shielded from it by these green strong hills. It's easy to ignore the what's-to-come when the only world you care about lies at your feet.

Unfortunately for me, the rest of the day is a repeat of this first experience: Walk to an historic ginseng stand, find no trace of the plants, then choose a likely tree, rock, or logging trail for a marker and plant seeds, in hopes of starting a new ginseng patch. It doesn't take long to realize that anyone interested in quick riches would be a fool to bank on ginseng. But I'm interested only in seeing the plant, not reaping a harvest—eager to ensure that I'm not being led on the vegetative equivalent of a snipe hunt.

We're nearly back to the truck after six fruitless, or rather rootless, hours when Kenny stops along a steep slope and opens his purse for a sack. My eyes search the ground around us, but I see no vegetation resembling a three-prong ginseng plant. Kenny senses my question before I ask it. "We're standing in the middle of a patch of wild ginger as large as any I've seen." he says happily.

I look at my boots to see them nearly covered in musty-green, heart-shaped leaves that would fit neatly across the palm of my hand. Similar in shape to those of a basswood tree, ginger leaves lie close to the ground, supported by a delicate, milky stalk. "Ginger roots can be used in cooking, or as tea, once they're dried," Kenny explains. "You can sell them, too. But you have to pick a bunch to make any money. I just like to dig a few for my own use each year."

Kenny pokes his digging tool deftly to one side of the plant, leans back on it to loosen the earth around the stem, then pulls the tool out and scratches delicately at the ground parallel to the drooping stalk. He pulls the exposed root from the ground with his index finger, brushes dirt from it, and snaps one end briskly between his fingers. "Smell that," he says, holding the soft root up to my face.

The ginger wafts tangy and aromatic, and a childhood recollection of my mother's spice cupboard surfaces. The wet root oozes slightly; closing my eyes produces memories of gingerbread and ginger cookies, and the aroma is so compelling I have to resist the urge to pop the dirt-covered root into my mouth. I hand the ginger back to Kenny, who stuffs it in the bread bag with a dozen others he has collected. "There," he says happily. "I have enough for myself from this patch. You can walk down here anytime in the fall and dig a little if you want some tea."

I take a long look at the wild ginger before we go. Another woodland bounty I knew nothing about had been growing only a quarter-mile from my back door. I also realize that when I leave the woods I must straighten slowly and allow several seconds for my neck and back to regain their normal set. It's a pose I'll strike with frequency in the next couple of weeks. "Next week you come to my neighborhood," Kenny winks as we part for the day. "We'll find you ginseng then."

* * *

The following week the weather turns fall-like as the damp, humid air of summer retreats from an autumn cool front. I poke my way to Kenny's on a Tuesday morning, my elbow sticking out the truck window, the rest of me grateful for the flannel shirt I'm wearing. Early September weather seems always in transition in the Mississippi Valley, the extremes of the just-past and the soon-to-arrive mingle and flirt with each other like nervous divorcees at a social dance.

Kenny and Spider are waiting when I arrive. One of the reasons Kenny and I clicked so immediately was our shared belief that hunting dogs need training on more than just game birds, and Cody and Spider are both devout trout spaniels, mushroom setters, and hickory-nut retrievers. As the dogs greet one another in the truck bed, Kenny directs me along the twisting roads leading to some of his best ginseng ground. No need to lead me on diversionary paths or swear me to secrecy; these valley routes are so remote I couldn't retrace the drive even if I knew ginseng grew like crabgrass on the roadside. Finally, we crest a huge, winding hill and park on the narrow shoulder. Kenny reaches into his sack, produces a chunk of cardboard with his name scrawled in large, black-marker letters, and places it in the truck window to identify himself. "Keep the owner from looking for a trespasser," he says.

We drop off the road and begin picking our way down the steep hill, leaning heavily on walking sticks. The bluff is rugged, thickly timbered with red oak, and full of rotting stumps from long-ago logging. Kenny pauses frequently, scanning up and downslope. We've walked no more than fifteen minutes when he stops, leans on his staff, and clears his throat as if he's about to make a speech.

"You'll hear 'shang hunters talk about how a plant 'lays' on a slope," he says, looking first at me, then shifting glances at the ground to the left and right. "And this is the type of place I look for. Sometimes when the place is right, you actually find the plant, too."

I'm searching frantically now; feeling like a kid in class who's been called on by a teacher I want to impress. Finally, I admit defeat. "OK, I know you have a plant spotted, but I can't see it."

There is no reply, just an obvious, downward stare that I follow until I'm gazing at a smoky-gold, three-pronged ginseng plant that I nearly stepped on.

I'm told there are people who can learn to identify wild ginseng, dig it, sell the dried root, and not lose their souls to the plant in the process. I am not among this sad number. The moment I saw that first plant clinging to that craggy, near-vertical Wisconsin hillside, I knew I was staring at a lifetime of Septembers spent on my knees.

Kenny brushed the leaves away from the area where the stem entered the dirt and pulled out his digging tool. "Watch how I do this on the first one, then you'll know what to do when you find your first one."

Kenny slipped the forked digging tool into the dirt a few inches away from the stem and pulled back on it, loosening the earth. Keeping the tines well away from the suspected lie of the root, he repeated the process in a rough circle around the plant. Then he probed the loosened soil with his index and middle fingers. "I'm feeling for the root," he says. "Trying to figure out which way it grows so I don't break it when I pull it up. Sometimes they grow so tight to a stone or tree root you can break them off. If they get too wrapped up you can't get them out. Leave those plants for seed stock."

Freeing the root with his index finger, Kenny pulls it from the rich loam. The gnarled, cream-colored main stem forks into two craggy, twisted shoots that taper into tiny fibrous root hairs. Kenny brushes most of the dirt from the crevices, then holds the root at eye level.

"Is that a big one?" I ask.

"No. Medium size. We'll find bigger today. Something to do before we look for those plants, though." Kenny holds the stem and plucks three cranberry colored berries from a small, star-shaped seed cup. "Break the skin covering those seeds between your fingers," he says, thrusting them at me. "Then press them into the dirt by that rotting log." Remembering the commercial seeds we sowed last week, I follow his instructions. Somehow this process seems more satisfying and I pat the ground affectionately when I'm done. Kenny nods approvingly, then uses his walking stick to pull himself erect. "Time to find some more."

I think I have the image of that first plant seared into my consciousness, but Kenny finds the next dozen plants solo; his stumbling apprentice only noticing the obvious, poinsettia-shaped leaves after he stops and leans on his walking stick. I relish the digging, though; the dank, humid mustiness of the forest dirt on my fingers as we ferret out the lie of each root. Kenny teaches me how to age plants by counting the bud scars at the top, and he points to scars on some roots that indicate their battles with drought or disease.

Then we find a true treasure: a two-foot-tall, four-prong plant that Kenny nicknames "Grandmother." We stand together and admire the thick, twisted root. "Some years she never showed herself above the ground," Kenny says. "They'll go dormant if the conditions are right or they're sick with disease. They're elusive that way—mysterious." As I plant Grandmother's seeds, Kenny bags the huge root, looks off into the woods and says softly, "When you find a big plant like this one, sometimes there's others around. Why do you think that is?"

"Because Grandmother has made seeds that started other plants."

"Sounds good to me. I'll head for that old oak over there. Call out if you see anything."

Two seeds remain in my palm, but I straighten before planting them. "Grandmother's seed made others," I mumble softly, the realization swelling in my head. I look in a rough circle around my feet, looking for the obvious plant. Zero. My gaze swings upslope;

nothing but prickly ash and oak seedlings. Finally it hits me: The seeds would roll downhill when Grandmother dropped them. I dig my boot heel in, turn right, and almost immediately spot a three-pronger growing twenty feet away.

"Found one, Kenny!" I crow softly, then stumble the seven steps and kneel like a penitent at the altar. I dig that root, stuff it in my bag, and instantly see another plant. It is a juvenile, a two-pronger, but I'm proud of the spot just the same. Making my way to Kenny, I do a cartoon double-take; there's another small one, the configuration and "lay" of the leaves unmistakable.

It's as if I've learned to solve a Magic Eye puzzle for the first time. These computer-generated holograms were wildly popular for a time, and they used to drive me batty. The muted kaleidoscope of colors and patterns contained a 3-D picture that others saw, but never me. Finally, after learning to stare and refocus and intentionally blur your vision just right, an image leaps into focus. Suddenly you can do most any Magic Eye placed in front of you—you've trained your vision and mind for that specialized purpose. Obviously it'll be a long time before I know ginseng, but after marking a half-dozen more plants, including one that Kenny misses, I feel I'm on my way.

Lunchtime comes after we've made a long, looping canvas of the hill and reach a small knoll overlooking the valley. Settling ourselves on a log, we eat sandwiches and take long pulls from a water jug. The dogs lie at our feet, letting the cool September breezes blow across their faces. We joke about training them to locate ginseng, imagining a wide-ranging, keen-nosed hound-pointer mix that would bark at every three-pronger he found. "You'd have yourself a valuable animal if you could do that," Kenny chuckles.

After lunch we make our way to a long, remote ridge. Kenny picks up the pace to reach the spot, barely scanning the ground as we walk. It's clear he has a destination in mind and I know it when he stops and leans into his stick. I follow his gaze to an ancient, gnarled white oak whose trunk grows vertical for fifteen feet, then arcs back earthward in a rainbow, the leafy crown growing nearly horizontal to its sprawling root system. "That tree's a marker," Kenny explains. "The 'shang growing round it is a stand my family's picked from for over sixty years."

The yellow beacon of ginseng leaves are clearly visible as we cover the distance to them. The stand is amazing: The plants grow so densely I have to watch my step as we enter it. Stopping by the sentinel oak, Kenny points to the few plants we'll dig: Large, robust, three- and four-prong plants full of crimson berries. We dig silently, bagging roots, stems, and leaves, burying every berry we can find. As we finish, I stop to look at the bounty around me— there are easily three hundred plants in my immediate view, certainly that many behind me and over the gentle slope. A digger with eyes on short-term profit could see a tidy sum in an afternoon of digging here. Kenny surveys the patch as we prepare to leave. "This is my retirement plan, if I need one," he smiles.

It's late afternoon when we return to the truck. We're silent on the ride home, letting stiff backs and legs melt into the truck seats, feeling the pleasant exhaustion of a day in the hills. Back at Kenny's we tend to our harvest, washing the roots under gently running tap water to remove the dirt, lightly scrubbing each with our fingers. When the day's harvest is clean and patted dry, we carry it to the attic where we place the roots to dry on old window screens suspended from the ceiling with wires. Drying will cost the roots two-thirds of their wet weight but make them more attractive to a buyer. Then, on a November day just before deer season, Kenny will drive downriver with nearly four pounds of dried ginseng and receive the highest price he's seen in four decades of digging: $550 per pound.

*   *   *

Ginseng season is short and, like most everything in bluff country, dictated by the weather. On a mid-September day we decide on one more hunt to cap the season. Kenny warns beforehand that the plants are dying for the year, their once-golden leaves wilting and falling one by one. Our outing is more a denial of time's passage than a serious quest, and after several hours of walking good ground, we're forced to face the truth. The final omen comes as we crest a small hill and find a monstrous, four-prong plant lying on its side, its once-golden leaves a wrinkled gauze moldering against the forest floor. We kneel beside the largest plant of the season, carefully brushing away leaf litter in order to find the bud stem that will reveal the root. But we find no trace and Kenny says simply, "We can't dig this one. Without seeing the bud stem, we could damage the root if we try." He reads the incredulous look on my face, jabs me with an elbow and grins. "Told you it's elusive."

It seems a fitting end to the season, and we leave the woods, a breeze with the promise of October against our shoulders. Kenny suggests we stop at the farmhouse of the landowner to say hi, and when we pull into the yard, I decide to let the dogs out for a drink. We've run hours in the hills and they look as parched as I feel. As I walk to the farmhouse, I notice Cody drinking deeply from a five-gallon pail, his graying muzzle dripping water. I smile broadly—not knowing the water is mixed with antifreeze that will kill him.

Cody's death shakes me as deeply as that of any loved one. I decide to bury him in the timberline behind my house, in a cover where we chased grouse and pheasants on many autumn afternoons. It takes me many minutes to dig the hole, many more to sit beside Cody's still, tranquil form and sift through my memories of him.

When I've shoveled the last spade of dirt to cover him, I place a round slab of stone to mark the spot. Worried that I won't remember this stone from the others I see, I search for another, more visible marker. Absently, I stick my hand in a coat pocket and my fingers close around a small snuff tin that rattles when I touch it. I recognize the sound instantly and fumble with the lid, a palmful of ginseng seeds tumbling into my hand as the cover slides off. There are easily three dozen seeds, plenty to start a small stand of plants that could last several generations if nurtured carefully. I can think of no better marker for this sad, quiet place in the woods. I press each seed carefully into the soil, pat the ground affectionately, then start the long walk across the field to home.

RAT TALE
Where Am I?

KENNY TELLS THE TALE: Ever been lost? Lost you say? I've been lost more times than I've got fingers and toes to count them on.

Take the time when I set out at the crack of dawn from our farmyard in the Buffalo County hill country to collect a couple of squirrels for the family cooking pot. I was about ten years old and feeling real adventuresome. My Pa's little single-shot .22 caliber rifle felt good cradled in the crook of my arm. My other hand was searching my jacket pocket for possibles: jackknife, five .22 bullets, big safety pin, medium-sized fishing sinker, a couple of odd-shaped pebbles, and my lucky penny. Yup, I guess I've got about everything I might possibly need for today's adventure. I was headed downhill for the Yeager's Valley Crick, which wound its way through an old cow pasture about five hundred yards from our barn. When I got to the crick I noticed there was a heavy fog bank settling into the valley. It was early autumn, and fog banks came and went almost every day this time of year so I paid little attention to it. My mind was on a couple of nice, fat fox squirrels I'd seen a few weeks earlier in a big, old cottonwood tree a-ways up the crick from where I was standing.

As I made my way along the crick bank, the fog got thicker, and several times I found myself veering off into the old pasture, and I had to stop to think which way the crick was. Twice, the crick was found by my listening intently for gurgling water tumbling over the rocky bottom.

Finally, I found the big cottonwood—or it found me, as I almost flattened my nose against the side of its trunk. Squirrels? Heck, I couldn't even see the tree, let alone a squirrel in it. So much for the fox squirrels today. I decided to cross the crick, which bathed the feet of a heavily wooded hillside.

The leaves underfoot were wet and soft and quiet. As I began to climb the hill, I thought the fog might be thinner up higher, but it was just as thick as along the crick bottoms. The huge oaks and hickories took on a ghostly appearance. They appeared then disappeared as the dense fog rolled and billowed among them.

An uneasy feeling came over me. I felt as though I should leave the woods—now! But the chatter of a squirrel found my ears from the hilltop. I went toward it.

At the top of the hill, I found no squirrel, only more phantom trees and fog, fog, and more fog. There were no familiar hills stretching as far as the eye could see, no farm buildings, no fields, no crick. Just fog everywhere.

Fear welled up inside me. My steps grew quicker, my breath came faster, my heart began to pound in my ears. I traveled along the ridgetop for a short distance, then dropped off of the crest and started down the hillside toward home. Before long, I was in the middle of a sizable blackberry patch. The berry bushes' long, tangly tentacles wound around my legs and arms and I began to fight them like I would those of an octopus.

Somehow I tripped and staggered my way through the patch. Momentarily, I stopped to pick the stickers and thorns from my clothes and skin. I remember thinking: There's no berry patch in the woods on the way home—I must be lost! Lost? How could I be lost? This was my own backyard. I'd fished and hunted, picked berries, romped and played along Yeager Valley Crick and in the hills since I was big enough to walk.

I hurried on a bit, but came up short when I realized my Pa's rifle was leaned up against a tree back at the edge of the berry patch. With a fair amount of difficulty, I was able to retrace my steps and locate the tree and rifle.

A great wave of tiredness swept over me as I slumped to the ground beneath that tree. My attention turned to a brilliant blue jay perched on a nearby windfall. It pecked at something held between its toes. In my mind, I began to beg of the bird: "Please, Blue Jay, tell me, where am I?" I knew that the blue jays were the town criers of the woods, they sounded the alarm whenever something was stirring about. Again, I asked the jay, this time in a hushed whisper of a voice that sounded like someone else's. "Please, Blue Jay, fly home to our little farm and tell somebody, anybody, where I am." The jay called raucously a couple of times as it flew off.

Tears welled up in my eyes but I held them from falling. A thought came to me—all I had a do was go downhill to the bottom, find the crick, and follow it downstream all the way home. I half-ran, half-stumbled, rifle clutched in my skinny little hand, the two or three hundred yards to the bottom of the hill.

No crick! Where was the crick and our old cow pasture? Through tear- and fog-filled eyes, I saw the outline of an old cow trail near the edge of the woods and began to follow it. Wait a minute! What was that I heard? My ears strained to hear that sound again. A cow bell? And it was coming closer. The clumping of heavy hooves could be heard and the rhythmic *dong de dong de dong* of a cow bell for sure. Within a minute I was staring at one of the most beautiful sights of my life: those big, dark, bulging eyes with the whitish circle around them that belonged to Betsy, a brown Swiss cow. Beyond Betsy was Ruby and then Molly on the trail. Whoa Nelly, was I one happy camper! These were Grandpa Adolph's cows. I was on a cow trail in Grandpa's lowland hay meadow, and if I followed the cows I'd be in Grandpa's barnyard right soon.

My tears tasted salty because my mouth was open in a smile as I followed the cows down the winding trail to Grandpa's place. Their slow, easy, methodical gait seemed to suit me just right, while the bell *donged* out one of the happiest songs on Earth.

Just within sight of the cow barn, I left my rescuers to trundle on down the trail on their own. I cut sharply toward the creek, below the meadow hay shed, where the cool, clear waters bathed away the blood and grime from my cuts, scratches, and abrasions as well as the sweat, tears, and the fear from my face. I adjusted my cap with a certain amount of precision, the bill slightly cocked over my left eye. I retied my shoestrings and neatly tucked my shirt inside my belt. I picked up the rifle, cradled it gently in the crook of my left arm and walked as nonchalantly as I could toward Grandpa Adolph and Grandmother Mary's rambling farmhouse. In the barnyard, I petted the cows as if I hadn't seen them in awhile. Betsy stared at me for some time, and I wouldn't have been overly surprised to see one of those big, dark, bulging eyes slowly close in a knowing wink, but it didn't. I ambled on through the barnyard gate, across the main yard, up the garden walk, and gave a couple of sharp raps on the screen door.

"Hah, who's out there?" Grandpa's voice boomed from his couch on the screened-in, wraparound porch.

I hollered back, "Kenny, Grandpa. It's Kenny out here." Grandpa ordered me in and I went, rifle and all, in order to show him what good care I was taking of Pa's .22. He promptly ordered me out, to put the rifle where it belonged, outside, and I did as he said.

I sat next to Grandpa on his battered couch. He told me how he'd killed over twenty flies already that morning with his homemade fly swatter, which lay even now across his lap at the ready for the next unsuspecting fly that came his way. That fly swatter was a formidable looking weapon if ever there was one. The handle was a smallish-size iron rod with a loop on one end for a grip. Attached to the business end of the rod was a chunk of car tire inner tube about six inches square, with holes punched through it so it didn't catch too much air when he brought it down against a fly. Flies were his mortal enemies until the day he died. Thistles were another, but we didn't talk thistles that day.

Grandpa asked me what I was doing that morning with Pa's rifle and all. I told him I was hunting squirrels up along the crick bottoms, but I didn't even see one.

"Too foggy," he muttered. I agreed.

He mentioned that Grandmother would like to see me. I jumped up and headed for the kitchen door while Grandpa wondered aloud, more or less of himself, "Funny thing how them cows came home this time of day, don't you think?" I didn't answer.

As usual Grandmother was glad to see me and I her. It was always so good to sit in Grandmother's kitchen. Somehow I felt safe, warm, loved, and content in that big, square, high-ceilinged room. Grandmother finished what she was doing over by the wood-fired kitchen range then went into the pantry and slid the cover off her clay-crock cookie jar—I could always tell by the little scratchy sound it made. She came over to the large oak table by the window where I was sitting and put a glass of strawberry nectar and a big, thick sugar cookie on a glass saucer on the table in front of me. Grandmother sat beside me while I enjoyed the goodies.

"Seems like you was hunting squirrels in the wild blackberry patch up here on the hill," she said as she straightened her apron. "Ain't nothing lives in there except rabbits in the winter and rattlesnakes in the summer."

I said nothing as I munched my cookie. She knew!

"It's pretty near noon. I better call your Ma before she worries herself sick over you. Person could get lost in the hills, being so foggy and all, couldn't they now?"

Oh boy, now the cat was going to be out of the bag for sure. I wouldn't be able to use Pa's rifle or get out of the house again for the rest of my natural life. I just knew it.

I listened closely as Grandmother cranked out three long and two short rings on the wall telephone. The smell of woodsmoke, coffee, and fresh-baked bread hung in the air.

"Hello, Melvina," Grandmother kept a steady gaze out the window as if she was studying something. "Yup, he's here, been here quite a while. He's fine. Got a little scratched up in the berry patch hunting rabbit instead a squirrels. Ain't that just like a kid for you?" Was she going to tell? I squirmed a little and the old wooden-spoked chair squeaked in protest.

"Yeah, he's just finishing up his cookie and nectar. I'll send him on home." Grandmother hung up the phone. I let out a long slow sigh of relief. She came over, put her arms around me, and gave me a great big hug. I looked up at her and said, "Thanks, Grandmother!" She winked at me and nodded her head.

I said goodbye to Grandpa, who was still swatting flies. As we left the porch, I picked up the rifle and carried it carefully in the crook of my arm. Grandmother and I walked side by side along the garden path. A blue jay cried out from an overhanging spruce branch, where it was pecking at something held between its toes. Then it flew away toward the rugged, wooded hills.

Grandmother said, "That darn, old, pesky jay's been around here all morning making a ruckus." I stared after it until it disappeared away up in the woods. Could it have been? I wondered. Naw! It couldn't be, I really didn't believe in such stuff.

OCTOBER

River Rat Almanac

IN OCTOBER, THE days dawn cool, and by noon the fogs and mists are burnt off by the sun. Savvy riverfolks are out and about fishing, hunting, birding, or just leisurely cruising the Big River. Here and there a turtle sits on a driftwood log soaking up some of the last warm rays of sun for this year. The savage white winds of late fall and winter are gathering to the north. Late summer rains drift down the river as quiet, clear waters almost as blue as the sky above.

The great river valley lies sparkling and shimmering with brilliant colors. Red, orange, yellow, and green adorn the bluffs: The colors of autumn jump out at us so vivid and alive that they almost burn their imprint into our mind. Walnut, ash, and basswood trees stand naked, adding a touch of dark contrast to the brilliantly painted landscape. The sky seems bigger, the air clearer, easier to breathe and lets you see almost forever. Where has the summer gone? Blown to the four directions of the wind.

Goose and duck talk is readily heard in the backwaters. The river is now a super highway for our feathered friends. Flock after flock form wavering V's as they follow their ancient pathways across the sky, heading south. They leave little sign of their passing—no trails, few footprints . . . only the whisper of their wings, the sweetness of their songs, and their ghostly images in our minds, until the spring.

Young critters disperse to seek their own territories. It's a time of preparation, hard work, and change on the Big River. October is the first full month of autumn and all things sense that the Circle of Life has turned.

Duck Hunting and
Duck-Hunting Dogs

Glance at the Mississippi River in midsummer and the river's purpose is ill-defined. Equal parts barge path, water park, boat venue, and fishing hole, the summer river is abuzz with activity and voices, its broad surface accommodating so many activities it appears as frenetic as a youngster's first state fair. But come October, when frost-rimmed nights and cold fall rains drive most folks inland, the river gets down to business once again. Now the broad ribbon of water winding through bluff country seems to serve a singular, important purpose, acting as a migration corridor for thousands of south-bound ducks and geese.

The waterfowl, of course, are looking for resting spots on their way south, quiet places to feed and dabble until ice and snow push them on again. The Whitman Swamp, full of sheltered lakes, tiny ponds, and flowing creeks, is such a haven. Wild rice beds offer food in abundance, as do the acorns of swamp white oaks. Nearby fields promise meals of corn and soybeans full of the proteins that strengthen wings for the long flights ahead. And enough water in the Whitman stays open through winter that a good number of ducks and geese decide bluff country—at least for this year—is far enough South for wintering.

When duck season opens in October, the hunting is rarely for migrants, but for birds that were hatched and reared in the Whitman itself. The swamp is a duck factory, full of food and nesting grounds that seem tailor-made for producing young wood ducks, mallards, teal, and widgeon.

When Kenny invites me for an early season hunt, the weather is not what is associated with classic waterfowling. Those outings take place on gray, late-autumn days, when you turn up the collar of your hunting coat against the sleet and pray the shooting happens before you shiver too severely to hit anything. The morning Kenny calls, the clouds drift high in an otherwise blue sky, and temperatures seem more suited for a bike ride to gawk at the changing leaves. However, I've long ago passed the stage where suffering is a required part of the outdoor experience, and I cheerily sign on for a fair-weather duck hunt.

Kenny is waiting at Big Lake Shack when I pull in, having just righted an overturned canoe from its resting place near the dock. Spider's tail waves happily in anticipation. In the background, Big Lake shimmers in the October afternoon sun. I couldn't see them, but I hear mallards gabbling from the stands of bulrushes on the sloughs stretching behind the lake.

"Afternoon, Kenny."

"Good afternoon, Scott. You bring your waders today?"

"I did. And a box of shells. I figure I'm good for one duck."

Kenny's hearty laughter rings across the swamp, but I am only half-joking. I've done just enough waterfowl shooting to know I am miserable at it.

"I'm sure we'll give Spider something to fetch today, you just wait." Spider's tail thumps happily at her name, and she joins me eagerly at the truck as I slip into my hip boots and slide some shells into the pocket of my hunting coat. By the time I've gathered my gear and made it to the canoe, Kenny is waiting beside it.

"You hop up front there with Spider and let me paddle, Scott. Just enjoy the day and look for ducks."

I don't have to work hard to accomplish either task. The silver maples are turning a pale yellow and the bulrushes have faded to a rich khaki. Soft sunlight caresses the swamp as Kenny's paddle dips and dribbles through the duckweed. As we round a dense stand of wild rice, a small flock of teal erupt from its confines. Spider whines eagerly at their flush, and I turn to smile at Kenny. "Not fair putting them so close to the landing. I'll start to think this'll be easy."

Kenny just smiles and leans into the paddle, pushing us across a shallow flat and toward a sparsely wooded point jutting into the west end of Big Lake. A twisted maple stands as a sentinel at the end of the point, and with a final push of the paddle, Kenny beaches us next to it. Spider and I hop out in unison, and I reach back and pull the bow of the canoe on shore, the warm muck pulling at the heels of my boots as I trudge toward higher ground.

As we pull the canoe onto the wooded ridge, more birds—a small group of wood ducks, a brace of mallards, a dozen widgeon—skitter out of nearby hides and launch themselves into the October sky. This is clearly a place that ducks like to be, and speaking softly, Kenny tells me to sneak toward the end of the point and sit among the swamp grass in a comfortable place. "I'll hide the canoe a little, then slip in beside you. The ducks will come back here. I've only hunted this spot a time or two this fall."

I settle onto a small, dry, sedge-covered hummock that offers some concealment, but also a good view of the water around me. Shortly after, I hear Spider and Kenny take positions slightly to my left, where Kenny can see and shoot a small sheltered bay. Within minutes, I hear the soft whistle of wings behind us. Knowing that ducks can see the upturned face of a hunter as easily as a rescue pilot spots a signal mirror, I resist the urge to look up and instead glance sideways at my companions. Kenny's gaze is directed not at the ducks, but at Spider, who is following every move of the circling flock through searching eyes. Spider's sleek ebony coat seems to offer no camouflage against the yellow-brown marsh grass, but she sits so still she appears as little more than an ancient, weathered stump. Of course, stumps don't whimper at the sight of approaching teal.

"Take them!" Kenny whispers, and I stand immediately, shouldering my pump gun and seeing the ducks in the same instant. The half-dozen greenwings are twenty yards out, wings locked, committed to land on the flat water directly in front of me. Struggling for balance as I swing on a single, the birds flare and my blast hits nothing but bulrushes on the far side of the marsh, smacking the marsh grass like a ball cracking a catcher's mitt after a mighty whiff. Strike one.

Kenny, who passed an easy shot at the flock before they reached me, offers an excuse. "Teal are the fastest flyers in the swamp, you know. You think you're leading them plenty and you hit a bird thirty feet back of your target."

The truth was, of course, that I'd forgot to lead the ducks at all, falling back on the snap-shooting I've used while hunting upland birds like grouse and pheasant. But upland shooting is nearly always done just as a bird flushes and its flight is the slowest. Even a duck that's putting on the brakes is moving so fast you have to shoot well ahead of it, swinging the barrel in front of its beak at roughly its flight speed, then continuing the swing even as you pull the trigger. It's a timing that can take years to perfect, and I remember my cousin—who missed an embarrassing amount of waterfowl when he started hunting—telling me he didn't realize how drastically you had to lead ducks until the boat he was standing in lurched violently as he shot at a streaking mallard one day. His barrel swung miles in front of the greenhead as he pulled the trigger, but amazingly, the duck tumbled out of the sky stone dead. Cousin Bob began copycatting the wild lurch and started dropping ducks with regularity.

Embarrassed at blowing the cake shot, I mumble an apology to Kenny, but he's used to such shooting displays. After all, he'd spent a good part of his youth guiding duck hunters, both on the open water of the river proper and in the wilds of the Whitman Swamp.

"I was in my twenties when I first started duck hunting seriously," he tells me as we wait for the swamp to settle down after my shot. "I was back from the army and had done some duck hunting on the river, but it was crowded in the good spots even then, with people shooting each other's ducks, fights between dogs and such.

"So I decided to hunt the swamp, which I'd been to as a kid with my parents. It was a remote and complicated place that took a lot of time and legwork to learn—that's why there weren't many people hunting in there. I spent many days, from dawn until dusk, walking from pond to pond, marsh to marsh, following the sloughs where they led. And I began to realize what a special place it was. There was every type of puddle duck living in there, including wood ducks, who nested in the hollow trees so common in the swamp. When I first started hunting there, wood ducks weren't so plentiful and you weren't supposed to shoot them. But soon their numbers began increasing and they opened the season again.

"About that time I got my first duck dog, Spook, a cross between a black Lab and a golden retriever. He was black, with longer hair than a Lab and a white star on his chest. He was with me all the time, and it was good training for both of us, because I loved to hunt ducks and shoot. At the beginning of every season I would order a case of shells from the hotel in Cochrane [Wisconsin]. They were a wax-paper shell with a paper wad and they cost two dollars a box. I was a young man, and it was important for me to shoot my limit, and many days I did. I figure in most years Spook would retrieve a hundred ducks or more.

"Somewhere in there I started guiding hunters, who would stay in houseboats at the Great River Harbor in Buffalo City. I would go out in the early morning and pick them up and guide them all day—sometimes out on the river for divers, but mostly back in the swamp—for forty dollars, and I'd clean all the ducks. Sometimes I would get a tip—usually ten dollars, or a box or two of shells. I hunted with a lot of people in those years, some were great shots, some great callers, some were just good storytellers. But there weren't too many that I wouldn't hunt with again. Most all of them were there for a lot more reasons than just killing a duck."

I'm grateful to Kenny for adding this last qualifier, especially in the aftermath of my bungled opportunity. I'm about to voice my thanks when I notice Kenny looking at Spider again, and I follow suit. While her sleek head remains still, Spider's amber eyes are searching the tree line at the far end of the swamp. I shift my gaze in that direction just in time to see a pair of mallards screaming in to us at eye level. I scramble to raise my shotgun and swing on the brace, pull the trigger, and watch them sail—unharmed—over our heads. Once again, Kenny has passed a shot in order to give me first poke, and in doing so, missed any chance at one himself.

"I guess it's time for the master to take his turn," I offer sheepishly.

"That's no problem, Scott. There'll be plenty of other chances for me. Just take your time, and forget about these two misses. The only shot that matters is the next one."

I appreciate the coaching and attempt to make my flubs disappear in my mind. As if to affirm Kenny's coaching, Spider walks to my side, presses her flank against my leg, and sits down, a wide grin spreading across her face. Leave it to a retriever to lighten the mood.

As we lay back and enjoy the October sun until the next ducks arrive, we discuss the richness that dogs lend to hunting. Like many waterfowlers, Kenny's enjoyment of the sport would diminish greatly if not for the intimate, working relationship he shares with a retriever. Kenny had a taste of that relationship with Spook, a hardworking friend he spent seventeen years with. Like most rivermen, Kenny believed in owning only one dog at a time, and the bond that results from the pairing of one man and his dog is hard to underestimate, the two achieving a harmony and understanding transcending words. Of course, when a hunter loses such a friend, replacing him becomes an even taller task. But in the wake of Spook's death, Kenny stumbled onto a dog of even greater ability and desire.

Her name was Joey, a purebred black Labrador with a pedigree as long as a canoe paddle. Bred for success in field trials, Joey was nearly three years old before her trainer, Kenny's friend Armand Snyder, decided she didn't have the right stuff for such intense competition. Joey had a wonderful nose, keen intelligence, and loved to hunt, but Armand thought her too soft to handle the razor-sharp concentration required for competitive trialing. So he asked Kenny if he was interested in a "started dog" to replace Spook. Still grieving the loss of Spook—but knowing he wouldn't enjoy life without a dog—Kenny agreed to adopt Joey.

"They say every man gets one great dog in his lifetime, and I guess Joey was mine," Kenny says as the October breeze brings the smell of duckweed across the swamp. "It was clear from the start she knew a lot more about retrieving than I did. She knew hand signals and was trained to the whistle. Field-trial handlers need that control to direct the dog to a 'blind' retrieve—a bird that the dog hasn't seen fall. It was good for her to know, but I had to untrain some of that for her to be a good duck dog. Dogs that handle can become too dependent on the trainer to tell them where to find birds, and I wanted her to be able to trust her own judgment, especially when hunting cripples. So I worked with her on that, but not right away.

"The most important part of training a started dog is gaining its trust and friendship. It's not as easy as it is with a puppy, who's known only you from the beginning. So we just spent time together: walking in the swamp, riding in the canoe, fishing in the summer. By the time hunting season came around, she knew how to sit in a boat and what I wanted from her.

"She turned out to be quite a hunter and many times made retrieves that I would have thought impossible. She'd dive far underwater to fetch a wounded duck, and at least a dozen times I saw her bring back two ducks at once—grabbing one by the wing and the other by the neck and swimming back. That's the kind of stuff they frown on at field trials, but makes perfect sense when you're hunting. A dog that's in the cold water all day long learns how to save energy.

"Over the years she made hundreds of retrieves and got better every season. She threw three litters of pups, too, and one of those dogs—a lab named Reba Rose—became one of the top field-trial labs in the country. Joey wasn't a big dog, only about sixty-five pounds, and I think that helped with her endurance in the swamp and in life. She lived to be thirteen, so I hunted her for ten and a half years."

Being a dog man, I know that every sportsman has one hunt in their dog's career that they remember above all others. When I ask Kenny to pick Joey's shining moment, he does so without hesitation.

"Armand Snyder and another friend, Dick Fleming, came down to hunt the swamp with me one weekend," Kenny recalls. "Joey was about eleven years old then, so her legs weren't as strong as they used to be. Armand had brought along a lab named Rowdy, a great field-trial dog, and Dick had Traveler, a one-year-old pup that was actually a granddaughter of Joey.

"We went out before light and I put Armand and Rowdy on a spot near Long Lake, and we put out some decoys. Then I took Dick and Traveler down the way a couple hundred yards and put out another set of decoys. Then Joey and I sat in between them on a wooded ridge. When daylight came the ducks were flying and a big mallard came into Dick's spread and he killed it with one shot. We had special rules in the swamp then—you could only load one shell at a time. That kept the area from getting burned out by too much shooting.

"Anyway, Traveler went out and picked up a decoy, but after Dick hollered at her, she dropped that and swam back with the duck.

"It wasn't long and a hen mallard flew past Armand and he shot, wing-tipping her. She sailed into a boggy area across the lake, and Armand watched where she landed, then sent Rowdy on the retrieve. Rowdy swam on a line to the edge of the bog, then stopped to tread water when Armand whistled. Armand gave a hand signal and hollered, 'Back,' and Rowdy plunged into that bog to look for the duck. He thrashed around in there for about fifteen minutes, and every once in awhile he'd pop out and look at Armand, who'd give a hand signal and send him back in. Finally, Armand gave up and said, 'We'll just have to write that one off, I guess.'

"Not long after that, a black duck flew past Dick and he shot and wing-tipped it. The bird sailed into the same marsh. Dick sent Traveler in there, and the dog thrashed around for about fifteen minutes and came out, exhausted. Armand asked Dick if he was done, and Dick said, 'Go ahead.' So Armand sends Rowdy over, and of course the whole process is repeated. Rowdy thrashes and swims around and keeps coming out, looking for hand signals. And after awhile, Armand shakes his head and figures they've just lost another one. It was getting to be about nine o'clock, so I holler out and ask if they'd like to come over and have some tea and a sandwich. They both said yes and head over to my dry bank, and we sit down and eat.

"All the while, Joey's been sitting on the bank, looking at that boggy spot and just quivering. Armand finally looks at me and said, 'What's with her?'

"I said, 'She wants to go over there and find those two ducks. Are you two through? If you are, I'll paddle her over there and pick them up.'

"Well needless to say, there's some guffawing and sneers—it'd been over an hour and a half since that first duck flew in there, and two dogs mucking around besides.

"But I went down to the canoe and Joey hopped in and we paddled over there. When we got to the edge of the bog I said, 'Go fetch, girl,' and she jumped out of the canoe and into the bulrushes. She'd been in there for about ten minutes when I could see the weeds whipping back and forth from her tail, and I knew she had something when I heard her snort. She always did that when she was on one. So I turned to the boys and I said, 'Well, fellas, she's got the first one,' and it wasn't long before she swam out with that mallard. She came to the back of the canoe, and I took it from her, turned back to shore, held up a finger and said, 'That's one!'

"I let Joey get back in the canoe to rest for a minute or two, then I said, 'Fetch it up!' and sent her back in there. This time she was gone for a long time. I took a long drink of water from my jug, then a nip of Copenhagen, and just waited. Pretty soon I heard a bunch of yipping like a dog chasing after a rabbit. And then I see this duck break into the open water, swimming with Joey right behind. She can't swim fast enough anymore to catch it. So I grabbed my gun—I was shooting an old single-shot then—put a shell in it and pulled up and killed that duck. Then Joey caught up with it and brought it back to the canoe. I grabbed the duck, pulled Joey in the boat, turned to the guys and said, 'That's two!'

"We were feeling pretty smart when we paddled across Long Lake and onto that bank. Joey was real tired, and she rolled herself dry in the leaves, then curled up in the sun to take a long nap. We all watched her do that, and then Armand turned to me and said, 'How much you want for that dog?'"

We both laugh long and heartily at the tale's irony: A devout field trialer knowing he'd been bested by the very dog he'd given away—and of his willingness to laugh at himself about it. And of course we laughed with obvious pride for Joey, a dog long-dead, but one that would live on in duck-camp tales for years to come. Every hunter dreams of such moments, and having not one, but four, witnesses see your dog make the greatest retrieve of its life is a surreal moment of the highest order.

But it's Spider who brings us back to the present. Her earnest whimpering causes us to glance at her once again, then follow her stare to find a lone widgeon circling our secluded point. Like the others, this bird seems intent on landing nearby, and should present an easy shot. Instead of comforting me, the thought makes me even more nervous as I struggle to keep my face down and think of the proper lead and follow-through. Kenny must sense my anxiety and whispers the only statement that can calm me down: "Don't worry about missing. I'll back you up."

Suddenly I relax, no longer worried that a miss constitutes blowing it for all three of us. The widgeon appears as a brown blur in the left of my peripheral vision when Kenny whispers, "Take her!" I stand, focus, swing, and shoot in one motion, and amazingly the duck tumbles out of the sky and splashes like a softball thrown into the marsh. Spider marks the fall and, swimming as gracefully and surely as an otter, makes the retrieve and churns back to us, holding the duck like a birthright.

There will be other memorable duck hunts as the fall wears on: A frosty morning just after Halloween, when chortling mallards pile into the decoys we placed near a wild-rice bed; a blue-cold, silent day the last week of the season, when we paddle a canoe up the only open creek in the swamp, jump-shooting fat greenheads as they flush. In each hunt I learn a little more about the swamp, about dogs, about ducks and geese and the places they love, and yes, even a little about shooting. But this day will remain in my head as the time, not just when I became a duck hunter, but when I fell in love with it.

RAT TALE
Old Spook and the Last Duck Hunt

KENNY TELLS THE TALE: It was late in the summer of my twenty-third year and I was standing with one foot up on a chunk of firewood, both elbows resting on top of a snow fence that formed a circle about twenty feet across. Inside the fence were two dogs: one a golden retriever, the other a cross-breed, long-haired, black mutt. Standing alongside me was an old riverman named Ottmar Probst. Ottmar wore bib overalls and chewed Copenhagen snuff. His fingers were the size of Polish sausages. Ottmar had hunted and trapped and fished for a living on the Great River all of his life. He knew about all there was to know about gill netting, seining, and setlining for fish. He knew about turtle trapping and hooking them under the ice. He knew the ancient art of net-making and mending. He knew about pickling and smoking fish and meat of all descriptions. Ottmar was one of the great old-time river rats, and I wanted to live like him.

My attention, however, was riveted on the black dog frolicking and jumping about. He was of medium height and weight, somewhat sinewy and thin in the ribs. "What's his name?" I asked.

"Spook," Ottmar grunted.

I called to the dog, "Here, Spook. Here, Spook." The dog came over to the fence where I stood. I reached down and petted him, scratched his ears. He sat down, closing his eyes with pleasure. I opened his mouth. My Pa always said a good dog's got a black roof in his mouth. This dog did. I patted him on the head and away he went. I asked Ottmar how much he wanted for the black dog.

Looking me square in the eye, he sputtered, "You want him? You can have him for nothing. If you don't want him, I'll shoot him first thing in the morning. Got no room here for two dogs!" As if to emphasize that statement, Ottmar took a three-fingered dip of snuff and spit a long brown stream of tobacco juice into the hot summer's dust at his feet.

I loaded the dog into my battered old car. I had long since removed the back seat because I needed the extra room for hauling trap stakes, canoes, and such. With the seat gone, I could easily slide these items in through the trunk and on into the space where the back seat was once fastened. Now, the inside of my car could smell like anything from beaver, muskrats, and ducks to catnip, wild ginger, and ginseng depending on the time of year. Might even find a chub or a creek sucker stuck in a corner from a fishing trip a week or two earlier. Spook was busy looking and smelling in every nook and cranny he could find. This pleased me for it showed he was aggressive and probably had a good nose.

We drove over to my father-in-law's place. Old Bill had a spare dog-house and chain. When I let Spook out of the car, he promptly got into a hell of a fight with old Bill's police dog. Though he was much smaller, Spook showed the toughness and determination that was to become his trademark. Old Bill and I got them apart and tied Spook up at his new home. We figured Spook to be about a year old, because he would fight and lift his leg to pee, signs that he was about full-grown.

The month wore on and soon it was the tag end of September. The autumn sun felt good to Spook and me as I threw the dummy out for him to retrieve again and again. We sat under a swamp birch and rested. I rubbed his ears as we looked into each other's eyes. Over the last three weeks since I got him, we worked on and off most everyday like this, working then sitting a spell, eating lunch together, and most of all just getting to know one another. Spook learned to sit and stay fairly well. He also learned to get the dummy both on land and in the water, showing great enthusiasm and desire to please. By now the young dog was a nice quiet rider in the canoe.

About ten days later came the opening day of duck season. Spook and I went deep into the Whitman Swamp where we chose to hunt on the Tent Camp Slough. Where there's water, shelter from the wind, and large oaks you'll find wood ducks feeding on acorns. Spook and I found a nice, dry place to sit at the base of an ancient, gnarled white oak tree. The bank rose gently from the water to about five feet in height. We waited for noon, which was shooting time.

Shortly after noon, a beautiful drake wood duck came flying down the slough, twisting and turning, making its way between the branches of the trees that lined both banks of the slough. Its iridescent head shone brilliant in the autumn sun. I raised my gun, started behind the flying drake, pulled up to him, saw the barrel go slightly past his head, then I pulled the trigger all in one motion. *Bang!* I saw the duck crumple. *Ka-plop*, it hit the water. I looked at Spook, every muscle was tense, every nerve quivering as he sat at the edge of the water. "Fetch!" I called sharply. He plunged hard into the water, green duckweed spraying in every direction. Quickly, he swam and lunged his way through the shallow water and sticky black mud until he reached the duck. He sniffed the bird. Swam around it once or twice. Sniffed again, then came back without it. Upon reaching the bank he shook himself off, rolled in the leaves, then turned, and looked at me as if to say, "That bird don't look or smell like something I want to carry in *my* mouth, pal!"

About that time I remembered what an old riverman had once told me: "You got to know more than the dog does in order to teach him how to hunt." So, I put the gun up against a tree, walked down to the edge of the water, pulled up my rubber hip boots, and called for Spook. Together we waded through that black, boot-sucking, Mississippi mud out to where the duck lay. I opened Spook's mouth, stuck the duck in it, and held his mouth shut until we got back to the bank.

From that day on, Spook was a swamp dog. A swamp dog is a working dog. It has to fight critters. Its face is scarred. Its ears are tattered, and it has to learn which critters it can tangle with and which ones it can't. A swamp dog has to know in which direction the camps are located on a black summer night with thunder crashing and lightening striking all around us. A swamp dog needs to get us home during a frigid, blinding snowstorm with January's white winter winds howling down the great river valley, sweeping across the open, ice-covered marshes, and leaving nothing untouched by their bitterness. After a few years of "ice walking," I will follow my dog across the thin, first ice of the season. I will trust my life to my dog, for they seem to develop a sixth sense about where the ice is safe to travel. A swamp dog has to keep on putting one foot ahead of the other, no matter how cold or hot, hungry or thirsty they are.

As the years passed, Spook and I became inseparable. Each September, we combed the hardwood forests of the hill country surrounding the Mississippi for roots and herbs. Day after autumn day we hunted ducks, squirrels, rabbits, partridges, and pheasants. In late fall and throughout winter, we trapped 'coon, 'rats, beaver, and mink. Come spring, we fished for trout in the many tributaries of the Big River, and all summer long we fished the Mississippi shorelines for catfish, sheephead, bass, and other assorted finned creatures. It was just the two of us touching, smelling, hearing, seeing, tasting, and feeling nature as if each day was the last on Earth.

One day my wife asked me to bring Spook into the house at night. "He's five years old and its cold and wet outside," she chastised me. Now, I was brought up on a small, dirt-poor farm in the hill country, a short distance from the river. We were not accustomed to having our dogs in the house no matter what the weather. But by now Spook was the best friend I'd ever had in this world, human or critter, so in the house he came. From then on Spook went wherever I did. Day and night we were together, working, playing, and living as family. Over the course of the years, we suffered the sorrows and hardships of making a living with nature as well as experienced the joys and delights.

* * *

After spending sixteen years with me in the backwaters and bluffs along the Mississippi, old Spook's face showed the scars of many swamp battles. His hind legs were withering. He walked with a limp. I could tell that as he lay by the cabin door, the autumn sun felt good to his old bones. I knelt down beside him and held his weary old head in my hands. Looking into his eyes I saw that gray, dull appearance that meant his spirit was fading. I murmured to him, "Old, Spook, it's time you and me had one last duck hunt together."

That next morning we were up before dawn. The dark air was cold and damp, but the woodfire made the old Big Lake Shack feel quite comfortable. After a hearty breakfast, we left the camp and walked down to the edge of Big Lake. As I readied the canoe, old Spook stood by the water listening to the sounds of the night critters and sniffing the air like old dogs will. I picked Spook up and set him in the bow of the canoe on an old coat. I stepped into the stern, picked up my old poling stick, and set off across the swamp. As we wound down through the slough, I remembered the thousands of times we'd passed by these same trees, islands, and beaver dams both by canoe and on the winter's ice. A half hour later, we came to the Tent Camp Slough. We left the canoe, walking down the east bank until we came to that same big, gnarly, old swamp white oak we'd sat by sixteen years earlier. I spread out a couple of gunnysacks and laid my tattered wool hunting coat on top. Spook and I sat there waiting for daylight.

A barred owl hooted its lonesome, eerie call from across the slough, signaling the end of another night's hunt. The trees began to take shape as a misty fog rose from the water in the haunting half light of dawn. Moisture fell from the trees. As the drops hit the water in a steady *drip-drip-drip*, they reminded me of the sands of time: steady, unrelenting, slipping away.

When it was light enough to shoot, I saw several small flocks of wood ducks trading back and forth along the slough. Suddenly, a single drake came dodging and weaving its way down the slough. I shouldered the gun, followed, swung through, then slapped the trigger. *Boom!* The bird cartwheeled end over end toward the water and splashed down.

Old Spook staggered to his feet, toddled down to the water, slipped in, and made his way slowly to the duck. He picked the bird up, turned, and brought it toward the bank. I picked up my gun and made my way to the edge of the water. I stood there, silently waiting for the dog to reach the bank. When old Spook got just close enough, I set the gun against a tree, reached down, and helped him up the bank. I patted his head and said, "Good boy, Spook, good boy!" I dried him off with a gunnysack for he was too weak to roll in the leaves.

I sat down under the oak tree. The sun began to burn the fog off the water. I laid the duck by my knee. Spook turned around once or twice then curled up between my legs with his nose close to the duck at my knee. He could smell the two things he loved most in the world: the scent of duck and me.

As we sat there together I remembered the pleasant days of summer, leisurely, long, and full of life; the bitter, snow-filled days when the swamp takes on the appearance of a white desert; the days of the thawing sun, a warm breeze, a blackbird, and the promise of spring. But now it was fall, the time of harvest and death for plants and critters alike. We heard goose-talk from a high flock following their ancient southern pathways in the sky. Across the slough, a pair of gray squirrels worked in the autumn leaves gathering acorns for winter. In years past, old Spook would have treed them for sure and then looked back at me to see if I was coming to get one for supper. Not today. No, today he lay quietly resting. I placed my hand on his chest, feeling it slowly rise and fall. From across the Great River in Minneiska, Minnesota, I heard a church bell toll its lonesome song. It was Sunday morning. In my mind's eye I could see the people, all dressed up, filing past the preacher at the door. Shaking hands, then hurrying on with their lives. The diesel engines of a towboat hummed as they pushed their way upstream in the river's main channel.

How long we sat in our special place I don't know. I recall wishing I could stop the sands of time like the sun had stopped the dripping of the dew and fog from the trees. But the Circle of Life must go on, so we loaded up our canoe and headed for camp.

A few days later, old Spook was gone. He died peaceably near the front door of Big Lake Shack. I buried him in a special place. There have been other swamp dogs since, and we have always begun our life together by visiting old Spook's grave where we sit a spell and remember the days gone by, the time that is now, and ponder what is yet to come.

Spook taught me many lessons. He taught me the true meaning of friendship. He taught me that when you start a job, you finish it no matter what. Old Spook helped me better understand the great Circle of Life. Death and life are one and the same, for without death there would be no new life. There would be no room for new life, nothing would be returned to the Earth. In order to have life we must have death. We cannot have one without the other. Most of all, I learned that the old saying "It is better to have loved someone or something and lost them, than to have never loved at all" is most certainly true. Even though the body is gone, the spirit is in the wind, earth, fire, and water. For as long as the mists rise from the waters at dawn and the whippoorwill calls at dusk, we will be there together. One day, I'll feel a cold nose nudge my hand, I'll look down and there by my side, sniffing the wind will be a dog called old Spook.

NOVEMBER

River Rat Almanac

THE NOVEMBER WIND sends clouds, chasing each other, tumbling across the steel gray sky which spits light snow and sleet. White capped waves relentlessly pound the shores and islands of the Big River as it seems to rebel against the notion of lying still and frozen by the approaching winter.

The restless and angry waters seem ready to sweep away all traces of summer, and indeed they do. Duckweed, driftwood, and fresh beaver chewings are driven into every nook and cranny of the backwaters by the fierce northwest wind and the waves that it creates.

Those ancient, slow-moving kin of mine, the turtles, are submerging themselves in traditional black, boot-sucking mudholes throughout the Big River's backwaters. The turtles will not see daylight, fresh air or food 'til Spring.

It feels good to sit down on a fallen log and listen to the blue jays and chickadees and the "goose talk" in the sky. The distant hum of towboat engines, no doubt pushing grain barges after an abundant harvest, can be heard now and then. But it is the song of the wind that I hear most as it drifts among the dry brown cattails, the tangled wild rice, and the mostly naked trees. It is haunting, mesmerizing, yet soothing, an ancient song of late autumn, harvest moons, frost on the pumpkin, woodsmoke and roast turkey and Thanksgiving. Certainly, I am thankful for family, friends, the harvest, and good health, but most of all for the chance to walk the Circle of Life in this most special place called the Upper Mississippi River valley.

Hunting the "Wet-Tail" Deer

If ginseng hunting forces you to look down and hunting ducks turns your gaze skyward, then deer season can only be viewed as merciful relief. Just when all that craning and stooping makes whip-lash a sure bet, along comes a sport that can literally save your neck. On the other hand, training your eyes on a Whitman Swamp whitetail is no easy task. With acres of willow, tag alder, bulrushes, cattails, prickly ash, dogwood, button brush, and more tree species than I'd care to count all acting as perfect camouflage for the soft, gray-brown coat of a whitetail, just seeing one of these wraiths can be a tall order.

I get my first proof of this one sun-drenched fall afternoon as Kenny and I drive toward Big Lake Shack. The narrow two-track snakes past dense underbrush, and whitetails are known to bed within feet of the trail. I nearly yell when the first deer, a yearling doe, leaps from a bed that seems to be under the front quarter-panel of my truck. As her white flag bobs away, three others—two mature does and a buck with spreading antlers on fire from the sun—rise and trot off. They run toward a tangle of deadfalls, prickly ash, and ironwood so dense that a man would have to crawl through it; the whitetails enter it as easily as kids slipping into a video-game arcade. It takes awhile for my heart to slow down as they disappear, and when I look at Kenny, he is smiling at me.

"That's one beautiful buck," I breath.

"Yes, it is," Kenny smiles. "He's been down here the last couple of seasons. You'll see his rubs all over if you look."

As if to confirm Kenny's statement, we pass a stout red cedar next to the lane. The orange-brown, shaggy bark is peeled from the trunk for a two-foot length. The yellow sapwood exposed by the scar gleams in the afternoon sun, small droplets of sap oozing from its surface. This is clearly one of the sites where our stag has been venting his testosterone.

Such sights are common in this area. Buffalo County, Wisconsin, is nationally famous for the record-class whitetails it produces every year. The steep timbered hills and rich fields of hay and corn provide, respectively, refuge to help bucks reach maturity and food that ensures easy calories for growing both muscle and antlers. In addition to the big ones, bluff country grows enough does and fawns to place the area among the state harvest leaders. Though the deer-hunting tradition is fairly new here—seeing a *deer track* was big news only fifty years ago—it didn't take long for bluff country to establish itself as a whitetailer's Eden. Folk have spent small fortunes to own hunting land here, and few have questioned their investment.

But most of that money is being spent in the hill country, where verdant fields adjoin oak-covered hillsides in scenes fit for a feed-store calendar. Down in the Whitman, deer hunters swat mosquitoes, struggle to free their boots from the mud, and curse at the omnipresent water, which makes straight-line, dry-foot travel a fantasy of the highest order. As Kenny once told me, "The biggest advantage of hunting the swamp is you don't have to drag a deer uphill very often." When I asked for another advantage, all I received was a blank stare. "I'll tell you when I think of one," he finally said. I'm still waiting.

Nevertheless, deer hunting in the swamp is a magical experience. I got my first taste of it not long after that first exposure to swamp deer—or as Kenny likes to call them, "wet-tails." I mention to Kenny that I'd been bowhunting a nearby farm for many years, and would he mind if I tried the swamp one day? "Not at all, Scott.

I'll show you a couple good places before we leave today," he says.

Less than a week later I was sitting in the first of those spots, the downed top of a pin oak lying within fifteen yards of two heavily used trails. Each of those trails led from a dense stand of marsh grass and cottonwoods (the bedding area), to a dry oak ridge (a funnel), and then dumped into a shamrock-green field of rye grass (the salad bar). The once-healthy pin oak grew near the junction of the two trails, and after dying, conveniently leaned over and made a perfect natural blind. Such positioning makes one wonder if nature is truly random, or if, perhaps, God just might be a deer hunter.

The swamp is relatively quiet for the first half-hour of my afternoon vigil, but it gradually comes to life. Two wood ducks whistle overhead. A nuthatch pecks at the bark of a nearby river birch. Eleven Canada geese leave the swamp, fly above my tree, and wing toward the bluffs, their necks craning back and forth as they gabble and *har-ronk* at each other. The geese are a black V on the horizon when I hear the marsh grass rustle behind me. I know without turning my head that deer are on the way.

The most obvious trait about swamp deer is that they all wear black socks. Except for a few months when the swamp freezes, whitetails are forever in muck, and the constant exposure gives them four semi-permanent leggings. The two yearlings that emerge from the bedding cover and slink past my tree toward the rye have been in bogs up to their ankles. When they hit the dry ground of the rye field, their *schmucking* becomes a prance, almost playful, as if they can feel and appreciate the lightness of their feet on the new surface. The lead deer kicks up its back feet and ducks its head down, scampers in a wide half-circle, then settles down to eat. After a curious stare at its partner, the second doe follows suit.

These are the only deer that will pass within range of my blind, but certainly not the last I'll see. By dusk, more than twenty wet-tails have joined them in the field. One is a fine buck, sleek and gray-coated, with eight points on his antlers and a handsome face sported by few mature animals. But he is not the big one Kenny and I saw last week, and while I trudge to the truck in the dark, I find myself feeling a little disappointed at not seeing the trophy.

It is not, I know, the way that Kenny would want me to feel about the hunt. His view of deer hunting—while no less passion-ate than mine—is much more utilitarian. Deer hunting is a special event to be shared with family and friends, a true highlight on the river rat calendar, but shooting a whitetail is all about laying up meat and thinning the herd. It is not about displaying hunting prowess by waiting for the biggest buck in the woods. As he said to me shortly after showing me the oak-tree blind, "I shot a lot of deer over the years, some for different reasons than others. I was into the horn thing for awhile. Also hunted with a group of guys for a time, and we'd walk the hills all day long, making drives to each other, sometimes killing three, four, maybe five deer in an after-noon. But after awhile, I wanted it to be more personal, more like duck hunting. So I went back to just hunting by myself or with another guy or two. I found more satisfaction that way, I guess."

In doing so, he also returned to his roots. Kenny's first deer hunts, ones he shared with his father on their farm in the hills, were soli-tary affairs that linger as magic memories. "I still remember the fall a couple of years before I could hunt," he recalls. "My Pa would go up to the woods for a couple hours in the afternoon, usually take a team of horses and a wagonload of manure to spread on the field. After he did that, he'd hitch the horses and go up to the woods. That day I stood in the yard and watched him walk up in the woods, and before long I heard a shot, and then another one. It took a long time for the echo to leave the valley, it was so still that day. But when it did, I hollered as loud as I could, "Did you get him, Pa?" and before long I hear, "Yeah, I did! C'mon up here and help me drag him out!'

"So I ran up there as fast as I could, and when I got to the woods he was standing over a beautiful buck with a huge, ten-point rack. It looked so big to me, and I studied everything about it—the coal-black nose, the black feet, the salt-and-pepper fur. And I knew I wanted to hunt deer myself. And two falls later I did.

"I didn't get one that first year, but the next year we were up in the woods and there'd been a big snow. The woods were like a wonderland, the trees flocked with white. I walked a hillside to where Pa was sitting, hoping to kick a deer to him. But nothing came to him, and he said, 'Stay right here, and I'll walk to you this time.' So I put myself right at the base of the tree where he had, standing in the little spot where he'd scraped away the snow.

"He'd gone a couple hundred yards up the hill when I heard something knock the snow off of a branch behind me. I turned, and there was a doe and fawn, running up the hill to me. It was like they were suspended in air, they moved so graceful. I was mesmerized as first, then it occurred to me that I should try and shoot one of these deer. So I picked up the gun and didn't even aim, just pointed the barrel like I would at a duck, and fired. The doe bucked down, then kind of cartwheeled onto the ground and slid against the base of a tree.

"Pa told me if I ever got a deer to walk up and poke a stick in its eye to see if it was still alive. So I did that, and she never blinked. So I called up to my Pa that I got one, and he hollered back, 'You did not.' But he came down and said, 'Well I guess you did. You got her right in the neck.' So we slid a rope around her neck, and I dragged her down the hill and across the fields to the shed by myself, and we hung her there, with a stick to hold her ribcage open and cool her off inside. I was so proud to show that deer to my Ma and the neighbors who would come over. There's always something special about the first deer you ever get. You never forget that hunt."

Kenny's passion for deer hunting would only grow with the years, as he went through periods of wanting to kill numbers of deer, then killing big deer, and finally, settling into hunting in the swamp, where taking a whitetail or two for a winter's worth of venison was all that mattered. It seemed that hunting on swamp time made success seem less important; that chasing whitetails in the same haunts where he enjoyed duck hunting and beaver trapping made for an easy, perfect logic. Like most hunters who've seen many falls come and go, the place where he hunted began to mean as much to Kenny as the hunt itself.

Not that he doesn't try to succeed. Shortly after my first bow hunt, Kenny shows me another area or two where I might try my luck. While we walk the autumn woods looking for deer sign, Kenny talks about whitetails in an almost mercenary way. "I think if I had to quit deer hunting today, I'd still eat venison as often as I could," he muses. "I don't care if I'd have to tag a deer someone else shot, or even pick up a roadkill when I could. I like to eat deer too much to quit. There's so many different ways to make it taste good—fried, smoked, jerked, roasted. . . . It's tasty, fat-free, healthy. I can't see going through a year without plenty of venison."

Our walk leads us to an oak opening not far from the rye fields. There are deer signs everywhere: blackened trails that wind through prickly ash, places where oak leaves have been pushed and pawed at to reveal acorns, densely matted beds where whitetails have laid down after feeding. On the edge of the feeding sign is another cedar-tree rub, the deeply gouged bark and height of the marking suggesting the big one has visited this area as well. "This'd be a good spot to sit some evening," Kenny says as I turn to him. He sees me looking at the rub and smiles, as if he can read my mind.

"Yeah," I breathe. "There have been some deer here. Maybe I could put a stand in that tree, there. I could shoot to a couple of these trails."

Kenny nods in agreement, but his eyes have left mine and shifted to the pawed ground nearby. As I move around the tree I've picked for an ambush, breaking off twigs that might deflect a shot, Kenny talks softly behind me. "You know if it weren't for her fawns, I think an old doe would be one of the toughest animals to hunt in the woods. They're as wary as any buck. About the only time they make mistakes is to warn their fawns of danger—they'll make themselves vulnerable for that, but not much else.

"One of the first things I learned about these swamp deer is they aren't as predictable as the deer in the hills. Up there, deer'll bed on the hillsides and come to the fields to eat. They might stop for an acorn on the way, but you can bet they'll hit those fields sooner or later. Down here, a deer has a hundred choices. Some'll come to a field like that rye, but not all. They can stay down in the swamp—eat browse, acorns, sedge grass, whatever's handy. One day they might bed near some cattails, the next in a clump of prickly ash, another they'll lay on some oak ridge. Don't have to travel on a trail, and water's no barrier to them; with their hollow hair they can swim good, just like a dog.

"Y'know, a few years ago in '93, the swamp was full of water. We'd had a heavy snow that winter, and come spring, the river was above flood stage for 108 days straight. That was tough on the critters in the swamp. Everything that needed dry ground to live had to move out, and for some of them, it meant swimming a mile or more. The animals'd crowd on the last spots of dry ground, and when those would flood, they'd swim to the next, until most of the critters that could had left the swamp.

"I spent about a week paddling a canoe in there just after it flooded, just looking around. One day I come on this doe swimming for high ground. Deer are strong swimmers, and this one was no different, except she had her fawn tagging behind her. The both of them were swimming just fine, their heads held high and the water just churning behind them. But I watched that fawn, and every once in awhile the water would quit churning behind it, but she never got any further behind. I saw that once or twice and I got real curious, you know? Like how could she quit swimming and still keep up? So I paddled until I come right behind them, maybe fifty yards or so, and then I could see it: When the water quit churning, the fawn would grab her mother's tail in her mouth and hang on. She was getting a free ride, I guess! I followed them until they got onto dry land."

I'm clearing the last of my brush as Kenny finishes the story, and I turn to him and smile. "That's pretty amazing. I wonder how often something like that happens."

"Good question. Probably more than we think. Those old does are smart critters, you know. And probably the best eating deer in the woods, besides a yearling."

I nod in agreement, but as we walk past the giant rub, I gaze at it longingly. What a thrill it would be to see the monster who made that again!

Three days later, I return. I quietly climb the tree we picked near the feeding area and hang a stand. Once again I see deer throughout the evening: a small group of does that linger out of range before scurrying to the rye, and later a young forkhorn who cruises past, his mind addled by the impending rut.

A half-hour before dusk a huge doe emerges from the brush and heads toward my tree. Unlike the family group that preceded her, this matriarch moves like silk, testing the wind before committing to a trail, scanning the woods before her for danger. I press my back to the tree and avert my gaze, convinced her finely tuned senses will pick me off if I make the slightest blunder. After many long minutes, she feeds within ten yards of my stand and, amazingly, stands and presents a quartering-away shot at her ribcage. I have an extra tag allowing me to shoot an antlerless deer, and I reach quickly for the bow, hoping to seize this perfect opportunity. And somewhere deeper I think, I want to please Kenny, convince him I've been listening to his talks that any swamp deer is a trophy.

My fingers are clenched on the string, and I'm tensing my back muscles for the draw when I see the gleaming rub out of the corner of my eye. What happens, I wonder, if I shoot this doe and her death run spooks the big buck, who may be on his way at this very moment? The breeding season is fast approaching, and I've hunted long enough to know the split-seconds it can take for such a bizarre event to occur. I look back at the doe, who has lifted her head to glance down the trail. It's a now-or-never moment, and when she snaps her head to gaze at the brush behind my stand, I relax my draw. Perhaps she sees the big one coming! The doe whirls and trots off, and I swing slowly but assuredly toward the source of her fright. It is the young forkhorn again, his stare fixed on the doe, confusion and lust swimming in his eyes. The woods darkens as he ambles past, and I crawl down from the tree, defeated now by two deer—the invisible, antlered trophy and one that presented herself to be taken and was foolishly rejected.

Kenny chuckles when I tell him the story the next time we meet in the swamp. "You'll have that," he muses philosophically. "That saying about 'a bird in the hand' is often true."

I prepare for another reminder that any wet-tail is a trophy, but instead, Kenny grabs a walking stick and motions me to follow him. We cover ground slowly, walking through fallen leaves until we've gone well into the swamp, to a remote peninsula where a huge swamp white oak he's dubbed—in honor of Sigurd Olson's book—the *Listening Point Tree*. It's a bluebird, early-November day, the calendar telling us that ducks and deer should be active, the weather reminding us that calendars are just numbers on paper. Kenny motions me to sit with him by the tree.

"A few years back I came to this very spot with my dog Joey, on a day similar to this one. We were just killing time—no ducks flying. Anyway, a boat comes up Indian Creek with four bowhunters in it. They go past me, up the slough, and to the far end of the island, where the boat stops. Two of the guys get out, and the other two come back here and land the boat across the crick from me. These two are going to drive the island to the other ones waiting.

"I watch the drivers start out, and they aren't gone but a couple of minutes when I hear a twig snap near that boat. I figure it's one of the hunters coming back for something he forgot in his hurry. But it ain't a hunter. It's a big buck, walking with his head low, sneaking through the willows. He'd laid down until those drivers walked past, then snuck back through.

"Once he gets by the boat, he goes right for the water and goes in past his belly, then just stands there. Some of the time he's looking across at me, but mostly back at his backtrail. The wind was blowing from him to me, so I knew he couldn't smell me, and I just sat real still. Pretty soon he starts across, and he swims that creek in about two seconds, holding his head back like he's afraid to get his rack wet. When the buck come out by me, he shook himself like a dog, and we were so close I felt droplets of the spray on my arms—could see the muscles on his ribs rippling as he shook. Then he gave a final look at that boat and walked back into that swamp like it was his. And I guess it was."

We're both silent for many moments, visualizing the big one

making his clean getaway. Finally Kenny stands and heads for Big Lake Shack and I tag behind, one question lingering in my mind.

"Is that the same deer that's making those rubs, you think?" I finally ask.

"I don't think so," Kenny sighs. "But I bet it's his son."

Deer hunters, of course, know all about the survival smarts of old whitetail bucks, but to witness such a crafty escape is a rare experience. And as we wander through the November woods, I find myself wishing I had been the one to see it. Interestingly, in my fantasy I not only don't carry a bow, I'm actually rooting for the buck. Strange stuff for someone who—because of a handful of savage rubs on some red cedars—can hardly sleep at night as he formulates plans and theories for foiling a trophy deer.

I manage to hunt several more days before the early bow season closes, starting each afternoon with the hope that a monster will appear, leaving the woods in darkness knowing I'd been fooled again. When archery hunting closes to give the gun hunters their turn, I yield the swamp to Kenny, Mary, and Kenny's father, who stay each night at Big Lake Shack, cooking stew or soup on the woodstove, then turning in to fitful sleep in the bunks. They rise early each day to prod the swamp for deer, sitting patiently for a few hours, gathering at the shack for a meal, venturing out again to make small, circling walks to each other, hoping to jump a bedded whitetail and push it to a waiting partner.

It is how deer hunting should be conducted: in a group small enough to allow an intimacy with the landscape and the quarry itself, but with enough friends that there is a camaraderie binding the hunters as firmly to each other as it marries them to the land. By season's end, four Whitman whitetails hang from the meatpole: the forkhorn buck I'd seen while bowhunting, two adult does, and a yearling. Each deer will hang for several days, then be skinned and quartered, the meat frozen and used through the year as needed. The memories and laughter will be stored in deeper places and used as soul food for many years to come.

Two weeks after the firearms season closes I return to the swamp. Bowhunters are allowed the month of December for a final chance at a deer, and for some reason I have always loved the cold, solitary effort of late-season hunting. A brief scouting run reveals that deer are beginning to bunch near convenient food sources, their no-nonsense trails easily read in the light snow cover. I find a worn path linking a remote bedding peninsula and a distant field edge, and crawling into a basswood tree that overlooks a junction of that trail and another, settle in to wait. December deer frequently wait until the last sliver of daylight before rising to feed, so I'm surprised when I hear the soft crunch of hooves on snow an hour before dusk. I rise slowly, bracing my hand against the tree as I stand, and catch my breath when I look down the trail. It's the big buck I've waited for, moving like an automaton toward feed. Tired from the rigors of breeding and evading hunters, his mind is now occupied with putting groceries in his belly and resting. With any luck, he will continue his course and walk within range of my tree. I reach for the bow, snug the arrow against its nock, and wait.

My breathing is shallow and crisp when the buck stops three steps from a small opening twenty yards from my tree. Whitetails, especially ones as large as this wide-racked ten-point, pause frequently even when they have a firm purpose. Nothing has to alert them; the pause is done simply on principle, like the ingrained stop we all execute before crossing even the most deserted roadway. As he stands, licking his nostrils and looking blankly left and right, my eyes scan his ivory horns, trace the line of his muscular neck, roam over his taut ribcage. There is a small, dark tuft of hair just behind his shoulder that I focus on: This will be my aiming point when he proceeds, an arrow hitting him there certain to end his life in seconds.

A lot can happen to a hunter's heart while he waits. In the long moments that pass as the buck surveys the landscape, my mind drifts off my aiming point and—for some reason I still can't fathom—to the sunlit spot by the Listening Point Tree where Kenny and I sat less than a month ago. I think of that buck, who probably sired the deer before me, and his ingenuity, his skill, and without sounding too anthropomorphic, his pride. After, all he could have just swam the creek and made a rush to the safety of the swamp. But instead, he stopped and looked over his shoulder at the boat as if to flaunt his victory. Someday he knew, as all prey animals must, that he would not fool the hunters. But on that day he had and saved his own life. He had also shown an onlooker just how extraordinary an animal a whitetail buck can be, and how much richer a woods are with him in it. That's a notion all hunters need to be reminded of from time to time.

The mental aside lasts only seconds, but in those few ticks I not only lose my concentration, but the buck resumes his march down the trail. He's through my opening before I can draw, so I hurriedly look for another within my bow range. There are none. The buck continues to walk, stopping briefly to browse a small willow. He reaches a gap thirty yards away, but this is five steps beyond the distance I know I can kill with my recurve. In another moment he is past me, weaving his tall rack through the cover and slinking toward an easy meal in the crisp December afternoon.

As I trudge to the truck in the darkness, my boots squeak lightly against the snow, and for some reason the sound pleases me. So does the feeling in my chest. I lost a chance at my buck, but found something bigger in those lonely winter woods.

RAT TALE
Monarch of the Swamp

KENNY TELLS THE TALE: The morning had dawned gray and misty. It was early October and the pungent smell of autumn—fresh acorns, fallen leaves, and damp earth—permeated the air. I'd been cruising the Big Lake Country, blazing trails, counting 'rat houses, and clearing portages for the hunting and trapping time soon to come.

I was halfway across a beaver dam when I saw them. I stopped walking then knelt down to get a closer look. They were deer tracks—the largest whitetail tracks I'd ever seen. Deer had been crossing this beaver dam since the first day it was built, maybe ten years ago. Now this is nothing unusual in the great swamp country along the Mississippi backwaters: Everything on four legs, plus humans, uses beaver dams as bridges in swamp country. In my many years of traveling the swamp, I'd seen a whole lot of tracks but this set of tracks was special. They were long and splayed out wide after the manner of big bucks, the dew claws sunk deep into the rich, black mud. I made up my mind then and there that I would lay a trap come November for this great Monarch of the Swamp.

Now a swamp buck is not quite the same as any other deer. A swamp buck is not accustomed to people for there aren't a whole lot of folk that venture deep into the swamp country. A swamp buck is smart, wary, and tough; they learn to live on acorns, swamp grass, and browse. Only under the cover of darkness will they come out to the edge of the swamp to feed in the fields, even in winter when the going is hard.

During the next six weeks I scouted out his home territory, finding that he bedded about three-quarters of a mile southwest of the beaver dam in the high marsh grass that covered a narrow spit of land jutting out into a lake. He left many rubs and scrapes between the beaver dam and his beds.

Some of the rubs were on big trees like I'd never seen a buck rub on before.

When at last opening day of deer season came, I was up two hours before shooting time. After a hearty breakfast, I dressed in layers of wool, felt shoes covered with four-buckle overshoes, and chopper mittens. I knew it might be a long, cold day.

After walking down to the edge of Big Lake, I stood my battered old gun against a tree, turned my canoe over, put my tea bottle, lunch, and my gun in the bow, and shoved the canoe into the water. I picked up my ash pole, stepped into the stern, and shoved off.

It only took about twenty minutes to get to the beaver dam. Upon reaching the dam I had to walk about fifty yards to an old deadfall that I had prepared to sit under. Once there, I checked the wind direction, found it to be in my favor, laid a boat cushion on the ground, and settled in.

In the pre-dawn stillness I heard a beaver drop a tree into the water far down the east side of Big Lake. A great horned owl flew to the top of a naked oak and hooted softly as if to say "It was a good night's hunt." Several flocks of ducks whistled their wings overhead; far out over the river channel I could hear some tundra swans calling their wild, lonesome call. All was normal and right in the swamp.

Dawn arrived as it always does, by surprise. One minute it's dark, the next you can make out shapes and forms, then suddenly it's light. I eased some shells into my Remington Model 11. It felt like an old friend in my hands, reblued twice but now worn and shiny again, the stock taped and scratched. I'd used that gun for everything from ducks and pheasants to partridge and deer. I knew full well if I missed the swamp buck, it wouldn't be the fault of the gun.

Within moments a doe and two fawns picked their way carefully across the dam, stopped once or twice to test the wind, then walked off toward the west. Good! They hadn't smelled me. Quietly I waited. The sun appeared like an orange ball in the east. It always seems coldest about this time of the morning and today was no exception. I wiggled my toes and fingers as much as I could.

To the east I heard blue jays calling raucously. When the jay calls, it's time to watch closely. Sure enough, within minutes I heard the crisp leaves rustle across the slough, then I saw him walking slowly toward the beaver dam, the morning sun glistening off his polished antlers. He stopped at the edge of the water, raised his head, and tested the wind, puffs of steam shooting from his black nose.

I seemed to live the next couple of minutes in slow motion. As I waited for him to take just one more step, the smell of fresh, black mud and frozen leaves hung in my nostrils. Out of the corner of my eye I watched the thawing frost run down the trunk of a small maple to my left. Time was suspended. I moved nothing but my eyes, the old buck did the same. He wasn't going to move. It was now or never. My hands were shaking and it wasn't from the cold. I took the safety off, raised the gun slowly, aimed for his neck, let out half a breath, and fired.

Now the spell was broken. In a split second I felt the recoil, heard the crack of the gun, and saw mud and water spray as the huge deer leaped into the air, swapped ends like a bucking bronco, and bounded off through the brush.

I knew immediately I had missed, for a hit in the neck will drop a deer in its tracks as a rule. I said a few choice words, walked over to the canoe, took my tea bottle out, poured a cup, and sat down. I noticed my hands shook, and I wiped a few beads of sweat from my forehead. Suffering succotash! That was one beautiful deer.

Upon checking, I found I had shot off a tag alder about the size of my thumb that sent the slug off its mark. For several days I replayed that morning over and over in my mind, what should I have done different? Tried to out-wait him? Shot for the shoulder? Cleared more brush? There were many "what-ifs" to run through my head, but life goes on.

* * *

Over the course of the next several years as I was fishing, trapping, brushing trails, or hunting, I saw that buck a couple of times, but only fleetingly. Many times I saw his tracks or his beds. Once in a while I'd take a walking stick and go critter and bird watching and maybe dig some roots or cut herbs. Whenever I was in the old buck's country I'd watch for him or his sign. When hunting season rolled around each year, I'd tell myself that maybe I'd try for him again. Then I'd think, "No, by God! I had a good chance and he won fair enough!"

Sometimes as I thought of that morning at the beaver dam I was almost glad I'd missed. It was good to know that the old swamp buck was still out here. On winter nights when the northwest wind howled and the falling snow pelted off the shack's windows, I thought of him lying, curled up, nose to tail in the thick, dry marsh grass and I slept better. Some mornings after a fresh snow I'd go out of my way toward his country to find his tracks. "Yup, he's still here," I'd tell myself and step a little lighter.

Another winter passed slowly until finally spring arrived. The ice was just going off the marshes, and the water was open around the edges, but the old ice of winter lay dying, honeycombed and blackish in the middle of the lakes. The sun was warm, but the shade was cold. A south wind was blowing; it felt warm and gentle. I could smell life coming back to the swamp.

My old traveling partner and best swamp friend Spook was riding in the canoe's bow. We were getting toward the end of spring muskrat trapping. On this particular day we were working the Maple Tree Pond country. A narrow strip of trees runs southeast almost to the middle of the pond; at the tip of this land stands a gnarled, twisted, soft maple. Spook and I usually stopped here to eat lunch and hang the muskrats to dry. On this spring day, we dragged the canoe up on land, unloaded the 'rats, hung them up in the sun, and sat down to eat. I bent the dry marsh grass down for a nice place to sit, poured a cup of tea, took some lunch out of my bag, and began to soak up the sights and sounds of the swamp.

A muskrat swam up along the edge of the cattails. On the far side of the pond, a beaver sat on the top of his dome-shaped house peeling a willow stick for his dinner and enjoying the beautiful spring day. A pair of Canada geese came flying in from the south, circled the pond once, set their wings, and landed with a loud *swish*. The geese honked back and forth for a few minutes, then swam into the bulrushes, probably to look for a place to set up housekeeping. Suddenly, a flock of blue-winged teal came in low over the water, banked in perfect unison like a squadron of fighter planes, then were off in a flash toward the west.

For the first time this spring, the frogs were beginning to sing their peculiar song; I guess one could call their melody the national anthem of the wetlands. A red-winged blackbird sat at the top of a cattail calling as he swayed gently back and forth in the breeze. A lordly great blue heron walked slowly along the edge of the pond, stopping occasionally to strike savagely into the water with his long, spearlike bill and another small fish was history.

Old Spook was moseying around in the marsh grass about fifty yards in back of the big maple tree. I walked over to see what he had found. There, lying stretched out under a small patch of dogwood was the old swamp buck. His life had run its course. He had made it through another long, harsh winter only to die in early spring.

I knelt down by his side. He looked like he'd been dead a week or two at most. My wind-chapped hand stroked his gray, grizzled head. His eyes had begun to sink back into their sockets. He was still a huge animal but gaunt. Even in death he looked proud and graceful. Soon, as is the manner of nature, the coyotes, foxes, 'possums, and skunks would devour his flesh; finally the insects, sun, wind, and rain would return him to the Earth from whence he came.

As I sat next to him I thought of that frosty, November morning so long ago when I'd have given anything to sit by his side. To saw off his antlers, to tan his hide, and eat his flesh. Now he was gone. No more would I see his tracks in the mud and the snow. No more would the signs of his life—the rubs, the scrapes, and the beds—tell me of his comings and goings like the pages of a book. The white winds of winter and the passage of time had taken their final toll.

Spook and I went back to our dry, grass bed, sat down together, and finished eating. The tea, so warm and aromatic minutes ago, now had lost its tang to my tongue. My sandwich seemed dry and hard to swallow. The wind that blew from the south felt cold and the song of spring had lost its joy.

When I finished skinning the dry muskrats, Spook and I loaded our canoe, shoved into the water, and poled off down the slough. A short time later a large, whitetail doe jumped from her bed and bounded off into the hardwood swamp, her tail bouncing from side to side as she ran. She was heavy with fawn. That's when it hit me.

I sat down in the canoe letting it drift as it wanted. That doe would give birth, probably to twins in a short time, and chances are one of those fawns would be a buck. "By golly, I'll just bet the old swamp buck was the father of them, too!" I told myself. Yes, the old-time Native American prayer was right: "We are all creatures of the Earth Mother. We know that some of us must die that others may live, so the one great Circle of Life may continue unbroken."

When looking back over the time I knew the old swamp buck, I've come to understand nature and my own self much better. That old deer and nature taught me not to kill something just for my own glorification, to show off the trophy and brag what a great hunter I am. To go out of my way to kill a particular deer does not make sense to me now. For one deer tastes just as good as another. I only need to kill a deer to help sustain my own life and for the good of the herd. Other reasons do not matter.

I also learned that bonds can be formed with any critter if one takes the time to get to know it. In getting to know nature and the critters, I was really getting to know myself. I also came to realize that while some critters seem to be more regal and glorious, in reality they are all special and precious. This is true of humans as well. Finally, I came to understand that just *seeing* nature in all its wonder and glory was every bit as exciting and wonderful as anything else on Earth.

Once again I picked up my poling stick and old Spook and I were on our way, plying our ancient craft of living with nature. But from that day on, we would do so with greater care and love, knowing full well that one day soon we would once again stop in awe at the sight of a set of huge tracks, a rub on a big tree, or the glint of the morning sun off wide, high-tined antlers. Then and only then would the Circle of Life be complete, and I would stand and look off across the swamp toward the Maple Tree Pond and realize that the Monarch of the Swamp lives on.

DECEMBER

River Rat Almanac

IN NATURE'S CALENDAR—the Circle of Life—December is an ending and a beginning: the tag end of autumn and the beginning of winter. The Mississippi River lies quiet. No waves lap against the shores; no whitecaps pound the islands. Boat traffic ceases altogether. A few "black holes" of open water stand in stark contrast to surrounding ice and snow. The water moves, but it is quiet and slow as though "Old Man River" is saying, "I might be sleeping, but I'm doing so with one eye open, 'cause I'm a round river, and there ain't no beginning, nor is there an end."

Now is the time of watching and waiting, patience and tolerance, rest and death. Muskrats and beavers sit in dark silence in their winter quarters. Scattered flocks of ducks, geese, and swans drift between the few patches of open water. Red-tailed hawks glide in ever widening circles on blufftop winds along the river valley. Bald eagles wait in a naked cottonwood near open water. The views are good below. Underneath the tree are parts of fish and bits of muskrat fur—the eagles are dining well. About the middle of December a great number of bald eagles gather to fish in the open water at the confluence of the Chippewa and Mississippi Rivers, near Reads Landing, Minnesota.

I'm always surprised by the first real snowfall. The snowflakes are beautiful as they drift through the bare tree tops, slowly twirling and whirling their way to a silent landing. I watch flake after flake cover the crisp, brown autumn leaves with a soft, white carpet. Good thing the critters aren't surprised or they wouldn't survive. Nature's storybook is open for us to read on the snow-covered ice of the backwaters. Here, fox and coyote tracks crisscross the sloughs. Rabbit and mouse tracks circle every thicket and deadfall—ah ha! That's why predators are cruising this area!

Making Meat

Perhaps one of the greatest wonders in a year spent in bluff country is the season's first snowfall. The inaugural sifting of snow always makes the river valley seem larger; the stark white hills suddenly appear taller and more grand as they stand watch over the Mississippi and its tributaries. The timbered hillsides of Wisconsin's "West Coast" stretch down to narrow bands of corn stubble and contoured strips of alfalfa, fields that seem to have doubled in size by donning a white mantle. It's as if someone has turned a huge light on bluff country, shining it into forested nooks and shaded dales that have gone unnoticed for months. Even the atmosphere takes on a different hue, shedding the haze that hangs over the river for much of the year. Now sunlight sparkles unfettered through cerulean skies, playing on ice crystals and drifting snow and making them shine as if they were jewelry.

On a smaller scale, winter snow reveals the season's most easily read animal tracks, and I've always been fascinated by the tales they tell. As Kenny and I wander in the swamp early one December day, we find the tidy, prancing trail of a red fox as it worked the edge of an oak thicket. We follow the track for a hundred yards before Kenny stops and gestures with his walking stick. "It's a male," he says, pointing to an orange-red stain sprayed in the snow. "See how he lifted his leg against this little clump of brush? Just like a dog that way, they are. Can't resist marking something to let other males know he's in the neighborhood."

The track varies according to the terrain the fox travels. As he entered a stand of river birch and maple, the track is a simple beeline of perfectly made, catlike prints. The fox slowed slightly as he made his way into a grove of swamp white oak, his tracks coming closer together and weaving now, taking advantage of this bush and that clump of reeds for cover. The reason for his wandering became clear as we followed: the bounding leaps of gray and fox squirrels who'd raced through the snow to climb trees, surprised in the midst of their acorn-hunting by the hungry fox. Scattered powder proved that the fox had made a frantic sprint at one squirrel, but his tracks pulled up far short of the bounding leap the squirrel made at the tree, indicating an unsuccessful attempt. "Sometimes fast food ain't so easy to get," Kenny laughs, pointing to the scattered powder the squirrel threw in the snow.

As the fox reached the wood's edge and was about to enter an expanse of cattails, he paused to sit on his haunches. Had he heard or sensed danger? Was he stopping on the edge of cover, as deer frequently do, just on principle and precaution? Perhaps he'd smelled prey ahead, for his lengthening strides indicate a quicker pace as we follow his trail into the marsh; his walk turning into a trot, the track suddenly banking hard right, then spraying snow next to a brushpile. The sun glitters on the fluffy mound where the fox piled snow as he dove. Mixed in with the crystals of ice and flecks of mud are purple-red stains. "He got lucky here," Kenny nods at the mound. "Going to sleep good tonight."

"What'd he catch?" I ask, peering down at the battle scene.

"Rabbit," Kenny says simply, then points with the tip of his walking stick. In the snow is a wet swath of gray fuzz with salt-and-pepper guard hairs. I crouch and peer intently at the snow for several seconds, looking for other clues: bones, hair, more blood. There is nothing. Just the simple, hard evidence of an incident that took place yesterday in the December woods. One creature died so that another could live. Or as Kenny is fond of saying, "The Circle of Life just took another turn." In the months I've known him, Kenny has used this term dozens of times to explain happenings in the swamp.

Most folks who've studied nature, modern ecology, or the Native American life, have encountered the term, "Circle of Life." Biology teachers give it a passing nod in their textbooks, explaining with arrows and diagrams how plants grow and some animals eat them and other animals eat the animals that eat the plants and how each population in the chain depends on the others for long-term survival. It's an impressive line of thought, but certainly not a new one; Indians and other "primitive" peoples who live close to the land had this all figured out centuries ago. Their knowledge came from hundreds of encounters identical to the one Kenny and I followed in the snow. And, of course, the simple knowledge that they, too, were members of the Circle of Life they watched every waking day of their lives.

Gradually, however, most of us have lost this feeling, this connection to our role in the Circle, and it's not hard to see why. Most folks live in large cities and spend less time with nature, getting small doses of it—if any at all—from neatly produced programs on television. They buy their food in tidy packages without knowing, or caring, where it comes from. And, in time, they're able to divorce themselves from their place in the Circle. They see themselves as being apart from Nature, rather than a part of it.

Of course, the life of a river rat offers no chance for such denial. The snow-track drama of the fox and the rabbit won't allow it. Nor does the hanging carcasses of a pair of deer killed during the hunting season last week. The whitetails, a sleek, healthy brace of does, were shot by Kenny and Mary as Kenny made a small circle of the downed timber and prickly ash surrounding Big Lake Shack. Mary waited by a known trail crossing as Kenny walked, and when the pair of does jumped from their beds and tried to sneak past Mary into the safety of the swamp, she raised her shotgun and fired once, killing the lead doe. Hearing the roar of the gun, the other doe doubled back on her trail and tried to slip around Kenny. But he'd anticipated such a happening, crouching next to a tree and aiming at a small opening in the brush he knew a circling deer would cross. His shot was true, and now two deer lay in the snow, a supply of winter's meat waiting to be made.

Kenny and I meet after the deer had hung for a few days, the early winter air working on their carcasses to cool and tenderize them. Kenny dressed the does shortly after the kill, then skinned each still-warm carcass after hoisting it to hang on a stout pole strung between two oak trees next to Big Lake Shack. The hides were saved and carefully salted, ready to sell to a local tannery, which offers five dollars cash per skin, or a merchandise voucher for a pair of leather gloves. But the focus with deer is always on the meat, and butchering is the main event following deer season.

Reducing a deer to a pile of meal-sized cuts of meat you'd see in a market is a daunting task to some, but it needn't be. Butchering may also be one of the most satisfying elements of harvesting wild game. Nearly all the meat markets in bluff country will process a deer for you—indeed, many small-town butchers make a great share of their annual wage from handling venison. There's certainly nothing wrong with a hunter using this convenience. But something notable is lost when you drop off a freshly killed deer at a butcher shop, then return many days later to pick up a box full of neatly wrapped steaks and chops and burger.

You've missed the process of making meat.

Kenny hauled the skinned carcasses into town, preferring to butcher at his home, where running water and clean working surfaces make the job easier. A small shed close to the house boasts a large table and an old counter top that is perfect for working on deer, and Kenny has the knives sharpened and ready for our work.

"I don't do anything fancy with my meat," he explains as we duck into the shed. "No gourmet cuts or butterfly steaks or nothing."

"Then you've got the right guy working for you," I laugh.

Prior to butchering my first deer, I was intimidated by the size of the carcass before even starting the project. But after helping on a whitetail or two, then doing one myself, I realize the project was much easier if broken down into smaller parts.

With large animals like deer, this is accomplished by first "quartering" the carcass into four sections by the front and hind legs. Kenny and I tackle the front quarters first, as they are the lightest and easiest to handle. After cutting off the lower legs near the first joint, the front leg is simply lifted away from the body and a knife blade slipped under the armpit. The front legs of a deer are only attached to the skeleton by light tissue and a shallow ball-and-socket joint, so they are easily separated from the carcass by simply running a sharp, stout knife blade around the perimeter of the muscle. While it seems this attachment is incredibly flimsy, the reverse is actually true. Since whitetails fleeing danger use short bursts of speed, jump obstacles, slam to sudden stops, and make nearly ninety-degree turns, the "floating" nature of this joint allows them to pull off such gymnastics without injury. If their front legs were attached more solidly to their skeletons, deer would routinely break their legs from the impacts they endure.

Once the legs are removed, a smaller knife is used to fillet the meat from the bone. There are no prime cuts on the front leg and shoulder of a whitetail, so most of the meat is placed in small pieces in a clean, special bucket. This scrap- or chunk-meat can be saved for stew meat or ground into burger, depending on the hunter's preference. Some hunters also like to make a roast from the front shoulder, but that is not our choice this day. As Kenny and I each work on a front quarter, we use the flexible tips of our knives to separate meat from bone, following the natural contours of muscle and sinew, and cutting off the white hard bands of tendon where they connect meat to other tissue.

One of the unique challenges of butchering deer is removing the fat and white tissue from the meat as you go. In a beef cow, for example, fat is a desirable trait, for it enhances flavor and texture. Indeed, in the weeks before butchering, a farmer will feed cattle almost strictly on corn, a high-fat food that will ensure steaks and other prime cuts are well marbled, or interspersed, with fat. But the fat on a deer appears only on the outside of the meat itself, and the flavor ranges, in Kenny's words, "from shoe leather to downright disgusting." In fact, many a first-time butcher has left generous portions of fat on his venison, then screamed about its taste. "I'm convinced that's why some folks can't stand deer," Kenny says, stripping a layer of white-silver tissue from a palm-sized chunk. "They treat it like beef, and can't believe it don't taste the same."

I can only nod in agreement, having known many people who quit hunting because they finally admitted they couldn't stand the taste of venison. One farmer I knew complained, "I grew up eating nothing but deer since I was a kid. Folk couldn't afford nothing else. Venison's poor-man's food to me. When the freezer's empty and there's no money in sight, that's when I'll start eating that stuff again." Faced with such a speech, I considered volunteering to cook a steak for my farmer friend, but thought better of it. I had free rein to hunt his land because he no longer cared to; if I made a venison fiend out of him, would he still let me on? I selfishly kept mum.

Ironically, those who've had whitetail prepared properly usually rave about it. My wife Shari, never much of a meat-eater, could go for years and not miss the taste of beef, but literally craves venison. The rich, dark flavor of deer meat is one reason, of course—but "head knowledge" is part of her preference, too. Venison steak, for example, is more than twice as lean as an identically sized cut of beef. It also has more protein and fewer carbohydrates. This is big news for my wife, a bona fide health and fitness nut. And, there's the additional knowledge that she knows exactly where the meat is coming from and how it's been cared for. Having a couple of friends with slaughterhouse experience, I've spared Shari the gory details but assured her this is no small consideration.

Kenny and I finish our respective front quarters at almost the same time. Peering into the scrap bucket, Kenny nods and smiles. "A good start on the stew meat and burger. Let's make some steak."

Just as on a cow, the best venison steaks come from a whitetail's hind quarter, or ham. The hind legs are separated from the carcass just as the front ones are, but with more difficulty; the bone and cartilage connections are stronger and require a saw cut to detach the quarter quickly. Once done, however, the butchering of a hind quarter is one of the most satisfying elements of cutting up a deer.

Whitetails in general, and mature does in particular, have wonderfully muscled back legs that yield some of the most flavorful steaks going. The meat is dense and dark, more red-black than a glass of hearty burgundy wine. We slice into our respective slabs of meat almost reverently, the knives cutting across the rich grain, creating thick steaks that would rival any found in a butcher shop. The boneless steaks are laid in a special pan, ready for wrapping.

One of the fun aspects of butchering your own meat is custom-wrapping the cuts to your specific needs. If you're cutting meat for a family, you'll want larger packages that will satisfy the appetites of several people in one meal. But if only a couple folk will be dining on steaks or burgers, it's easy to wrap the meat in smaller amounts. Or, of course, mix and match the amounts for a variety of occasions.

As I place the last of the steaks I've cut in the pan, I take the time to lift one to my nose. There is something uniquely aromatic about fresh-cut venison, and there are hints of so many whitetail foods in their firm, red flesh: the light, sweet odors of the corn and winter wheat that grow on the edge of the Whitman Swamp. The rich, heady whiff of acorns from the white oaks growing in the Big Woods near Tent Camp Slough. The spicy tang of sedges and browse the does nipped while they lay in their beds near Big Lake. All these scents mingle and, taste being one of the strongest senses associated with memory, I recall the heady smoke of the last whitetail steaks I'd cooked on our charcoal grill.

Cooking venison differs from beef in one key regard: the time the meat is left on the grill. The liberal fat found in a cut of beef allows for a variety of cooking times and degrees of "doneness." But with venison, less is always more. The trademark leanness of the meat fairly screams for a quick cooking time, especially on the more delicate cuts like the steaks we're working on. For folks who'd order their steak medium-well or more, leaving the meat with a hint of pink in the middle will ensure a satisfied diner. For those who like their meat in the redder categories, searing a steak is plenty of cooking. If the steak is left on the grill too long, you'll have just created one more person "who never got used to the taste of venison" and compared the dry, tasteless, stringy slab to cardboard, shoe leather, or worse.

Once the front and hind quarters of each doe are taken care of, we turn special attention to the thin band of meat lying on the side of each deer's backbone. Venison butchers usually refer to this dense, dark strip of meat as the "backstrap." This flavorful cut is so valued among venison connoisseurs that poachers throughout time have made it a point to carve this prime cut from a whitetail carcass before abandoning the rest. Kenny directs me to slice each backstrap delicately from the carcass and leave it intact for wrapping. Cooked whole on the grill or sliced into small chops or cutlets, backstrap is a special-occasion meat, one you'd serve only on holidays or special occasions, or to dignitaries worthy of the honor.

The final step in butchering is processing the neck area. This is similar to the front quarters in that the neck typically holds more fat, especially in a doe, that must be removed before eating or freezing. As on the other sections, Kenny and I work diligently to separate the meat on the neck from all fat and other tissue, a labor-intensive and time-consuming process. This meat joins the other in the scrap bucket and will be used in making stew, ground into burger, or made into sausage. Kenny's future plans include the construction of a smokehouse, which will allow him to make his own sausage. Carefully wrapped and stored in the freezer, this chunk meat will preserve well until the smokehouse project is complete.

After two hours of working on the quarters, neck, and loins, all that remains on the deer is the ribcage. We trim some of the easily accessible meat from the flanks, but leave the rest. Rib meat is maddeningly laced with fat and time-consuming to separate, a clear case of low return for great effort. "We ain't getting carried away with those ribcages," Kenny avows. "I got friends who're particularly fond of that meat."

"You're kidding! I don't know many people who mess with them past what we're doing. Who do you give them to?"

"The chickadees, juncos, and nuthatches that winter in the swamp," Kenny grins. "I hang the ribcages in trees around Big Lake Shack for them. Takes them most of the winter to clean them up, but I figure they deserve it; most songbirds peel out of here for the winter, but they stick around and tough it out. They need that meat more than I do."

Hanging ribcages for the birds is the perfect use, of course; an act of recycling you won't find in an ecology textbook, but one that makes perfect sense to an Indian—or a river rat—tuned into the Circle of Life.

We finish the last of the butchering, then carry in trays of steaks, chops, and roasts to be wrapped and stored in the freezer. Kenny decides to leave the meat in the scrap bucket outside, dividing it later into smaller portions according to the amount of stew meat, hamburger, or sausage he and Mary will want in the months to come.

We emerge from the shed and suck cool winter air into our nostrils, stretching backs and arms sore and cramped from working over the butchering tables. Ours is the pleasant tiredness that comes from work with a tangible, meaningful end. We have converted raw flesh into meat that will sustain us through the winter and beyond; strengthening us as we hike and bird watch, paddle and fish, wait and hunt. A week ago, two vibrant, breathtaking whitetails from the Whitman Swamp died to sustain our lives. Their sacrifice is not one taken lightly.

Of course, deer are not the only creatures that the Whitman provides for river rat sustenance. There are the ducks we shot in October and early November: sleek, quick-flying teal and wood ducks, plump and gorgeous mallards and widgeon. The fish we caught last spring and summer: muscular, gorgeous brown trout and the strong and tasty catfish. And even the animals we'll trap in the months to come: tender, fragrant beaver and lean, succulent muskrats. Each are dressed and prepared according to their unique properties, then cooked and eaten with reverence and appreciation. We find ourselves at the top of the food chain, a position of unquestionable power and dominance. How we conduct ourselves may not affect our stature in that cycle, but it speaks volumes about acknowledging our good fortune and our thankfulness to the creatures who sustain us.

On the afternoon that Kenny and I trailed the fox to its successful kill, we encountered another winter scenario that was more subtle, though just as telling. We were less than two hundred yards from Big Lake Shack, and the long shadows of the December evening were quickly claiming the Whitman Swamp. We'd stopped to rest for a moment before crossing a frozen slough, and I'd taken the moment to daydream, leaning heavily on my walking stick and thinking of simple things—the smoky aroma of Big Lake Shack after a cold day in the swamp, the warmth of my truck cab on the ride home, the pleasant tiredness I'd feel well into tomorrow.

Suddenly, Kenny touches my sleeve.

"Look at that owl up there," he whispers.

That we hadn't spooked the monstrous great horned owl in the white oak before us was testimony to the soft, silent snow underfoot. Or perhaps it was the bird's focus on some prey below its perch. Owls are the most sensitive of raptors, capable of detecting sound or motion where other birds notice nothing. This particular owl is looming over a chunk of forest floor with the intensity of a chess master, and the tension is so palpable we pause and hold our breath to watch its next move. The bird is hunched at the shoulders and leaning forward as a skydiver ready to hop from an airplane, and we follow its gaze to the snow-covered duff below. Though we can't see it, we know the owl somehow sensed dinner down there.

The bird pitches so suddenly from its tree it seemed to have been shot from beneath, but it comes down in a controlled dive, wings spread and talons outstretched, the move as silent as death. But just before touching ground, the bird shifts and pulls up, retracting its huge claws like a fencer sheathing an épée. Just as quickly, it swoops back skyward, finds a bare branch, and perches again.

"He missed," Kenny whispers.

We remain silent, watching for the bird's next move. The owl swivels its head once toward us, then away again before focusing once more at the ground beneath it. Suddenly it tenses for a moment, then dives again.

"Another miss," Kenny hisses. "He's after the same mouse each time, just can't catch it."

This time the owl's momentum carries it closer to us, and it settles into a nearby silver maple, lifts and resettles its wings over its back and suddenly stares at us, aware of our presence for the first time. However tempting the mouse beneath him, the owl hadn't counted on company. Launching himself from the branch, the great horned sails into the gathering blackness in search of a better, safer hunting ground. He had not made meat and would need many more minutes, perhaps hours, to know that he would survive another night in the Whitman Swamp.

Rat Tale
Making Wood

KENNY TELLS THE TALE: My first taste of making wood came early on our family's small farm deep in the hill country a half dozen miles east of the Big River. We had one of those old-time woodboxes mounted on hinges along the kitchen wall. When the box was empty, we went outside, took a hold of an iron handle, and flopped open a small section of the wall, which was the backside of the woodbox. Now we could fill the box with firewood. This was my job from the time I was big enough to carry a couple of pieces of wood. The bigger I got, the less trips I'd have to make from the woodshed to the woodbox, and I soon learned to carry as much as I could because the house got real cold in a hurry with the woodbox standing open. Once the box was full, it was pushed up and tipped inside, where the wood was handy to get at. More than once I got blood blisters and black and blue fingernails by slamming them in the crack between the wall and the box. I'd scream like a cat with its tail caught in a washing-machine wringer, and Ma would push from inside the house to get my sorry little self released. She'd say, "Stick your finger in the snow right away, that'll help some!" It did, but I still snuffled and sniffled about hating to carry wood. I wanted to do real wood making with the men in the woods, not this piddly boy's work.

One day when I was coming up on twelve years old, and the sun was bright and the snow soft and mushy, Ma said, "Kenny, put on all the warm clothes you can find. Pa wants you to go along up in the hills making wood."

Making wood! Wow, did I fly upstairs, two at a time, threw on some clothes, jumped back down the steps, and ran out to find Pa. He was hitching Sally and Daisy, our team of sorrel workhorses, up to the "sleigh wagon." This strange contraption was sort of a wooden wagon box set on runners. Pa allowed me to "drive" the rig to the toolshed. I proudly held the harness lines and softly said, "Giddy-up." The team just stood there. Pa told me to talk up a little and flop the lines against their backs. I did and this time the team's muscles stiffened. The tugs tightened against the load and we were off; the horses plodded and the wagon creaked and groaned. At the toolshed, I reined back with a long loud "Whoooaaa" the way I heard Pa do so many times, and we actually stopped. I looked at Pa for approval. He nodded his head with a wink in his eye.

Pa headed for the toolshed door with me following. As we passed in front of the team, I patted each one of their soft, moist noses and told them what good girls they were. They muttered and snorted and stomped their heavy hooves in reply.

Inside, Pa said, "I've got to sharpen the ax, so get on the wheel." The "wheel" was a giant whetstone. A round sharpening stone about two feet across and five inches thick was mounted on an iron frame that had a seat and pedals like a bicycle. A metal can filled with water hung above the stone. I hopped on and began to pedal with a nice, steady gate while Pa held the ax to the stone. The faster I pedaled, the faster the wheel stone turned, with the water steadily dripping down upon it so the steel ax head wouldn't overheat and lose its temper. I loved to ride the wheel, watching Pa turn the ax this way and that to get the edge just right. He motioned for me to stop pedaling, and then ran his thumb along the edge of the ax to check its sharpness.

Pa handed me a pail with several steel wedges in it, which I carried outside and placed in the wagon. Next was the double-bit ax: "Careful you don't slice yourself, son. Put it in so's the blades don't touch no metal; don't want to dull it," Pa reminded me. Back and forth I went loading tools for the day's work: a single-bit ax, two-person crosscut saw, splitting maul with a taped-up handle, cant hook, and finally a log chain so heavy it took all my might to lift it.

I ran for the house to pick up the lunch Ma had made for us while Pa brought the team around. As I was leaving the front porch door Ma wrapped a long woolen scarf about my neck. "Aw Ma, it ain't that cold out today," I whined. "I don't care, the wind blows strong this time of year," she answered firmly.

I crawled up beside Pa on the wagon seat. He made a clucking sound with his tongue against his cheeks, slapped the harness lightly on the rumps of the horses, and we went forward in the open field next to the house. We both turned to wave at Ma who was doing likewise on the porch.

Sally and Daisy took up a good clip across the snow-covered field toward the wooded hills. When we were at the edge of the woods, Pa said we'd rest the team for a spell. The horses were puffing and blowing, and their backs were wet with sweat. A few moments later he urged them on, straight up the bluffs on an old logging road that wound between the trees along a sharp hogback ridge. On either side of us the woods dropped almost straight down into a steep ravine, and I clutched the seat tightly. Short, quick puffs of steam shot from the horses' nostrils, and they chomped and ground their teeth on their bridle bits as they nervously climbed the bluff.

Pa stopped the team in a tiny clearing. We wiped the horses down with burlap feed sacks, then tucked the sacks under the harness straps and collars to soak up sweat.

We unloaded the tools onto a flat stump in the clearing. Wood cutting had been done here before, and the odor of fresh-cut red oak and working horses filled the air. Pa picked up the double-bit ax, laid it across his shoulder, then started walking up the hill with me tagging along behind. He stopped beside a dead oak about as big around as I was, which wasn't much. I asked him why he picked that tree out of all the others. He explained that he preferred red oak over any other kind of tree that grew in the hills because it split easy, burned hot, and didn't leave as much ash as most. The dead one we were about to cut was the best of all on account of it already was dry with no sap in it, and it wasn't too big so we wouldn't have to split most of it. He went on to say that dead trees already on the ground weren't as good, because they'd have soaked up moisture and would be "punky" inside—soft and half rotten.

"Stand back now, Kenny," he ordered. He went to chopping a V-shaped notch into the downhill side of the tree. When I again asked him why, he told me the notch would help the tree fall in that direction. Then he moved to the uphill side and began taking long, hard swings with the ax. Chips and chunks flew everywhere, and the ringing of his ax broke the silence of the woods like a low-pitched bell. Once again he began with a notch, wider than the first one, that tapered narrower as the ax bit deeper into the tree. Now with each blow the tree's top began to shiver and shake; a few more swings and the tree tilted downhill. Pa looked over his shoulder to make sure I was standing up hill behind him. "It'll only take a chop or two now. Stay back there and watch the butt end of the tree; sometimes they jump off the stump, so be ready to move fast." A couple swings and the tree started falling, slowly at first, then it picked up speed as it fell downward through the surrounding trees' branches, taking twigs and small limbs from them as it went. When the tree hit the ground, it made a dull thud muffled by the deep, wet snow; the sound echoed through the woods, across the ravine, and beyond. The tree's butt end bounced head high in the air, then settled back to the earth to move no more. Once again the late winter woods fell silent, except for the scream of a high-circling red-tailed hawk, the shake of a horse's head, and Pa's heavy breathing.

As Pa sat down on the fallen tree to rest, he asked me to get the bucksaw from the "tool stump." By the time I got back, he was trimming branches. He showed me how to stand on the opposite side of the tree, reach over the top, and cut the branches from the butt end toward the top. In this way, the tree was always between the ax and me; a misguided swing wouldn't gash my leg. By cutting from the bottom up, the limbs wouldn't split as easily. We cut some of the larger limbs off about four to six feet from the trunk with the bucksaw. The bucksaw was maybe two feet long with smaller teeth then a crosscut saw. It was set into a squarish wooden frame with a threaded rod across the top of the frame for adjustments.

Next, we cut the tree into three pieces with the bucksaw. Then we un-hitched Daisy, hooked the log chain onto her harness tugs, and drove her to the fallen tree. Sally stayed where she was, but whinnied loudly after her partner, as if to say, "Where are you going, friend? I want to go too!" At the tree, the chain was strung out with the big hook end of it toward the piece we wanted to pull. Now the cant hook was used to roll the log onto the chain. It had a four-foot-long, hand-hewn hickory handle with a heavy curved metal hook loosely bolted to it. When the handle was pulled in the direction of the hook, it sunk into the bark and gave great leverage for rolling the log. A backward push on the handle loosened it and another grip was taken. I asked if I could try it and I did, but the hook kept slipping off. Pa chuckled, "That's why it's called a cant hook, because some folk can't get the hook to grab."

When the log was moved far enough, the log chain was cinched up and Daisy leaned into the harness slowly. Ever so easy she tightened the chain until the log began to move through the snow. Pa didn't drive her at all; the lines were free as she picked her way between the trees down the hillside to the little clearing, where she stopped next to the wagon. Sally, her part-ner of twelve years, greeted Daisy with a snort and a toss of her head as if to say, "Good job, pal!"

We unhitched Daisy, grabbed the bucksaw, and began to "buck up" the log into short chunks that would fit into our wood-burning stove. This took a lot of arm strength and stamina—both of which I lacked—so Pa did the sawing while I moved a small piece of wood under the log on each cut so the blade wouldn't pinch.

When the log was cut up, Pa asked me for the splitting maul and wedges. "Show you how this is done," he said as he swung the maul blade side down. *Whop!* The thigh-sized log spilt in half. Now we rolled over the biggest log we had. Pa took a steel wedge and began driving it into the chunk of wood with the hammerhead of the maul and the hills echoed with the steady, high-pitched ring of steel striking steel. Gradually the log began to split, until with a *pop* it fell apart. While he split more wood, I tossed the split pieces into the wagon.

When Pa needed a rest I tried my hand at the splitting job. Several times I struck the chunks with the handle instead of the maul head. Pa cautioned me: "Don't swing so hard. Let the maul work. Make sure it lands where you're aiming. You hit that handle a time or two more and it'll bust for sure." I split a few chunks after a fashion, but I was glad to get back to piling.

"Time to eat," Pa announced. There were several old blocks of wood standing next to the tool stump. We each took one for a seat and the tool stump became our table. In the lunch bag we found big, thick slices of venison summer sausage along with fresh homemade bread and apple pie. The battered old thermos held piping hot water with a little milk and sugar added. We chewed and smacked at our sandwiches, sipped and slurped down the hot milk-water while Daisy and Sally munched loudly on mouthfuls of hay. Pa looked across the stump: "Darned if our little eating gang here don't sound like a bunch of hogs bellying up to a slop trough, aye?" I laughed and kept right on chewing.

The rest of the day was spent making wood. Always the same process was followed until finally Pa pronounced the wagon full. We loaded our gear, hitched up the team, clambered aboard, and started down the hill on the same trail we came up on.

Going down that hill put a fear into me like I'd never known in my entire life. Pa sat quietly on his wool mackinaw with the harness lines held loosely in his callused hands. From under the brim of his sweat-stained felt hat two dark eyes stared intently at the team in front of him and the trail under their feet. The hill was slippery, greasy with ice and wet snow, slick as a gob of lard on a tin roof in July. It was as if everything was happening in slow motion. The horses' iron-shod hooves slammed down hard for extra footing. Daisy and Sally pulled and grunted and strained with all their might against the pushing load. Every muscle, tendon, and vein in their heavy bodies bulged as if fighting to escape the hide that covered them. As we straddled the narrow hogback ridge, Pa began to talk to the horses in a quiet, gentle, reassuring way, "Easy now, Sal. Hold her back, Daise. That's the way, girls, that's the way." I closed my eyes, bit my lip, and held my breath. One misstep, one slip, and us and the whole caboodle would end up down in the bottom of the ravine 150 feet below to either side.

Finally we came out of the wood and stopped in the open field to rest the team. "You look a little green around the gills, Kenny," Pa patted my shoulder. "I had to swallow my heart a time or two up there myself. But you never want to have fear in your voice. The horses will sense that right away, then they get scared and we're all in for a heap of hurt."

At home we piled the load in the woodshed; piece by piece the fresh spilt wood was stacked in "ranks." At the supper table, I did a whole lot of eating and not much talking. And that night I dreamed in peaceful sleep of fresh sawdust, horse sweat, axes, wedges, and splitting mauls.

On that long ago day, I became a full-fledged wood maker. And I have remained one to this very day. Daisy and Sally have gone on to that lovely, lush, green pasture beside a cool, shady, meandering crick where there ain't no harnesses, no horseflies, and no cause to sweat. In their place is the Black Bomber. A hulking, rusty pickup truck, which, when asked to pull a heavy load, belches, coughs, sputters, and backfires in defiance of the task at hand. Everything about this metal monster from hell is noisy: To shut the doors on the end gates or drop a piece of wood in its box is like hitting a tin sheet with a post hammer. A pat on its fender, a kiss to its nose, a kind word means nothing to this black beast of burden. Horse-smell at its worst is like sweet wildflowers compared to the Black Bomber's exhaust.

The only other change in my wood-making life has been at the sawing end of it. The crosscut and bucksaw have been hung on the cabin wall as reminders of days past in the woodland workplace. A chainsaw does the felling, brushing, and bucking up these days present, and it's faster and easier, no doubt about it. But there is a price to pay for these conveniences. That motorized metal piece of ingenuity bellows from hill through hollow like an enraged bull on the wrong side of a fence full of cows. It chatters and shakes and vibrates my body from my fingertips, up the arms, through the chest, across the teeth, and right on out the top of my head. My nostrils are singed, throat parched, and eyes watery and bleary from the aroma of burning oil and gasoline.

Needless to say those two newfound tools do not allow me to hear and see near as many birds and critters as I did when making wood years ago, but then that's progress, I guess. Yet much about making wood remains the same: Steel wedges, splitting maul, cant hook, log chains, and axes are still my regular tools.

The wood-making procedure has not changed either. Fell a dead tree. Trim the limbs and buck it up to fit into the stove. Split the logs into firewood. Load them all up for the ride home. Pile them into ranks where they can air-dry. Carry them to the house in a wheelbarrow or small sleigh. Put them into the woodbox inside the house. Pitch them into the stove as needed and enjoy the kind of heat that penetrates a body clean through to the bone. Clean the ashes from the stove. Clean the chimney soot out. Wow, how else can I warm myself eleven different times using the same quantity of fuel?

Of course there's the added bonus of being forced out into the woods on winter and early spring days to make wood. It's a time when the sun begins to climb higher in a crisp, clean, blue sky and the winds are flavored by a hint of spring. The birds and bunnies, whitetails and woodpeckers, grouse and groundhogs are all gearing up for the seasonal rebirth. There's something about the smell of fresh sawdust, sweat, and soaked leather boots, the aches and pains, the bruises and blisters that prove that a hard, honest day's work has been done. At night the food tastes better, the woodsmoke smells homier, and the bed feels more comfortable than ever before.

JANUARY

River Rat Almanac

JANUARY IS ONE of the quietest months of the year, when most wild things are down to the deadly serious business of survival. Some, like the white-tailed deer, herd up to beat down trails and bedding yards in the deep snow. Wild turkeys form gangs for easier predator detection and more feet to scratch for food. The ducks and geese that stay in the North flock together in the few spring holes and open water patches. Songbirds, grouse, and pheasants also form flocks. Coyotes hunt in small packs as well. For these wild ones there is strength in numbers. But other critters, such as foxes, rabbits, squirrels, mink, and otters, live alone or with a very small family group.

The critters that aren't dormant move around just enough to survive. They don't want to pass a point of diminishing returns—spending too much energy for too little food. They hunt just enough to live, the rest of the time waiting stoically, silently, for spring. Each wild creature has its own time-proven method of dealing with winter. Yet all have one thing in common: Food is energy. Energy means warmth and life. They spend as little energy as possible to find their food, and their kitchens are usually quite close to their bedrooms. This time of year I find that concept very appealing indeed!

Silence, sweet silence, seems to be the decree of the Big River in January. Its waters have become heavily laden with layer upon layer of ice growing thicker with each passing moment. Silence reigns on shore as well. The absence of bird calls sets January apart as the quiet month. In a day afield, one might hear only a handful of songs—chickadees, crows, blue jays.

Winter Trapping

Bluff country winters don't get the hype that those in northern climes do. Hurley, Wisconsin, for example, might get more than two hundred inches of snow in a year. Kids in International Falls, Minnesota, learn their negative numbers by reading thermometers hung outside the school. You can hardly get through a winter without reading some newspaper account of these "Winter Capitals" and the badge of courage the reporter got by filing a story from them.

It's natural to brag about your winter, and we do it here, too. Trouble is, the severity of the season is so indefinable. We measure our snow in inches, not feet. Temperatures don't sink below zero for more than a couple days in a row. But as Kenny is fond of saying, "There ain't no cold like the cold in the swamp." It's a damp cold, a creeping ache that seeps into your neck and slips in around your wrists, subtle and sweet like a slow-acting poison. It's a cold that doesn't register on any wind-chill charts. You don't think you should be shaking so badly—the thermometer back home read only twenty-five degrees. But another hat could've made a difference, and wouldn't a scarf feel nice right now? Next thing you know, you've resigned yourself to wetting your underwear if the need arises, because operating a zipper is simply out of the question.

There's no better way to discover how frigid a dank, windswept, backwater can get than by running traps. Kenny hosted a northwoods logger on the trapline a few winters back. This logger was a hearty guy, worked in the woods all day, every day; sawed timber with his sleeves rolled up at twenty below without batting an eye. After a half-day checking muskrat traps in the Whitman, he looked Kenny in the eye and confessed he'd never been so cold in his life.

Kenny just nodded and smiled, then pulled his beaver-fur hat further down on his forehead.

But enough bragging. Trapping is not about proving your toughness in the face of adversity, though that's part of the game. Trapping is one of the simplest, most fascinating ways a river rat has of wresting a few dollars out of a country that gives them so begrudgingly. And trapping, Kenny reminds me as we set out one day, is the continent's oldest profession. Pondering that statement as a stereotypical male, my first thought is of a trade requiring a lot less clothing, but Kenny reads my mind. "That's the *world*'s oldest profession," he says. "I'm talking North America. The voyageurs and the Hudson Bay Company were here looking for fur long before there was anything else."

I make a mental note to verify this claim by checking a history book when I get home, but for now I'm busy helping load the canoe. Scanning the bluffs as I walk between the car and boat, it seems the river valley has been flash-frozen. The hills are snow covered and Alp-like, their sharp ridges joining the few cumulus clouds hovering over them. The sloping oaks seem ready to snap under their own weight. Woodsmoke from a distant farmhouse looks like a column of coral you could shatter with a gentle tap from a handsledge. Despite the frigid temperatures, Rose Valley Creek—which flows through a wide flat between the Mississippi and the bluffs—remains free of ice, and Kenny has traps to check and more to set. With the canoe's midsection loaded with traps, stakes, and a rucksack full of gear, Spider and I crawl into the bow. Kenny shoves the boat off the shore, poling us through the shallows at the mouth of the creek, then sits and switches to a paddle as we enter deeper water. We'll run the line upstream first, then let the current take us back to the landing.

The primary target on this outing is beaver. Kenny has been hired by the city of Cochrane to remove some of the abundant critters, who've proliferated in the creek and caused some problems. Chief among these maladies is flooding; the rock-solid dam they've built has raised creek levels drastically and channeled water into places village folk don't appreciate. The beavers also neglected to consult with streamside landowners before starting a vigorous and thorough logging operation. No one wants the beavers cleaned out; they'd just like to throw some cold water on their party for a couple of seasons.

A slight northwest breeze pushes against us as we slip through small stands of silver maple, alder, and willow. Cattails and bulrushes crowd the stream channel, their dirt-brown stems bent and broken by wind and current and frost. We cover a couple hundred yards without speaking, the only sound the rhythmic dribble of water off the canoe paddle after each stroke. The snow and cold seem to have numbed the landscape around us, but the open stream is an oasis. Deer tracks enter and exit the creek at a busy crossing. A pair of chickadees greets us from a cattail stem, picking at the withered stalk. Rounding a bend, we startle a wintering flock of mallards, who flush and quack their displeasure at having to fly on such a cold morning.

Five minutes after the ducks we reach the beaver dam, a formidable jumble of mud and sticks that seems even more stout because of the ice covering its surface. As a boy, I once spent the better part of a summer afternoon dismantling a beaver dam with a friend. It was difficult, backbreaking work that left us exhausted. Nevertheless, we put a sizable hole in the dam, and thousands of gallons of water were pouring through it when we left, inundating a dry marsh and dropping water levels in the lake. We thought we'd done a pretty handy piece of work, until we returned the next morning to find our destruction neatly repaired. Clearly these beavers dealt with know-nothing boys all the time and viewed plugging a damhole with about as much distress as my mother did bandaging a cut on my knee. We gained a lot of respect for the beaver that day.

I relate this story to Kenny as we pull up to the dam, hop out of the canoe and onto the barrier, then tug and pull until our boat slides into the water on the upstream side. "Yeah," he says, motioning Spider back into the bow, "they're a pretty amazing critter."

The beaver, Kenny explains, is one of the only creatures capable of manipulating its environment to survive. Dams are the most obvious example of this ability. Beavers build dams, of course, to raise water levels on a stream or river. Upstream of the dam, the water rises until it spills over the river bank, flooding the surrounding shoreline and creating a small lake. This expanding water allows the beaver to swim to new and better food—young aspen, willow, and alder saplings—which they chew down with incisors designed for battle and mandibles that could power a chainsaw. As beavers prepare for winter, they swim the saplings to a "food pile"— sort of an underwater silo or grain bin—that sustains them through the cold winter months. While beavers don't hibernate, they do minimize winter activity, limiting themselves to trips between the food pile and lodge, which is another marvel of rodent construction made entirely of sticks, mud, and grass. All in all, a pretty admirable system showing incredible industriousness, ingenuity, and foresight.

The trouble comes in spring, when the female births between two and six (usually four) kits in the lodge. Suddenly, the beaver couple (they often mate for life) is now a bustling family with mouths to feed. To procure food, the adults go chop-happy, felling trees that they haul to the dam to raise and fortify it. The new and improved dam holds back even more water, so that now the lake not only spreads further inland, it also reaches further upstream. When the second winter comes, the same process is repeated, and the next spring there are ten beavers where once there were two. Of course, if beaver colonies grew unchecked every year, their dams would resemble Grand Coulee and their lodges adobe townhomes, but nature slows this growth; in the third spring, the male and female drive off the young of their first litter, who disperse to find territories of their own.

So while it's unusual to find a colony of more than ten beavers, it's also pretty rare to locate such a family that hasn't made a big mess out of its surroundings. And if those surroundings are close to a town, people start to complain until something is done about "the beaver problem." This is somewhat of a modern dilemma, as natural controls—wolves, in centuries past, and in recent millennia, trappers—used to kept beaver populations in check. Both predators enjoyed a healthy, respectful relationship with beaver, but nowadays most folk view dealing with an active beaver colony like they would eliminating rats from a garage. Many towns or individuals take the law into their own hands, and the results are about the same as you'd expect in any war against an overgrown rodent. Firearms and explosives have been employed, sometimes with the consent of authorities.

Of course, such overkill doesn't sit well with Kenny, who has run a trapline every year of his life since age six, through boom markets and soft ones. His respect for the animal and the long traditions of ethical trapping have kept him busily at it every winter, long after people in it to make money reckoned their profit margins and took a job at the local Kwik-Trip. Like so many other river rat activities, Kenny traps because it's in his blood, as essential to his being as plucking a trout from a stream or digging a ginseng root from the earth.

After settling into the canoe in the water above the dam, we paddle to the first of the beaver sets. A small marsh lies just off the right bank, separated from the stream channel only by a thin strip of swamp grass and bulrushes. Beaver have established several active runs leading between the marsh and the creek, and Kenny has placed two sets near these runs, hoping to capture an animal using one of the routes.

The first set has not been tripped, the large #4 trap is visible and empty underwater. (Traps are assigned sizes according to numbers, the smaller the trap, the lower the number. A set for muskrats, for example, would call for a #1, raccoon and fox a #2.) But when we reach the second set, Kenny cannot see the trap where he placed it in the run. Grasping a stout pole, he searches underwater near a stake he pushed in the bank until he finds the chain connecting it to the trap. Following the chain into deep water, he hooks into one of the links and begins pulling with obvious effort. The canoe sways with his work, and when the trap appears, the front foot of a dark, sodden, female beaver of about forty pounds is attached to it. Since she has been dead in the current for several hours her fur is soaked, causing her to weigh far more than her actual bulk.

Kenny is a "water trapper," a title that indicates not only where, but how, he places a trap. The water trapper, knowing the behavior of most furbearers when they realize their foot is being held, uses that information to make their death as quick and humane as possible. For the beaver—as well as an otter, muskrat, mink, or raccoon—water is safety, an escape from all sorts of danger that they've encountered since birth. So the first response of a trapped beaver is to swim for deep water. But that's exactly where Kenny has placed a strong stick at an angle to the bank and a couple of feet midstream from the trap. When the beaver makes its dive, the trap chain catches on this "tangle stick" and prevents the animal from resurfacing for air. The beaver quickly loses consciousness, drowns, and dies. In nature, it's about as quick and painless a death as any creature can hope for.

Hauling the beaver into the canoe is no easy task. Beaver are bulky, ungainly animals out of the water, and the soaked carcass could upset the canoe if dragged over the gunwale carelessly. Spider senses the awkwardness of the moment and rolls her eyes at the beaver, then at Kenny, not sure who to place her bet on. After a good grunt and a strong heave, Kenny gains the upper hand, and the carcass makes a loud thud as it hits the bottom of the canoe. Kenny resets the trap, and we are on our way upstream.

I admire the beaver as Kenny paddles. They are impressive animals; their dense, dark fur one of the most beautiful grown by any animal. The beaver was the hallmark animal of the fur trade that spawned exploration of this continent, and it's easy to see why people were so fond of the luxurious pelt. At forty pounds the female seems huge, but represents only an average-sized animal. Kenny has caught beaver weighing well over seventy pounds, and has heard of several animals topping a hundred.

We check two other beaver sets just above the dam and find nothing, but a muskrat set contains a nice animal. While Kenny has trapped every type of furbearer that calls the river valley home, he considers the muskrat his favorite. "I guess they've always been my bread-and-butter animal," he says, shaking the 'rat to dry its fur before laying it in the bottom of the canoe. "They're abundant, fairly easy to catch, and I like their fur; it's beautiful in its own way."

Virtually every river-bottom furbearer gets more respect than the muskrat. Otter have a sleek panache and outrageously gorgeous fur. Raccoons are like miniature black bears—common but adored. Mink are a cunning and savage predator with a dark mystique. And while beaver are big bumblers, their incredible size and storied reputation always make them a great catch. So why does Kenny hold his adoration for the lowly muskrat?

"There's something special to me about the muskrat," he sighs. "Maybe it goes to why I trap in the first place. I've never been a trophy hunter or a trophy angler, and I guess the same goes for trapping. I've always done those things just to live. If I had to make a living trapping trophy animals like otter or fisher or bobcat, it'd be tough to do. So I prefer to stick close to home, in the areas that I know the land and the critters well."

Muskrats are the most prolific furbearers of the Whitman Swamp. Unlike beaver, female muskrats may have up to three litters of four to six kits in a single season, and members of that first litter—born in April or May—may bear their own first young before the snow flies. Kenny calls them "the rabbits of the swamp" for their breeding prowess.

"They're incredibly tough, too," he says. "The males will fight viciously for territory and females. I've skinned them and found fresh wounds that would have killed a lesser animal. If the beaver had the tenacity of a muskrat, I'd be afraid of them." Part of that muskrat courage is a defense mechanism that comes from being picked on, as muskrats are fodder for virtually every predator going: fox, eagle, hawk, mink—even a snapping turtle will take a young muskrat on occasion, tugging it underwater and drowning it as the female 'rat swims on, unsuspecting.

The next several traps we check affirm that muskrats are among the easiest animals to trap, as well. Kenny finds a 'rat in each of the next three sets, goes empty on the fourth, then hits again with traps number five and six. All are animals in the two- to four-pound range, with rich mahogany fur and long slender tails. After removing each muskrat from the trap, Kenny shakes the carcass vigorously in the air to dry it, as wet fur is difficult to work with. Tossing each 'rat onto the growing pile in the canoe, Kenny resets the trap before we press on.

Each set is amazingly simple. An unbaited, #1 long-spring trap is placed in a narrow run or cut-bank that acts as a funnel for a muskrat on the move. The trap is staked with one of the simple willow whips we peeled in August just for this purpose; the butt-end of the stick fed through the trap chain's ring, then shoved into the soft mud of the stream bottom. Kenny makes each set in a couple of minutes, leaning over the side of the canoe, one foot dug into the bank for support. Then we are off and paddling upstream, looking for the next stake that indicates a set.

The system is one that Kenny has perfected in over forty years as a long-line water trapper. Long-liners, as the name implies, run lengthy traplines containing dozens, if not a hundred or more, traps. Long-line trappers are most often veterans looking to make some money. A hobby trapper, on the other hand, may limit himself to a handful of traps that he can tend in his spare time. While magazines and trapping manuals often contain elaborate sets designed to fool the cagiest individual of a species, the long-line trapper has little time for such fussing.

And as Kenny and I reach the end of his line on the creek, I get an obvious reminder why this is so. Looking to the southwest, I see the sun beginning its descent to the horizon, a handful of hours away from cloaking the river valley in the reds and oranges of dusk. Even with our early start, we've been on the water for six hours and are several miles away from the landing, with equipment to stow and animals to tend to. Though I have helped with some menial chores and tended to Spider, my main task has been to watch and learn, and I can still feel the strain of the day and hours of cold working on my muscles.

Kenny turns the canoe, and we head back downstream, the wind now at our backs and pushing us gently toward the landing. As we pass the willow stakes that indicate each water set, I wonder which ones will hold animals tomorrow, which will be empty, which Kenny will give up on. We have made a decent catch this cold winter day, but by week's end, more traps will be barren than full, and Kenny will pull the line, content that he has removed a reasonable surplus of animals, yet not hurt the overall population. Then he'll run another string of traps through a different section of the swamp— perhaps even setting them under the ice of a secluded backwater marsh—and begin the process again.

There is plenty of evidence that trapper numbers are declining in the river valley and, indeed, nationwide. Pundits who analyze such things point to declining fur prices and the pressure of animal-rights groups as the reason for the downswing, but I'm not convinced. While trapping has, at times, been lucrative, I've met few trappers who were in it to make serious money. Most kept at it for the same reasons Kenny gives: the intimate relationship with animals that most people never see; the hard-won knowledge of where a mink or otter, muskrat or beaver will place one foot out of thousands of possibilities; and the lonely comfort of wild places when the ice and snow and cold has driven away every other human. Such intangibles can't be paid for by a booming fur market or robbed by people who get their nature lessons from storybooks. These are secrets only the trapper knows.

RAT TALE
The Grandmother Tree

KENNY TELLS THE TALE: Almost smack dab in the middle of the Whitman Swamp encircled by a narrow ring of large trees sits a shallow, oval-shaped body of water called Schultz's Pond. Just west of the pond is an old tree lying on the ground that I call the Grandmother Tree. She was once a silver maple. Now she rests, sinking into the ground. Rotting. Decaying. The bugs, rain, sun, and wind are returning her back to earth.

When I first came to the swamp, the Grandmother Tree was even then already ancient, but she still stood proud, green, and healthy. Her "helicopter" seeds whirled and twirled about in the early summer; quite a few sprouted as saplings at her feet but most ended up in the mouths of hungry critters and birds. She fed them well. In the autumn, her leaves cartwheeled upon the wind in gay yellow and gold profusion and finally rested against the forest floor. By spring her leaves had given minerals, nutrients, and energy back to the Earth. Her lifeblood would once again pulse strongly, and her naked branches would hang heavy, pregnant with plump, fresh buds.

As the years went on, she began to lose a limb here and there. She started to dry out. Woodpeckers drilled holes in her to make a home. When the woodpeckers were through, the possums and 'coons enlarged the holes and made homes for themselves. The Grandmother Tree was never selfish. She gave of herself: shade in the summer, shelter in the winter. As time went on, she became even more fragile, until one day during a hard windstorm the Grandmother Tree crashed to the ground, and most of her limbs broke off. That's when I noticed her trunk was hollow with about a two-foot-wide cavity. The outside measurement of the tree was some ten feet.

Over the years I sat upon her trunk and ate lunch. Every time I went by, I touched her in reverence. I would stand and look at her and take a moment to reflect back on her life and mine as well. One early spring day in March, I was canoeing the swamp, trapping muskrats. At noon, I stopped at a place called Devil's Elbow, a sharp bend in Indian Creek, to eat my lunch. It was a warm and balmy day. The wind blew mildly from the south, and waves lapped gently along the side of the canoe as my dog Spook and I stepped onto a dry, grass bank.

As I sat eating my lunch I noticed to the west a huge, dark cloud rolling in across the main channel of the Mississippi River. I thought to myself, "It's going to rain some." I got my raincoat out of the canoe and finished my lunch. Spook and I went on our way. In about half an hour, that huge black cloud was directly over us. Thunder boomed loud and deep, and lightening struck all around us. It began to rain hard. The wind began to blow harder. The rain changed to sleet. From sleet to heavy, wet snow, the kind of sticky stuff that sticks to everything, even the canoe paddle and the sides of the canoe. The water was cold and it began to slush up. The harder I paddled, the less headway I made. There were whitecaps on the narrow slough. The wind howled; now it blew from the north. The waters and the sky were angry.

My eyes began to freeze shut. Each time I took off my gloves and held my hands over my eyes to thaw off my lashes, I'd lose control of the canoe. Quickly I'd put my gloves back on only to find it almost impossible to grip my paddle. A strange urge to lay right down in the canoe and go to sleep overtook my entire being. A sense of lightheadedness, fatigue, and a dream-like trance overwhelmed my brain. But the crashing of the icy waves as they sprayed across me somehow kept me awake.

I began to look for a place to pull the canoe out on the bank. Then I realized I was close to the Grandmother Tree. I maneuvered the canoe onto the bank, hauled Spook and myself out, quickly tied the canoe to a nearby tree, and turned it upside down. I took my soaking wet body, my dog, what little tea I had left in my bottle, and an old sandwich and made my way to the Grandmother Tree. I stopped before I crawled inside of her and I took note at how her arms—her limbs—were raised up toward me just as a grandmother would welcome a child to her bosom. I crawled inside the old tree. The wind didn't seem to howl as bad. It was dry. Inside the dark, confined space, I found crushed leaves and grass that were nice and dry. The critters had used the Grandmother Tree for their home. Now we would use it for ours.

Spook and I both fit inside. We stretched out and I lay with one arm under my head. I listened to the storm and I rested. I thought it wouldn't be too long and the sun would come out, the wind would quit blowing and we could go on home. But that didn't happen.

When darkness came on, I realized we were going to be staying there because the storm wasn't going to be stopping any time soon. And stay there we did. It was a little cramped to be sure, but I guarantee you one thing, when morning came I was mighty glad I'd found the Grandmother Tree. As we climbed out of the trunk at daylight, Spook and I couldn't believe what we saw. Everything was white: The swamp was sunk under snow and completely frozen over. I probably would have frozen to death had it not been for the Grandmother Tree. I owed her my very life and that of my dog's as well.

Today, she's still there, but just a shell of what she once was. But even now she still provides a little shelter for some critters. She's returning back to the earth, part of the Circle of Life. She will always share, give comfort, give of herself until there is absolutely nothing left to give. Isn't that the way with all grandmothers?

FEBRUARY

River Rat Almanac

NOW IN FEBRUARY, the dead of winter, the silence of the great river and its backwaters is seldom broken. Occasionally one hears the raucous cry of a blue jay or a crow, and as the ice thickens and shifts about on the coldest days, one sometimes hears a sharp crack like a rifle shot. But mostly it's quiet, except for the homeless winter wind moving through the dry cattails, bulrushes, and wild rice.

These same winter winds make beautiful, sparkling patterns in the snow, while the trees above stand naked against the crisp, cloudless sky.

This is surely a time of rest and silence and death. All things are either sleeping or fighting to survive, yet a keen observer will note the spring-time call of the chickadee. Cut a hole in the ice along the backwater bays and you'll see minnows, insects, and plants thriving. As the sun climbs higher in the sky, you know that winter's icy grip will soon loosen. Like the old saying goes, "If we can't stand the winter, we don't deserve the spring."

Fur Processing

I don't recall the temperature on the mid-February day when I skated my pickup toward Kenny's house in Buffalo City. But I do know when I skittered down the stairs to the Salwey root cellar—our designated meeting place for the day—I was moving with the single-minded purpose adopted by all critters that stick out winter in the river valley. The air was pin-drop still, and yet my ear lobes were nearly numb by the time I'd made my way past the iron gate surrounding Kenny's yard. There might be warmer places to meet than a root cellar, but any place was a damn sight warmer than the cab of my truck, where I'd spent the last twenty miles realizing what it feels like inside a frosty beer mug. Besides, I was scheduled for a lesson in skinning and stretching fur; what better way to warm one's frozen digits than a stack of thick, swamp-raised pelts?

Kenny is sitting in an old chair when I poked my head in the cellar door. He reaches to shake my hand with his right hand, then waves an old, tarnished knife at me with his left.

"Feel this," he winks, pressing the blade into my palm. I hesitate, the wide, browned blade warm and greasy against my skin. "Ain't nothing but an old butcher knife with no edge on it. You could ride to Chicago on this thing and never cut your butt!"

I chuckle as my hand closes gently against the dull blade before Kenny pulls it toward him again. On his lap are a muskrat skin stretched on a wire frame. Two other unskinned 'rats, as well as the carcasses of a mink, a raccoon, and a beaver, are lined up on a small wooden table.

"This knife is my scraper," Kenny explains as I take off my coat, the small, dirt-floored room feeling suddenly cozy. "There's all kind of factory scrapers made for this same purpose, but I haven't found one that works good as this. Let's me apply pressure where I need it; makes for a cleaner job, fewer cuts in the hide."

What most non-trappers don't know about the profession is the amount of work that goes into preparing an animal hide for sale. After an initial skinning job to remove the hide from the carcass, each pelt must be fleshed. Fleshing is a process of scraping away excess fat or muscle tissue remaining on the skin. The next step is to stretch the pelt over a frame. The skin is then left on the stretcher for several days and allowed to dry, at which point it is then ready for market. Processing fur is a time-consuming, labor-intensive process that is equal parts art and drudgery. It can also dramatically affect the dollar value of an individual skin, and seasoned trappers take great pride in their skill as fur handlers. Which makes simple tools like an old, dull butcher knife as important to a trapper as a set of precision socket wrenches to a budding mechanic.

It had been a while since I worked fur. I ran a modest trapline in high school with a friend and did some skinning, fleshing, and stretching of hides, but I'd never worked the variety and volume of animals that Kenny did. As a long-line trapper who made a substantial portion of his annual income from his catch, I knew Kenny had ways of handling fur that emphasized speed and efficiency without sacrificing quality. I was anxious to learn some of his techniques.

Fur handling starts, of course, with the skinning of the animal itself. On most species—muskrat, mink, otter, raccoon, fox, or coyote—the animal is "case-skinned": A single, lateral cut is made that starts on the back of one of the hind legs, continues under the tail, and ends at the other hind leg. From this initial cut, the skinner works the hide forward, separating it from the carcass with a series of gentle knife cuts, or ideally, simply pulling it loose with his hands. "The trick to skinning is to leave as much fat on the carcass as possible, but still not damage the hide itself," Kenny explains as he settles back down on his chair. "Generally, the fatter the critter, the easier this is to do. So you can do a lot of pulling on a 'rat or a 'coon, less on a lean animal like a mink or otter, and almost none on a fox or coyote. Those leaner critters make you use your knife a lot, and the more you do that, the longer it takes."

"Well, I've watched you skin a muskrat, and you're pretty darn fast," I note.

"Used to be a lot quicker, when I was younger and had more to skin," Kenny sighs. "When I trapped for a living I could do a 'rat in a minute and a half. I skin them over my knee, make that one cut along the hind legs and get the fur started, then do most of the rest with just my hands. When you're trapping 1,500 'rats a year, you learn to speed things up just by practice."

Once the hide is worked over the carcass and up to the head, some careful cuts are made to free the skin from difficult spots near facial features like eyes, ears, and mouth. Individual animals require varying amounts of time in these trouble spots as scars, leanness, and hide quality is unique to each creature. When the pelt is finally worked over the face and mouth it is freed from the carcass and essentially inside-out: the leather, or flesh-side, on the outside, the fur in.

After skinning an animal, the fleshing begins. Kenny's large, callused hands grip the knife blade, then lay it at an angle to the leather. Leaning the stretching board between his lap and the table in front of him, Kenny begins to make small, gentle scraping motions— like a pastry chef scratching scrap dough from a cutting board—to remove the small pieces of fat clinging to the hide. Kenny turns the stretched pelt four times, fleshing a strip of hide directly in front of him, then giving the stretcher a quarter-turn before starting on the next side.

"You learn to skin them right in the first place, with as little knife work as possible, and your fleshing job on a 'rat is much easier," Kenny emphasizes. "The less fat you have to remove now, the less chance you'll nick the skin, and that can mean a deduct in price. If your knife is too sharp, or you work the hide too hard, you can get what they call a 'paper rat,' one where the leather's so thin it makes a light papery sound when you tap it with the end of your finger."

After the fat has been removed to his satisfaction, he stretches the pelt on a wire frame made locally by Peerless Chain Company in Winona, Minnesota. The frame is a simple, heavy-gauge steel wire bent in the shape of an ironing board. Kenny slides the pelt nose-first, fur side in, onto the frame, which has a small, adjustable bar on the bottom that allows the handler to adjust the size of the stretcher to the dimensions of the pelt. Too loose and the fur simply sags on the frame; too tight and the pelt is stressed and over-stretched, damaging its quality.

"One thing most people figure about fur is that you judge a prime pelt from the fur itself," Kenny says as I lean in to watch him work. "That's part of it, but the main way buyers grade for prime is to look at the leather side. You get these darkish, blue streaks in the leather—like this 'rat has—that means the pelt isn't as prime. The whiter the leather is, the more prime the fur, and then it gets a higher price. All critters come into prime fur at different times. The first are fox and coyote, in late fall in a normal year. Then it's probably 'coon, beaver, mink, otter. 'Rats actually come last, far into winter and almost spring. Because some of my areas are located on fur farms, I can trap 'rats later than the regular statewide season. Those are some of the best-furred critters of the season. I can sell them at a good price."

Then he hangs it—stretcher and all, nose-upright—on a nail pounded into a ceiling rafter. The pelt is left to dry there for several days, until most of the oils present in the skin have dried, and the leather itself is dry to the touch. When the fur is done drying and ready to be sold, the stretching frame is removed, and the fur is stacked—still with the skin-side out—with others of its kind. When the pile of pelts numbers a hundred, the next pelts are stacked on top of that, but turned ninety degrees. This allows both trappers and buyers to quickly count and sort fur when making a sale.

The second clue that fur buyers look at to determine pelt value is, of course, the fur itself. To determine fur quality, buyers look at a "window," a small trimming made by the fur handler at the base of the stomach side of the leather. The buyer will lift the leather here and peek at the dense fur on the back of the animal. This allows them to inspect the dense guard hairs, the longest, most luxurious fur on the animal. If the guard hairs are long, full, and undamaged, the fur commands a higher price.

"Lots of things can damage the guard hairs," Kenny says as he fits another muskrat skin onto a metal stretcher. "Fox and coyote will be prime until their breeding season begins in late January and February. Then their fur can get rubbed—that's when the guard hairs get broken or pulled out—from breeding. Critters like 'coon can get rubbed fur just from crawling in and out of a tree hole, or from sleeping in their den, pressing their neck against wood or stone. Since they don't really hibernate, but come out on days when the weather's warm, they can get pretty rubbed by mid-winter and their pelts aren't worth as much. Beaver and otter fur can actually 'singe' late in the season, when the days are longer and the sun hits that dense fur for a longer period of time. The hair actually lightens, curls, and splits a little on the ends, like you'd held a match to it. And of course, muskrats can get rips and tears in their hide toward the spring mating season."

In less than the time it takes him to describe this process, Kenny has fleshed the next muskrat. Having fleshed a few pelts in my trapping days, I can truly appreciate the speed and efficiency with which he accomplishes the task. When I mention this to him, he only smiles and nods. "I should hope I'd be fairly quick. When fur prices were high and I was trapping to make money, I might bring in 1,500 'rats in a season. I'd get so busy, especially during the spring, that I'd have to hire skinners to work for me just so I could keep up. Ottmar Probst and his wife Ann used to help out once in a while. Those two could skin a 'rat in a hurry.

"I was getting close to seven bucks for a big 'rat in those days, and even an average one'd bring five. Interesting thing about the fur trade: When the prices are high, they'll buy most anything, because they know they can get rid of it. When prices are low, the buyers get really picky; won't even touch some furs that aren't first rate. Those years, back in the seventies and early eighties, you could pull a fair check if you trapped hard. I ended up paying off this house with just four years of 'rat-trapping, so I guess that was OK."

Selling furs hasn't changed much since the trade opened up on this continent centuries ago, the exception being that few fur companies employ trappers, as happened when the first Europeans came to North America. Virtually all modern trappers are independent contractors whose only payment comes when they sell their furs, and they can conduct business with whomever they choose. "I've sold to most every country fur buyer in the Midwest," Kenny explains as he sets into the next muskrat pelt. "The advantage of doing that is they pay you right now, and some'll pay cash. The disadvantage is that they're less able to pay a premium price, especially when the market is down, like now. They usually have to get rid of their furs all at once to a bigger buyer or auction, so they can't give you as much for yours, not knowing what they're going to get themselves.

"The alternative is to sell them to a big auction house. I've sold quite a few to the North American Fur Company up in Canada, the largest fur dealer on the continent. You have to package and ship your furs up to them, and pay an insurance premium in case your furs are lost or damaged in a fire or something. It sounds like a lot of work, and it is, but it can be worth it, because you're probably going to get a higher price than a country buyer can give you. That's because a big auction house pulls in up to two hundred fur buyers from all over the world who come there to buy big lots of fur at one time, and they're bidding against each other to get the best ones.

"That makes it a better way for a seller, especially if he has good fur and handles it well. Once your fur arrives at the fur company, they sort it according to size and quality, then put it into 'lots' made up of hundreds—even thousands—of furs of similar quality. So let's say I send them one hundred 'rats that make it into the 'large-select' lot. There may be eighty thousand 'rat hides in that lot, and the fur company won't sell them below a certain value. If the bidding gets going for that lot, the price can get pretty high, and when it sells, they just mail you a check for your share, minus a percentage, of course. The disadvantage of that system is you can sometimes wait a while to get paid. I've got a premium, double-extra-large possum that's been sitting up there for over three years now. But I guess I don't mind waiting. When fur prices are this poor, holding on for the best price you can get is worth it to me."

Predicting the vagaries of the fur market is a voodoo science involving the macroeconomics of world trade, the health of the stateside economy, and the ever-fickle trends of the fashion industry. I began trapping about the time Kenny was making his best money, and fur prices were as high as any time in recent memory, with muskrats going as high as seven dollars each, raccoons thirty to fifty dollars, and a prime red fox as high as eighty dollars. My small trapline provided a decent income, running it only on the weekends as my partner and I did. But in the mid-1980s, fur prices began to slide, then nosedive, due in part to the advertising campaigns of various animal "rights" groups, who swayed fashion designers to buy their "fur is dead" philosophy. Print and television ads decried the use of leghold traps, and the resulting backlash trickled into the side-industry of fur farming, and even up to the high Arctic, where certain native peoples made a significant portion of their living harvesting fur from a variety of furbearers, including immature harp seals. Domestic demand for coats and other products made from fur dropped precipitously and affected stateside fur prices.

There are, thankfully, other markets. Demand for fur has generally remained high in some European countries, as well as China and Russia, where most folks don't harbor any illusions about our long-standing use of animal products for human comfort and sustenance. Unfortunately, the economies of these countries—and their trade relationships with the United States—are not always stable enough to ensure a constant demand for U.S.-produced fur. There have been minor spikes and drops in fur prices, but overall, the market has been relatively soft in recent years. There are hopeful omens on the horizon: A number of fashion designers now yawn at the politically correct blathering of their colleagues and are including fur in their clothing lines again, and there are hints that expanding world trade policies will open new, lucrative fur markets and revitalize the industry. As Kenny finishes the last of the muskrats and turns his attention to the lone raccoon before him, I ask him his thoughts about future fur prices.

"I don't think we'll ever see the kind of prices we did twenty years ago, but you never know," he reflects. "I know this much: It was always a tough living, no matter what the prices were. It's demanding, back-breaking work that's cold and exhausting, even on the best days."

"But what do you think about the people who want to see the end of professions like trapping?" I ask, hoping to provoke a response. I'm staring at the raccoon that Kenny is now working onto the stretching board as I say this, remembering a similar-sized 'coon we encountered while duck hunting last fall. The animal, obviously sick with distemper, was sitting listlessly on a streambank, its eyes weepy, its legs trembling and weak. We decide to kill the raccoon and end its misery, but it is not the only one we'll encounter. Before the snow flies, we'll see six more, some suffering as the first one, others who've already succumbed to the disease. It's a classic case of nature weeding out the surplus of an animal population, and the waste saddens me. If such an animal is to die anyway, and they surely will, why not use whatever part of them we can? And, as one who sees—as Kenny does—humans as a part of nature, rather than apart from it, I see no reason why we shouldn't participate in this cycle. I expect a circle-the-wagons, it's-us-versus-them tirade from my mentor, but I'm surprised by his response.

"Most of the people against it ain't a lot different than you and me," he says, looking up from his work. "They love the swamps and the hills and the river just like we do. Problem is, there's damn few of us seeing the big picture. We got to set aside our differences as to whether we should or shouldn't kill critters and form a coalition of people who care about wild places. That's what's really important: places for wild critters to live. Because the whole time we're fighting about whether we should or shouldn't hunt or trap animals, their homes are being destroyed, and if that happens, all our arguments ain't going to be worth the breath we use slinging them. Once we protect the places that need protection, we can always go back and decide what to do with the critters.

"We need to get some folks on each side of the fence to crawl through the wire and start working together, pooling the brain power and money we got in common to work on protecting wild places. Then we could really accomplish something. Right now, most of us are thinking of our own self-interest—we can't see past the end of our nose. We got to switch that and start thinking about the long-term plan for nature and the critters living in it. Because what happens to them happens to us. That's the biggest thing. It's not as if we're standing outside the Circle, watching—hell, we're in there with them!"

"Do you really think that can happen?" I ask, struggling to disguise the pessimism in my voice.

"Yes I do," Kenny says, waving the fleshing tool for emphasis. "And you know why? Young people. Most of us old ones are set in our ways; we can't, or won't, extend a hand or a heart in order to make happen what we know should happen. It's almost as if we enjoy being enemies. But today's young people are better educated. They know more about the environment than we ever did. I've been in the schools with them; I see how they care for nature if they can learn about it. If anybody's got a chance to do what needs to be done, they're the ones who can."

Listening to Kenny's philosophy has taken my mind, and eyes, off of fur processing, but I'm brought back to reality by an acrid, musky smell. I look down at the skinning table and see Kenny returning my gaze with a twinkle in his eye. "Time to skin the mink," he says. "Figured we needed a little perfume in here!"

"Is that what's making that smell?"

"Eau de mink!" Kenny chuckles. "About an even race with a skunk for odor, don't you think?"

"Especially at close range!"

"I ain't even punched the little musk sac they got by their tail. You do that and your eyes'll water. Mink are the same family as skunk—weasel family, you know. That explains the similar smell."

"I never had much luck with mink on my trapline," I say, sheepishly. The sleek predator with its mahogany fur is one of the trapper's trophy species, and I'd always been a little embarrassed by my failure to catch one.

"Probably didn't leave your traps out long enough. Mink ain't like a beaver, 'coon, or 'rat, living in one place all the time. Especially a buck mink. They'll have a big territory that can take them a week, ten days, to cover. So most guys are trapping an area for 'rats, beaver, whatever, and they do good for three, four, five days, then it starts to slow down, so they decide to move and not overtrap the spot. No mink in the set they've made, so they pull it, too. Big mistake. Got to be patient with them; leave that trap a week, ten days maybe. Give them time to find it. Make it a drowning set that'll kill the animal quickly, but put it in a spot you can check every day.

"Mink aren't that difficult to trap because they're curious—they'll investigate any hollow log, any little pocket hole, any muskrat run—and they're a vicious predator. They'll find the breathing hole on a muskrat house, dig themselves in there, and kill the whole family. You can use those traits against them to make a good set, but like I said, it takes patience to catch them consistently."

"And a clothespin for your nose when you skin one!" I say, breathing through my mouth.

"Almost done. Mink take a little time to skin—they're lean and muscular, so you got to use your knife constantly to skin them."

Kenny slips the fur onto a wooden stretching board, fleshes it quickly, then slides a long wooden shim under the fur. "These wooden stretchers aren't as slick as the metal ones, but I like them for mink. I use the shim here because the hide is fairly tight on the stretching board, and if I leave it dry without the shim, I'll have a heck of a time getting the pelt off the board. This way, when the fur's done you just slide the shim out and the pelt comes off nice and easy."

The last pelt of the day is the beaver, another glamour species for the trapper, especially in the early days of the white settlement of this continent. Demand for beaver pelts was so strong for so long that the species was extirpated in some regions due to a lack of game regulation and an insatiable demand for their gorgeous fur. But beaver populations have swung back since modern game management principles were used to regulate harvest. And in recent decades, the sluggish fur market has so eased trapping pressure on the huge furbearers that many local governments pay a subsidy—the modern equivalent of a bounty—for trappers willing to take them.

Beaver are the only species skinned "in the round." Kenny makes a cut from the beaver's tail to its chin in the middle of its body, then begins removing the hide with the help of a skinning knife. Because of their unique body shape, a beaver skinned in this fashion will produce a perfectly round pelt. The skin is carefully nailed to a circular-shaped "beaver board," where it is then fleshed and dried.

"You'll notice these circles marked on the board I have," Kenny says, turning around and grabbing a large wooden board leaning against the wall behind him. The fleshing boards sports a series of black, evenly spaced concentric circles that reach to the edge. "Each of these circles indicates a pelt size in a system the Hudson Bay Company made way back in the time of the voyageurs. They decided that, for trading purposes, any beaver pelt that measured a total of sixty-five inches—thirty-three by thirty-two inches, for example—would be worth one of their famous wool blankets in trade. So a sixty-five-inch beaver is known as a 'blanket beaver.' There are other sizes, too, of course. Fifty inches is a small, fifty-five is called a medium, a sixty-incher is an extra large, and a seventy-inch fur is a super blanket."

After Kenny frees the pelt from the carcass, he stretches it across the board, revealing a beaver that will qualify for "extra-large" status. "I've caught them up to eighty inches," Kenny recalls as he pulls out a small tin box full of short, dark nails from a nearby drawer. Taking a small hammer, he gently pounds one nail through the edge of the hide and into the board, a process he'll repeat every couple of inches until the pelt is stretched smoothly. "And I've heard of guys with ones up to a hundred. I'll tell you, an eighty is big enough for me."

With the size of this pelt, I can't imagine a critter half again as large. I watch Kenny as he patiently scrapes the fat and tissue left on the pelt from skinning, revealing the prime, white leather below. Kenny's dark, strong, hands move the fleshing tool gently and effortlessly across the pelt, and the easy rhythm has a hypnotizing effect for my winter-weary mind. Upstairs, I recall, is another beaver pelt, this one stretched on an ash frame and hung on the den wall, in the manner of the Ojibwa, Hochunk, and Lakota Indians that once called this valley home. Fancy beading, hawk feathers, and decorative strips of leather decorate the ash frame, forming a totem of respect to this industrious creature of the backwaters and tributary streams.

It strikes me then, what a show of respect it is for us to use animals in this way: their meat strengthening our muscles, their hides and furs serving as our clothing and blankets and necessary gear. But they also serve another, perhaps higher, purpose as a reminder of our deep connection to the wild creatures that inhabit the same Circle of Life that we do. There are other artifacts gracing the walls of Kenny's den: photos, paintings, memorabilia. But front and center is a beaver hide, an emblem of the wild and lonely places that keep him whole.

Rat Tale
Beaver Lodge Fracas

Kenny tells the tale: On a late winter's day, I was traveling the rotting ice. It was a warm, sunny afternoon and the ice was becoming honeycombed. It was black in spots and there was water on top of the ice. Old Joey, my trusty fellow traveler of many years, and I were setting out with an ax and a walking stick. We were going to look over some beaver lodges. We crossed the ice on Big Lake without any major mishaps, and as we traveled the game trails out into the marsh, I saw old Joey hit a fresh track. She let out a yip and her tail began wagging back and forth. Joey was a swamp dog. She had scars on her nose, her ears were split, and she walked with a slight limp. She was a veteran of many years of swamp living. When old Joey set off on a trail, there was no question in my mind that she'd catch up with the critter sooner or later.

I soon realized Joey was after a 'coon, as the tracks were plain in the melting snow. Old Joey ran a little faster. I kept up the pace as best I could, huffing and puffing. I heard her bark tree. She was out on a place across from Big Lake called Dark Slough. It was so named because the silver maples grew thick as the hair on a dog's back on both sides of it. They tilted and hung to the middle of the slough where their top branches formed a twisted, tangled canopy way up in the air. Each year, come autumn, most all those silver maple leaves fell into the water, causing it to take on the color of strong-brewed tea. Along the banks of Dark Slough was an old abandoned beaver house with some dry sticks and a big mound on the bank. It sounded to me like that was where old Joey was barking tree.

When I drew close, I couldn't see no 'coon, no dog, no nothing. I guessed that she'd already caught up with the 'coon. I followed their tracks to about a two-foot-square hole—the old beaver's entrance to the abandoned lodge. Man, there was a heck of a ruckus going on inside there. Fighting. Barking. Growling. Snapping. I began to fear for the safety of old Joey. She was getting along in years, and her teeth weren't what they used to be. The longer I waited, the more impatient and worried I got. It just wouldn't end in there. Probably an old boar 'coon, I figured. Swamp wise. Tough.

Finally, I couldn't take it any more. I got down on all fours. I took out my little hand ax, and I crawled inside that beaver lodge. It was pitch black in there. You couldn't see the hand in front of your face. I hollered, "Here now, Joey!" thinking she'd come to me. Something came to me, all right. I could feel a tail swishing across my face but I couldn't tell if it was dog or 'coon. I disregarded both. I was already beginning to think of my own safety about that time.

There was no let up in the fighting. What a melee! Soon, they began to bump against the sides of the beaver lodge. The sticks were poking me. The 'coon and Joey both rolled over the top of me a couple of times. I knew now that all three of us was looking for some relief; all three of us wanted to see some daylight. There was no way of getting out of there now. I thought about taking my hand ax and swinging at what I thought was the 'coon, but then I got to thinking I'd hit Joey so I held myself back from swinging the ax.

I tried to see where the daylight was. A couple of times I did, but I couldn't work my way over to it. Finally, I more or less rolled up into a deep crouch with my head and hands between my knees and just kind of let it all happen. Hoh! The smell in that place was something awful! 'Coon and dog, mud and blood, stagnant water, and it smelt like something might have died in there over summer, too. Then I got to hoping that a bunch of snakes wouldn't have took a notion to spend the winter in that hellacious dark, dank tomb. To have some cold, slithery reptiles start to crawl across me would have brought me altogether unglued about then.

I was still thinking on the snake thing when all of a sudden it was quiet. All I could hear was heavy breathing. A low guttural growl. Was Joey the one that was quiet, or was it the old boar 'coon? I was afraid to find out. I crawled over on my hands and knees and stuck out one hand hesitantly. By golly, it felt like Joey was the one doing the breathing.

She wouldn't let go of the old boar 'coon. She had him by the throat. I found daylight and I crawled out through the small opening. I reached back in and drug both Joey and the 'coon back out with me. Finally, with some coaxing from me, Joey let go of that 'coon and I hung it up in a tree. Old Joey and I sat down in some dry marsh grass for some overdue rest. We both had some cuts and scratches, I guess her more than me, but none of them were serious.

Wow, did that fresh air feel and smell good! The bright sunlight shone into the grass against us and began to warm our old bones. Joey licked herself clean from one end to the other while I lay back and watched a couple of wispy white clouds drift across the otherwise blue sky. A flock of crows were hassling an owl beyond the Dark Slough country to the west along Indian Creek. A chickadee flitted up into a button bush and began to pick at its seeds.

I looked over at Joey, who was stretched out beside me in the dry grass, and said, "Ain't no way I'm ever going to try to help you out in such a beaver lodge fracas again, you hear?"

She looked up at me with those soft chestnut-colored eyes and ran her tongue long and slow along the side of my hand.

I amended my statement: "Well, at least not today, old girl."

MARCH

River Rat Almanac

THE WILD, UNTAMED winds of March are upon us suddenly, as if from out of nowhere. Skunks, possums, and 'coons venture forth on thawing nights in search of food, mates, and freedom from cabin fever. The feathered harbingers of spring, Canada geese and red-winged blackbirds, arrive in the great river valley via their ancient pathways in the sky. Holes appear in the black, water-covered, honeycombed ice along the backwaters. The river channel is icing out in a big way. Walleye and sauger anglers dodge mini-icebergs below the locks and dams.

Is spring here? Yes and no! Warm south breezes and bright sunshine one day can be replaced by icy north winds and snowfall the next. Nevertheless, my friend, all the signs along this ancient waterway seem to say "Spring is coming!" We answer "Great balls of fire!" and throw our hats into the air with joy. It's been a long, hard winter.

An Affinity for Turtles

Our culture doesn't quite know what to make of the month of March. It has been earmarked for tragedy, as Julius Caesar's betrayal and death came on the Ides of March. Sports fans, however, revel in "March Madness" and follow their favorite basketball teams through tournament time. As a child, I always knew March as the kite-flying month. It was the time of the year when gray, windy days made most outdoor play impossible, but lofting a colorful kite into the breeze always seemed an antidote to the long funk of winter and the interminable wait until spring.

Things aren't a whole lot different in the Whitman Swamp. In this last month of the river rat year, strong northwest winds can howl across the cattails, bringing snow and cold and even death to creatures who've burned their winter fat and forage in a land nearly barren of food. For them, March may be the cruelest month. It's so close to spring, yet so full of gales and snows and freezing nights as to seem the heart of winter itself.

March can be kind, too. Southerly breezes prod pack ice from the ponds and sloughs. Clouds are swept away, allowing a higher, stronger sun to soak the land. Buds emerge from trees and green shoots poke through the forest duff. Sit by a creek full of snow melt and you'll smell the rich, unmistakable odor of spring. It's too cold for shirt-sleeves and too warm for a coat, but you shuck off your jacket anyway, relying on the joyous beating of your heart to warm you. Amazingly, swamp creatures share the excitement: Red-wing blackbirds return to hang on cattails and trill; the season's first geese and ducks gabble in pockets of open water; and muskrats and beaver emerge from winter quarters and swim through rivers of ice-melt. The swamp, for months a sleeping giant, is awaking from its slumber.

We had cruised through several days of such sun-kissed March, then been smacked in the face for a week of harsh treatment by its evil twin, when Kenny calls me.

"Got your feet propped by the fire?" he asks, a hint of mischief in his voice.

"I would if we had a woodstove. It's damn nasty out there." I poke my nose past the curtain as I talk, confirming the weather report: hard-steel-colored skies, pelting flurries, winds out of the north at freeze-your-cheeks-and-then-some. Leaving the window, I turn to my calendar and look at the weeks ahead, assuming Kenny would want to set up an activity when a kinder, gentler March returned.

"What are you doing tomorrow?" he asks.

"I . . . uhhh, don't know. What did you have in mind?"

"Thought we'd follow Spider through the swamp for a day. Hit some turtling spots I know. Might find one. Might not. Can you be at the shack about ten o'clock? You'll want to dress warm. Not supposed to change much between now and then. We'll spend the day walking, though."

My response, as genuine as I could make it, is as see-through fake as a used-car salesman's pitch. "Sounds . . . umm, great, Kenny. I'll see you then." Hanging up the phone, I sneak another peek out the window, searching the horizon for a hint of change. There is none, and with a sigh I wander toward my closet, searching for the layers of wool I would need to stay warm tomorrow.

As expected, the next day offers little relief, and at first glance the swamp looks much like it did in January and February, when we paddled along frozen stream banks and chopped holes in the ice to set our traps. There is a slight but insistent northwest breeze lashing our cheeks as we set off from Big Lake Shack into the swamp. Spider leads the procession and I bring up the rear, following Kenny as he drags a small plastic child's toboggan loaded with "turtling gear": an ice chisel, a small ax, an army-surplus backpack, a steel spud to break through the ice, and a "turtle hook"—an ash-handled, four-foot-long stick tipped with a J-shaped metal hook just about large enough to fit an apple into. Kenny's turtling tools hadn't changed in the decades since he'd practiced the craft, but the toboggan is a nod to modern materials. The durable plastic tub replaced a traditional wooden sled, whose runners could bog down in soft snow and hang up on limbs and debris.

I dressed for the weather, but as we plod along the wooded ridges leading toward Tent Camp Slough, I tug my stocking cap down hard over my ears and pull my collar up against the wind. I am walking like a workhorse, not noticing the ethereal beauty of the swamp in transition from winter to spring. Thankfully, as happened on so many walks before, Kenny gently nudges me back into awareness.

"See the ice on that slough?" he says, using his walking stick as a pointer. "This cold snap's kept it safe to walk on, but not for long. See how the ice is pockmarked, or honeycombed, beneath the surface there? That's a sign it's getting weak from that warm spell we had a while back. Another one like that and it'll be done. No more walking on it, unless you're ready to get wet."

There are other omens as we trudge deeper into the swamp. Silver maple buds sag from limb tips, ready to burst into tender leaves at the next southerly breeze. Tracks of possum and 'coon are perfectly cast in the frozen mud along the bank, proof that their makers had taken advantage of the last thaw to emerge from their dens and hunt. The icy breeze and leaden skies prove winter hadn't quit the fight, but these smaller, telltale signs hint that the cold season is on the ropes. While birds and mammals made tentative stabs at spring travel, the snakes, frogs, and turtles of the swamp aren't so easily fooled. They are still buried in swamp-bottom muck, relying on a long-term temperature change to wake them from their stupor.

Our quarry this day is the snapping turtle, as true a creature of the backwaters as ever existed. If the flathead is the signature fish of the Upper Mississippi River, then the snapper is its reptilian equivalent. Heavily armored and tenacious, the snapper latches on to swamp life early and refuses to let go, ready to face adversity of all types. There are flashier, more glamorous creatures that call the swamp home, but none more suited to life here.

And, fittingly, there is also no critter more symbolic of my mentor than a big old swamp snapping turtle. Indeed, Kenny reveres turtles, calling them simply his "slow-moving friends." From our first meeting, it was clear to me that Kenny was in no hurry to get anywhere: Although he is strong, weathered, and unquestionably hearty, he never seems to have speed in mind as he travels. Whether he adopted this life's pace from watching turtles or it was just a coincidence, I was never sure. Now that we are searching for the wintering grounds of a swamp snapper, it seems an appropriate time to ask.

"Your eyes are getting keener," Kenny grins at my question and, somewhat predictably, stops to lean on his walking stick. "I've been fond of turtles ever since I was a child. I guess that ain't much different from most kids, if the reactions I get at some of my nature talks tells me anything. Like those kids, I'd watch turtles walking with their 'mobile homes' on their backs and felt a real closeness to them. Seems there's kind of a universal fascination with turtles, but it fades with most folks as they get older. Never did with me.

"In fact, the older I get, the more I see myself in them. Turtles ain't ever in a hurry to get somewhere, and as you know, neither am I. I tell stories slow, eat slow, walk slow, paddle a canoe slow, even drive slow—if you need proof of that last one, just ask the folks in the big cities I got to go to sometimes. They're honking at me like a flock of geese when I come to town! I been that way all my life, so it must be hereditary, like it is with turtles. They seem to be at home wherever they're at, and so am I—or I try to be. Guess the nights I've been forced to stay in the swamp in one of my out-camps, or tend a fire in the middle of nowhere, just trying to make it through a night are proof enough of that.

"There's something else I admire about turtles, especially the snappers we'll be hunting today. They don't die or give up easily. You won't find a more tenacious critter in the swamp, for my money. And over the many years I've spent living in this swamp and these hills, I've had more near-death experiences than I'd care to recall. Whenever I've went through something like that, I'd try to think about turtles and their toughness, their refusal to give in. Thinking on that tenacity has helped me through a lot of them times."

The strident honking of a Canada goose stops Kenny for a moment and we both look skyward. A small flock of birds, either fooled by the false spring or simply eager to get on with their seasonal trip north to mate, nest, and hatch a brood, are sailing low over the treetops. Their great wings seem to touch the high branches of a nearby giant cottonwood, and they crane their necks right and left, searching for open water to land in. "They'll probably head to the main channel," Kenny says, following their flight. "Hang there until things open up back in these sloughs and potholes."

Hearing a soft sequence of swishing and tapping, I look down to see Spider, her black, otterlike tail thumping against Kenny's leg as she gazes at the departing geese. "That's right, girl," Kenny smiles. "Time to go."

We set off again, following the familiar path toward Tent Camp Slough, but as we near the landmark, Kenny veers suddenly to his right. I follow as he walks across one frozen slough, then another.

We stop near the bank of a third slough. It looks no different to me than any of the others we've crossed on our walk in, but Kenny has pulled the toboggan up next to him as if to say "this is the spot." Spitting a small stream of snoose onto the snow, he drives his walking stick into a snowbank, then leans over to grab the ice chisel from his toboggan.

"We're standing on what I call a 'drain,'" Kenny explains. "Those are places where one pond or lake trickles very slowly into another one through a spot that's thick with plants or vegetation. Little or no current here, more of a seep than anything. The mud's rich and deep, though: good place for a turtle to dig himself in for the winter."

"When do they come to these places?"

"Start in the fall," Kenny says. "Late October maybe, November. The spots tend to be the same from year to year. Like lots of critters in the swamp, they follow the traditions of their ancestors, one generation following the next. This place is good for snappers, but other turtles—soft-shells, box turtles, map turtles, painteds—will pick different areas to winter in. Don't know why, but they separate themselves that way. Each one has its own way of making it through, and they know the things they need to do it. Snappers like these drains, but they ain't the only place they'll winter. Sometimes they'll take to an abandoned muskrat or beaver den. That way there's already a hole burrowed in to the bank; makes a nice room for them to spend the winter in."

"How can you tell there are turtles down there now?"

"We're about to find that out!"

Taking the spud in hand, Kenny taps gently on the ice in front of him and toward the bank. A testing prod here, another poke there. On the third tap, the ice sounds hollow, like Kenny had tapped on an empty wooden keg. Raising the spud again, he brings it down hard on the same spot. The chisel punches through the ice, and a small gush of air belches from the hole. Kenny turns and winks at me. "Should be a turtle down there, somewhere. That air coming out of the hole is a good sign."

With a series of sharp, rapid chops, Kenny uses the spud to make a foot-and-a-half-square hole in the ice. "It's got to be this big in order to get a nice-sized turtle up through the hole," he explains. "I won't take a snapper unless his shell's at least a foot square, so I need to know I've got room to work him up if we decide to take him." The water below the hole is clear at first, but the chopping action has roiled up some of the bottom muck, leaving the impression that we've just tapped a vein of oil.

Once the hole is cleared to his liking, Kenny lowers the spud gently back down, prodding the muck bottom below. "I do this carefully," he says, almost whispering. "Don't want to hurt them or wake them up if I don't have to. Just seeing if one's down there, and how big he is. I only take one a year, and I want it to be a nice one. Let the little ones go, and don't disturb them from their nap." The spud sinks easily into the slop the first four or five probes, then suddenly *thunks* gently against something hard. Kenny turns toward me and smiles. "There's one."

"How do you know it's not a rock or a tree root?" I ask.

"No rocks here. It's a turtle."

Kenny straightens up, then moves to the toboggan and fishes a long black-rubber trapper's glove from the army rucksack. "Water's shallow here, no more than a foot or so. I can use my hand to fish for him down there, then. If it was deeper, I'd use the turtle hook. But I'll feel him out, see how big he is, before making a commitment."

I am incredulous. I know that turtles go into a deep sleep in winter. So do black bears, and you wouldn't catch me crawling into a den unless I'd seen a thoroughly trained professional inject the sleeping bear with enough chemicals to put a small village out for a winter night. I don't have Kenny's experience with snapping turtles, but I'd seen enough of them to know their business end was nothing to mess with. I don't care how dopey they get while dozing in primordial goo, you wouldn't catch me fishing down there with a gloved hand for all the turtle soup in the world.

I'm amazed at Kenny, too—especially when I recall a tale he told me months ago, when we were working the backwaters for catfish. Checking a setline many summer mornings ago, Kenny pulled in a big-bodied snapping turtle that had attacked one of his baits. Snappers weren't unexpected on a setline; indeed, Kenny viewed the turtle's presence as a real bonus and happily hauled him into the canoe. The big snapper would provide several hearty meals, and after coaxing him to let go of the bait, Kenny popped him in a burlap sack and tucked him under the seat. Normally he carried two washtubs in the canoe bottom: one for any catfish he caught, another for bonus turtles. But today he toted only one such tub, and that one was full of writhing fish. When he snagged the big snapper, he figured the dark, cool confines of the burlap sack would keep him calm until he finished tending his lines and made it back to camp. Besides, he'd flipped the snapper on its back, a common method of keeping them disoriented and largely helpless until more permanent measures could be taken.

All went well until Kenny hauled in a line that held a deeply hooked catfish. The aggressive flathead swallowed the setline hook, and in order to free the fish and add it to the washtub, Kenny needed the small set of pliers he always kept under his seat for just such an emergency. Naturally, he'd forgotten about the turtle, which, in the many minutes since its capture, had managed to not only right itself, but had also poked its head out of the burlap sack that served as its prison for a short, but irritating, stay. When Kenny's bare hand reached under the canoe seat for the pliers, the snapper decided to live up to its name.

"The problem with a snapper," Kenny told me that day, "is that little hook, or beak, they have on the top of their mouth—lets them latch on tight. That, and of course the tremendous power they got in their jaws.

"He latched onto my thumb like it was the last thing he was ever going to bite in this world. It was damn uncomfortable, let me tell you. The harder I pulled against that turtle, the harder he pulled on me. I tried putting my foot on his shell and pulling up. I tried relaxing my grip and seeing if he'd let go out of boredom. Nothing doing. He was in it for the long haul and my thumb was the loser. I had me a mess, no doubt about it. Setline is weaving back and forth across the water; canoe's bobbing like a cork; I'm using language you don't hear outside a tavern fight.

"Eventually I managed to get the boat over to the shoreline and stick a leg over the side of the canoe and get enough grip to slip out of the boat. Snapper was still dug in like a wood tick, so I was able to get to my pack and fish out the only knife I had along. With him gripping that hard, I was able to pull on my thumb, stretch his neck out, and cut him clean through, right next to the shell. He was dead, but you couldn't tell it from his head. He still clung to me like I was a free ticket to somewhere special."

So this story is running through my cold-addled brain as Kenny kneels by the hole in the ice, then reaches his hand gently into the soft mud beneath the surface. I'm about to question my host's sanity; instead I take a deep breath and ask just what he intends to do to this creature who, only moments ago, dozed the deep slumber of an animal ready to wait out days like this one and not come out until he knew the summer sun was here to stay.

"Trick to it," Kenny says. "Need to feel around the entire shell, just to see how big he is. I do it with my fist closed, else that sleeping giant could hit me with his business end, and we'd be shaking hands until long after I got him onto the bank. The key is to always keep your fist closed and wait until you're sure it's the right size before hauling him up. That way you can wait for a bigger one. Soon's I 'bump' a turtle I slide my fist to the top of his shell, then work my way to the edge, always keeping to the top as I go. If it seems too small, I leave him where he is and keep looking."

Kenny grimaces as his hand moves along the shell, and then just as quickly as he slid his arm through the ice, he pulls it back out. "Little one. I tucked him back in. Let's go find his grandpa."

We reload the tools on the toboggan and head out in search of another drain. We pass a section of the swamp known as the "Big Woods" for the large, unbroken stand of swamp white oaks growing there. "This can be a good deer hunting spot when the acorns come in," Kenny says, hinting for me to make a mental note. "Last year there were no nuts, and you couldn't buy a deer in here. Just past this next bend is another drain; I've found turtles in there before. We'll check it out."

But the second spot yields no sleeping snappers, despite several explorations with the ice chisel. Another long walk, this time through marsh grass, young willow, and scraggly cottonwoods. We wind up at the edge of a slough that looks exactly the same as the first drain we checked. As Kenny stoops to pick up the spud, I look around for our tracks or a hole we've already chopped. For all I know, Kenny could have led me on a big circle—the backwater equivalent of a snipe hunt—just to see if I was paying attention to my surroundings. Usually when he pulls such a stunt, however, he hints at his own mischief with a wry grin or an arched eyebrow. But Kenny's face is serene and focused.

"How do you keep track of all these spots?" I finally ask. "They all start to look alike to me."

Kenny laughs. "Don't they though! I felt the same thing when I was learning this swamp. Did a lot of stumbling around. That's why it took me ten years before I knew it well. Learned a little section one year, another the next. It's a slow method, but a sure one. "

I study the lay of the land, grasping for clues to our location. Nothing seems familiar. Taking in the horizon, I notice the distant line of bluffs that I assume are Minnesota. "That must be west," I announce, pointing toward the line of hills.

"East," Kenny smiles, then points to an identical ridgeline behind me. "That's Minnesota, over there. Common mistake, since they both look the same. Another one is listening for trains, but there's tracks on both sides. Wind can be a better clue. Remember it was blowing from the northwest when we came in?"

I stick my face into the breeze again and slowly begin to pick out familiar landmarks: a line of tall cottonwoods here, a rust-brown expanse of swamp grass there. "I guess I'm not learning very fast," I say sheepishly. "I thought I knew this a little better than that."

"That's because you're following me, not navigating for yourself. Easy to lose track. As you spend more time down here alone, you'll learn it quicker. Only way to know it for sure."

Kenny points to a section of ice in front of us that looks softer than what we're standing on. The spud raises once and drops, punching easily through the ice. Kenny clears out the proper-sized hole, then trades the spud for the turtle hook and lowers it into the muck. He probes the oozing bottom only twice before the hook makes a solid tap. "This might be the one we're looking for," Kenny says, kneeling again by the toboggan and sliding on the long trapping glove.

For some reason, the anxiety I felt on the first turtle hole has vanished and is replaced by a keen anticipation. Perhaps this time my fear has been replaced by something more predatory, and I'm reminded of the words of a big, rugged man who guides bear hunters in the northwoods every fall. "I take out lots of hunters every fall who want to shoot a bear," he told me once. "Problem is, they don't really want to see one." Suddenly, I desperately want to see a snapping turtle, and I watch intently as Kenny slides his fist through the ice and feels his way around the snapper's shell.

"It's a good one," he announces simply, his face parallel to the ice. "When I find one like this, I got to work my hand along the edge of the shell. I can tell I'm by the tail by the bumps and protrusions along the shell. Then you just reach under the shell there, grab him by the tail, and . . . "

Kenny begins to pull his arm from the hole, hesitates for a moment as he gathers his strength, then heaves a large, dark-shelled snapper onto the snow-covered ice.

I catch my breath in a gasp. The snapper looks prehistoric. Its craggy, armored shell looking as primordial—and formidable—as a triceratops. The heady odor of fish and muck and long-dead swamp grass hits my nose like I'd fallen in the turtle's hole myself. Green-brown water spreads around the turtle, turning bone-white snow crystals into a dark slush. The snapper's head withdraws slightly into its shell, then emerges slowly, like a battering ram from a turret. In that instant, Kenny's reverent claim—that snapping turtles fear no creature that lives in the swamp—becomes suddenly and irrevocably clear to me.

It seemed a moment frozen in time as surely as the ice beneath us, but Kenny had been busy as I gawked and stared. Grabbing a set of pliers from the rucksack, Kenny pokes it carefully in front of the turtle's face. The snapper blinks slowly once, then grabs the pliers in its hooked jaws, clamping down on the hard metal instinctively and without hesitation. Reaching behind him for the hand-ax lying in the toboggan, Kenny slides it next to his leg, then speaks softly to the turtle in long shadows of the winter afternoon: "Dear brother or sister, I know you were sleeping well. I'm sorry for waking you and putting you in a winter world you've never seen. I'm sorry, too, for what I'm about to do. I'll eat your meat and use your claws and shell and breastplate with the respect they deserve. I thank you for your life."

I look closely at my friend for a second, and in that moment I hear the dull thud of the ax hitting ice. When my gaze shifts back to the snapper, the ice has turned red beneath it.

We load the turtle on the toboggan and spend several quiet moments gathering gear and brushing snow from our pants. The marsh, which moments ago contained only two men and a turtle on a small patch of ice, slowly grows larger. The raw wind rattles branches in the treetops. A flock of chickadees chuckle and gab from a nearby grove of river birch. Spider bumps Kenny's leg with her nose, urging us to finish our tasks. We chuckle, softly at first, then with more gusto as the dog splays her legs and bobs her head like a sparring boxer. "Time to go, girl?" Kenny asks, then tugs at the toboggan rope, rights it for the long walk back to Big Lake Shack.

Later that evening, after watching Kenny carefully clean the meat from the turtle and prepare the shell and claws for preserving as ornaments, I enjoy the quiet drive home. Without thinking, I drive far slower than the speed limit, reflecting on our long search for the snapper and the reverent harvest that followed. Like all successful hunting, turtling is a bittersweet mix of elation and sadness, but something felt different to me. While our harvest is a non-event in the backwater Circle of Life, it seems somehow more significant than, say, killing a swamp whitetail. Did my knowledge of Kenny's deep personal connection with turtles affect my thoughts about harvesting them? If a hunter kills the animal he or she acknowledges as his totem, is that animal's death more significant than that of one less revered?

I grapple with these thoughts in the months ahead, as the swamp sheds its winter clothing and blossoms into the verdant growth of spring, then summer. On a June day that hints at the midsummer heat to come, Kenny calls and asks me to join him in a backwater paddle. I had not seen the swamp since our turtle hunt, the weeks after that day passing in a blur of work and family commitments. "We'll have some soup from that snapper we caught," Kenny promises, "then poke around, see how the wild rice is coming."

My truck is less than a mile from the turn off to the Whitman when I see a large, dark form on the edge of the road as the blacktop dips toward a creek. From a distance, the profile is nearly frightening in size and appearance: a huge humped back; long, thick legs; a snout as strong and stout as an ax head. It is a snapping turtle as big as a spaniel; easily twice as large as the one we pulled from the swamp three months ago. I brake, gently at first, then slow the truck to a stop as the giant snapper plods sluggishly across the road and pauses on the other side. The stream, I know, flows through a mile of bottomland farms, through willow thicket and swamp grass, before finally dumping into the Whitman. The turtle is likely a female, swimming toward an area her ancestors used for millennia to lay their eggs and birth the next generation.

An old car approaches, then stops in the road, its driver following my gaze as I stare at the roadside turtle. The snapper balks as the vehicle approaches, starts to pull her head into her shell, then stops to face the noisemaker. There is no fear in her, and finally, after a long moment, she takes a few plodding steps off the shoulder and plunges into the dark water of the stream. The car pulls away, and I coax the truck toward Big Lake Shack, anxious to tell Kenny what I'd seen.

He shares in my wonder and admiration at the huge turtle, which I describe as we savor the meat of one like her. That meat sustains our muscles as we lean into our paddles and canoe the quiet swamp, our minds full of the vision of the next generation of turtles that will inhabit the Whitman Swamp. The Circle of Life was complete for another year.

RAT TALE

Life Along the Big River

KENNY TELLS THE TALE: When I was a young boy at the middle of the last century, river rats were considered "poor folk" by the rest of society. Our old-time rivertowns used to have at least several families who lived off of the bounty found along the Big River or its backwaters. You could generally spot the river rat families' homes by several telltale signs: gigantic wooden reels or spools wound full of homemade, hand-woven, tar-rubbed fish nets; a gaggle of low-profile, extra-wide, flat-bottom johnboats; and handpainted signs announcing "Fresh Fish 4 Sale" or "Smoked Fish on Order." These folk lived by the skin of their teeth—and their outdoor skills had been passed down from one generation to another.

It was that knowledge of the outdoors that intrigued me as a young boy. Oh, how I longed to be one of them. To my mind, their's was an adventurous, exciting way of life. River rats held a number of things in common: an undeniable love for the "free life" of self-sufficiency and independence and an irresistible urge to see what lay around the next bend in the river, the next hook on their setline, the next trapset, and the coming of a new day at dawn. Some of my ancestors were "one of them," and I knew at an early age that I would be as well.

I have made my choice to live in this land and make my living from the Big River, the backwater swamps, and the hill country. I wanted to be a river rat from the days when I was a young boy, and being a river rat is all I've known for most of my life now. I wouldn't trade this life for the world. I've worked the river through each year, from the first days of soft and gentle springtime in April to the slow pace of the hot summer in August, from the shimmering autumn colors of October to the last winter winds of March. My life has been rich and full, and I could not ask for more.

Yet in a strange, unforeseen twist of events, I was given more by an old-time game warden who had the foresight to urge me to share my experience with others. Because of him, I learned of a most peculiar paradox: If I am to see the natural world remain as I know it, I have to give it away. I have to share it in order to keep it.

This I now do with pleasure and hope. There is no question that my river rat lifestyle has almost completely disappeared; still, that does not diminish my new hopes and dreams. Humankind has two great assets: our natural resources and our human resources, the future generations. By sharing my knowledge of nature, my hope is that folks will be inspired to live their lives close to nature, to take better care of it, and be good stewards of the land. When youngsters hear my stories and respond with questions, queries, and fire in their eyes, I am heartened. Chances are they will never be able to live my lifestyle, yet their interest in nature has been awakened, and that is what counts. Once they are interested, they will become inspired, and learn to love and respect nature, and the Circle of Life will turn smoothly.

It is then that my second set of hopes and dreams will have been realized, and there will be little to lament about the passing of the last river rat. For there is no beginning in this land of river and hills. Nor is there an end. The Circle of Life does not stand still. An old saying among riverfolk is that each time you step into the Mississippi River, you never step in the same river twice.

ABOUT THE AUTHORS

J. SCOTT BESTUL is a regional editor for *Field & Stream* and a contributing editor for *Sporting Classics* magazines. He was born in Madison, Wisconsin, where he grew up loving the outdoors, hunting, and fishing. After graduating from Winona State University in Winona, Minnesota, he taught English in secondary schools for four years before he decided to pursue his dream of writing. He is now a full-time writer for a variety of magazines. He lives in southeastern Minnesota with his wife Shari and their young twins, Brooke and Bailey.

KENNY SALWEY IS the last river rat. He cut his milk teeth on a canoe paddle and seasoned it with Mississippi mud. He's a hunter, trapper, outdoor guide, self-sufficient woodsman, and storyteller. Born in the Mississippi River hill country of West Central Wisconsin, he dreamed from childhood of becoming a river rat. He has dedicated his life to the survival of our two most precious resources: our natural resources and our children. He lives in Buffalo City, Wisconsin, with his wife Mary Kay and their two dogs, Webster and Spider.